Supreme Court Economic Review

VOLUME 12

Supreme Court

THE UNIVERSITY OF CHICAGO PRESS
Chicago and London

Economic Review

EDITORS

Francesco Parisi and Daniel D. Polsby

Sponsored by the Law and Economics Center at the George Mason University School of Law

INTERNATIONAL STANDARD SERIAL NUMBER: 0736-9921
INTERNATIONAL STANDARD BOOK NUMBER: 0-226-64594-0
The University of Chicago Press, Chicago 60637
The University of Chicago Press, Ltd., London
© 2004 by The University of Chicago. All rights reserved.
Printed in the United States of America

The paper used in this publication meets the minimum requirements of American National Standards for Information Sciences—Permanence of Paper for Printed Library Materials, ANSI Z39.48-1984.∞

Supreme Court Economic Review

The *Supreme Court Economic Review* is an interdisciplinary journal that seeks to provide a forum for scholarship in law and economics, public choice and constitutional political economy. Its approach is broad ranging and contributions will employ explicit or implicit economic reasoning for the analysis of legal issues, with special attention to Supreme Court decisions, judicial process, and institutional design. The use of theoretical and empirical economic models is permitted, but papers are expected to be accessible to a general audience of judges, academic lawyers, and economists.

Peer review is an important feature of this publication. Accordingly, manuscripts should be accompanied by a cover letter indicating that the submission is being made on an exclusive basis. Electronic submission of manuscripts can be directed to the Editor, Supreme Court Economic Review, at the following e-mail address: *scer@gmu.edu*

Other correspondence can be directed to

Editor, Supreme Court Economic Review
George Mason University School of Law
3301 North Fairfax Drive
Arlington, Virginia 22201-4498

Supreme Court Economic Review

Table of Contents

The 2000 Presidential Election: A Statistical and Legal Analysis

*Richard A. Posner**

*In this article, Judge Posner summarizes and updates his pre-
vious analysis of the failed 2000 Presidential election in
Florida, and the ensuing litigation that culminated in the
Supreme Court's decision in Bush v. Gore. The article uses
multivariate statistical analysis to demonstrate the causes
and consequences of the numerous spoiled ballots and evalu-
ates the claim that Al Gore won at least a moral victory in
the Florida election. The article then analyzes the litigation
over the election, and concludes that there are pragmatic justifications for the Supreme Court's controversial decision that
gave the Presidency to George Bush.*

I. INTRODUCTION

The deadlocked Presidential election of 2000, and the breaking of the
deadlock by the Supreme Court in *Bush v. Gore,* have given rise to in-
tense debate,[1] and raise fascinating questions two of which I address
in this lecture: Was Gore the "real" winner of the election? And is the
Supreme Court's decision defensible? I have already published a book

* Judge, U.S. Court of Appeals for the Seventh Circuit; Senior Lecturer, University
of Chicago Law School. This is the revised text of the lecture that I gave on November
24, 2003, in the Distinguished Lecture Series in Law and Economics 2003-2004 of the
James M. Buchanan Center for Political Economy of George Mason University. I thank
William Baude for his very helpful assistance with the revised regression analysis presented in this paper, the lecture audience for many stimulating questions, and Professor Charles Rowley for inviting me to give the lecture and for his many courtesies.
    [1] With Alan Dershowitz, for example, charging that the decision was actually cor-
rupt. See Alan M. Dershowitz, *Supreme Injustice: How the High Court Hijacked Election 2000* (Oxford, 2001).

about the election deadlock and the ensuing court battles,[2] and a chapter in a subsequent book in which I consider the case in relation to democratic and jurisprudential theory.[3] I draw on these previous publications here, but refer the reader to them for additional detail and a fuller elaboration of my views, as well as discussion of other issues raised by the election deadlock and its litigation aftermath. The statistical analysis in the present essay is new; it updates and revises the statistical analysis in my book.[4]

II. WHO "REALLY" WON IN FLORIDA?

On November 18, 2000, after the ballots cast on election day (November 7) had been counted mechanically and then recounted mechanically, after a few completed hand recounts had been factored in, and after late-arriving overseas ballots had been added to the tally, Bush was ahead in Florida by only 930 votes out of the almost six million votes that had been cast and counted in Florida for a Presidential candidate. And by then it was clear that whoever obtained Florida's electoral votes would be the next President. The secretary of state of Florida, Katherine Harris, wanted to certify Bush the winner by 930 votes. But as a result of the litigation discussed in the second part of this essay, additional hand recounts were conducted that shrank Bush's lead, although they did not eliminate it completely. The hand recounts were stopped by a stay granted by the U.S. Supreme Court on December 9 (by which time Bush's unofficial lead had fallen below 200 votes), and their resumption was precluded by the Court's decision on December 12 in *Bush v. Gore*, which forbade further recounting.

A margin of 930 votes out of six million made the Florida Presidential election a statistical tie. Because the counting of millions of ballots by any method is liable to error, a razor-thin margin of victory such as Bush received establishes merely a probability—and not necessarily a high one—that the victor actually received more votes than the vanquished. That is what I mean in calling the vote in Florida a statistical tie.

The initial count of the Florida vote was by vote-tabulating machines, and (at least as corrected by the machine recount) it was fairly accurate. In Broward County, for example, where the hand recount was conducted in a way calculated to maximize the number of votes missed by the machine count, fewer than 2,000 out of more than half a million votes cast were deemed not to have been recorded for either

---

[2] See Richard A. Posner, *Breaking the Deadlock: The 2000 Election, the Constitution, and the Courts* (Princeton, 2001).

[3] See Richard A. Posner, *Law, Pragmatism, and Democracy*, ch. 8 (Harvard, 2003).

[4] Posner, *Breaking the Deadlock* at ch 2 (cited in note 2).

Gore or Bush as a result of the failure of the tabulating machinery to count an undervote[5] that "should" have been counted as a vote for one of the Presidential candidates. This was fewer than 0.5 percent of the votes cast, a rate that if projected to the state as a whole would mean that only about 30,000 votes statewide had been erroneously not recorded for a Presidential candidate. If those missed votes were representative of the entire Florida vote assumed to be a tie, then counting them accurately would be very unlikely to change (and of course should not change) the result; there would be only a 5 percent probability that the statewide vote for Bush or Gore would change by more than 174 votes.[6] Gore would have needed to pick up approximately 51.75 percent of the 30,000 undervotes to have overtaken Bush's 930-vote lead.

That would not be out of the question. But the 30,000 figure is too large, not only because Broward County method of recovering countable votes from undervoted ballots was questionable (more on this shortly) but also because undervotes are much more common in counties that use punchcard voting machines—as do 40 percent of the counties in Florida, containing 63 percent of the state's population. A punchcard ballot is tabulated by being run through a computer that trains a light or other electromagnetic beam on the ballot and records a vote for the candidate whose chad (a perforated area, usually rectangular, next to a candidate's name in a punchcard ballot, which the voter punches through to record a vote) has been punched out, permitting the beam to pass through the chad hole to the sensor that records the vote. The other counties, with minor exceptions, use the marksense ("optical scanning") system. The voter marks a paper ballot with a pencil. The ballot is then inserted into an optical scanner (very much like those used for the SAT, the LSAT, and other mass tests), which records the vote—and usually is programmed to reject an overvote. If the scanner is located in the polling place itself, the voter will have an opportunity to revote correctly when the scanner spits back his ballot because it is overvoted. But if the scanner is located in the county election office—that is, in the terminology that I will use, if the ballots are county-counted rather than precinct-counted—the voter will not have the opportunity to revote, because his ballot will have been placed in a sealed envelope at the polling place for shipment to the county election office.

The marksense method reduces the problem of undervoting be-

[5] An undervote is a ballot in which no vote has been recorded for a candidate for a particular office; an overvote is a ballot that contains votes for two or more candidates for the same office.

[6] Imagine flipping a fair coin 30,000 times. There would be a 95 percent probability that the number of heads and tails would be 15,000 plus or minus 174, since any greater deviation would be more than two standard deviations from the mean of 15,000.

cause it is easier to fill in the oval or circle on the marksense ballot than to punch through a chad on a punchcard ballot cleanly. But marksense technology solves the overvote problem only when the optical scanner is located in each precinct, which is not always the case. Punchcard votes can be counted at the precinct level as well, but this is less commonly done than when the marksense system is the one used.[7]

The Florida supreme court eventually ordered some 60,000 ballots recounted—twice my estimate of the number of recoverable undervotes. But the 60,000 figure is an estimate of *all* the Presidential undervotes statewide, and some of them were either deliberate or so inscrutable that no machine tabulator (or for that matter hand counter) could have extracted a vote from them. In addition, however, some fraction of the estimated 110,000 overvotes statewide, which the court decided not to have recounted, were, as we shall see, votes that a fair and competent hand counter, but not a machine, would have awarded to one or another Presidential candidate. Suppose that half the estimated statewide total of 170,000 undervotes and overvotes were votes that such a hand counter would have recovered from the ballots (that is, would have awarded to one of the candidates). Again, if those 85,000 votes split evenly between Bush and Gore, Bush would still have won. And though Gore would have had to win only a shade over 50.5 percent to have overcome Bush's lead, it is doubtful that a 50 percent recovery rate for undervotes is realistic. It is based on Broward's recount, which as we shall see used inappropriate criteria. And the use of the same recovery rate, indeed of any recovery rate, for the overvotes is complete guesswork, because there was no recount of overvotes—Gore did not want one.

So far—and critically—I have assumed an *infallible* hand counter. Whether the margin of error would have been narrowed by an actual recount of the votes by hand depends in part on the accuracy of hand counting compared with machine counting. Neither method is categorically superior to the other. Machines can be poorly designed, defectively manufactured, inadequately maintained, or poorly operated, and as a result of any or all of these shortcomings make many errors. There is, as we shall see, little evidence that the punchcard voting and tabulating machines in use in Florida are defectively manufactured, inadequately maintained, or poorly operated. But they are unforgiving of human error, and this could be regarded as a defect of design. Human counters, however, can be fatigued, biased, or simply unable to infer the voter's intent with any approach to certainty from a ballot that the machine refused to count; so they can make many errors

---

[7] The correlation between county-level (versus precinct-level) vote counting and use of the punchcard method is a highly significant .60.

too—some deliberate, which is beyond a machine's capacity. Republicans were entitled to be concerned about hand recounts by canvassing boards dominated by Democrats, and Democrats about hand recounts by Republican-dominated boards. A further problem is that both machine and hand counting can dislodge chads, which means that the very process of recounting introduces new errors even when the recounters, human or mechanical, are careful, competent, and neutral.

The closeness of the statewide results made it unlikely that hand counting, even if more accurate than machine counting, would break the statistical tie unless it produced a very large margin for one of the candidates. Suppose that hand counting correctly resolves half the errors in the machine count without introducing any new errors, so that the probability of error would shrink from 0.50 to 0.25 percent in a hand recount. (This is still assuming that the Broward County hand recount yielded an accurate estimate of the number of votes missed by the machine, and still defining errors curable by hand recount to include voter errors.) In other words, only about half the 30,000 undervotes statewide that I am assuming were miscounted by the machine would have been accurately counted as a vote for a Presidential candidate. Gore would have had to receive more than 53 percent of these 15,000 recovered votes to overcome Bush's 930-vote lead. (At 53 percent to Bush's 47 percent, Gore would have picked up a net of 900 votes.) Even if the 85,000 figure is used, and it is thus assumed that 42,500 votes would have been accurately counted in a hand recount, Gore would have had to receive more than 51 percent to have prevailed.[8]

This is possible, of course, but unlikely, and not only because of the uncertainties already discussed. The fact that Gore did not request a recount in any counties besides Broward, Palm Beach, Miami-Dade, and Volusia is evidence that he didn't think a recount in any of those other counties would have yielded net gains. It is true that he offered to agree to a statewide recount if Bush would agree to abide by the results. But he must have known that Bush would refuse, since agreeing would have entailed the surrender by Bush of options that he possessed to thwart a recount that went against him, notably the Florida legislature's appointing its own slate of Presidential electors pledged to Bush.

It is also true that in not seeking a statewide recount initially, Gore may have been concerned with the delay that such a recount would cause. But this could not have been his reason for asking for a recount in just four counties, rather than in five or six or eight or some other

[8] Assuming the other half of the undervotes or overvotes (those erroneously counted by fallible hand counters) were distributed randomly between the candidates, Gore would have won the election with an even lower percentage; but that would not have been a win based on an *accurate* recount.

number larger than four though well short of 67, the total number of counties in Florida. Since the recounts in the counties in which Gore did not request one would not have produced perfect ties, it is a fair inference that he thought such recounts would have produced a net gain for Bush, though maybe a smaller one than the gains that the recount in the Democratic-selected counties produced for Gore. "Maybe" becomes "probably" if we assume that Bush would have requested a statewide recount had he expected it to favor him; but the assumption may be erroneous. Bush may not have made such a request because it would have tended to validate the hand-recount method, and he could not be certain how a statewide hand recount would turn out, whereas he was certain that he had won the machine-tabulated vote. From his perspective, he had won the toss and now his opponent wanted to toss again, using a different (but not a more balanced) coin.

Still, the possibility that Gore would have received 51 percent of the miscounted votes statewide, or even 53 percent, cannot yet be excluded. Indeed, Gore probably would have overcome Bush's lead had the recounts been confined to the four counties picked by him—but only if those recounts had been administered in accordance with the criteria used by Broward County's board.

A number of alternative criteria for recovering a vote from an undervoted ballot by a hand recount, that is, by human inspection or interpretation, are possible. Surprisingly, there seems to be no agreement on which are proper. I array the alternatives in ascending order of liberality:

1. Count dangling (that is, hanging or swinging) chads but no dimpled chads.[9]
2. Count any chads if light can be seen through the chad hole.
3. Count dangling chads, plus dimpled chads, provided there are no fully punched chads.

---

[9] Some readers may need help with terminology at this point:

Hanging chad—A chad attached to the ballot by only one corner.
Swinging chad—A chad attached to the ballot by two corners.
Dangling chad—A hanging or a swinging chad.
Tri-chad—A chad attached to the ballot by three corners.
Dimpled (also known as pregnant) chad—A chad that, while bulging, indented, or marked, remains attached to the ballot by all four corners.
Pierced chad—A dimpled chad that is pierced. The term "dimpled chad" is sometimes reserved for an unpierced dimpled chad, and when that is done "pregnant chad" becomes the only designation for all chads, pierced or unpierced, that are attached to the ballot by all four corners.

A tri-chad is almost as equivocal as a dimpled chad, and I shall discuss the two types of chad together. I shall also not distinguish between pierced and dimpled chads (the two types of "pregnant" chad), although some pierced chads will pass a light test.

4. Count dimpled chads only if there are no fully or partly punched chads.
5. Count dangling chads, plus dimpled chads, provided there are several dimpled chads.
6. Count dangling chads plus all dimpled chads.
7. Count dangling chads plus all dimpled chads plus chads that are near an indentation or other mark (maybe made in pen or pencil rather than with the stylus that the voter is given to vote with), provided the counter feels able to discern the voter's intent from the character or location of the indentation or its relation to other marks on the ballot.

Palm Beach County seems to have moved from (2) to (1) to (5). Broward County used either (6) or (7), probably the latter. It is unclear which criteria Miami-Dade and Volusia Counties used.

Gore's net gain of 582 votes in the Broward County recount represented 0.15 percent of his total votes there. If the votes he received in the machine count in Palm Beach and Miami-Dade Counties are multiplied by the same percentage and added to his net gain in Broward, his aggregate net gain from hand recounting is 1,480 and overcomes Bush's 930-vote lead.[10] But the 1,480 figure is unreliable as a guide to who "really" won the election. To begin with, it is based on Gore's recovery of votes in the county in which he had his highest margin (67 percent) and so could be expected to obtain his highest percentage of recovered votes. Next, Democrats dominated the canvassing boards of all four counties. Close calls were therefore likely to favor Gore, and close calls were inevitable if the criteria used by Broward County were used in the other counties as well. The canvassing boards' political complexion also made it likely that they would use criteria (namely the Broward criteria) that maximized the number of votes recovered from the ballots that the machine tabulation had not counted. For as long as the recovered ballots divided in roughly the same proportions as the machine-counted ballots, the more ballots that had been rejected in the machine tabulation that were recovered in the hand recount, the greater would be Gore's net gain. Suppose that in some precinct Gore had received 7,000 votes in the machine tabulation and Bush 3,000, and 300 had been rejected in the machine tabulation, so that Gore led Bush in the machine-tabulated vote by 4,000 votes. If now the 300 were counted as votes, and they split in the same proportion as the votes that had been included in the tabulation, Gore

---

[10] Volusia County completed its hand recount before the November 14 statutory deadline for the completion of recounts and as a result the 98-vote net gain that it produced for Gore was included in calculating Bush's 930-vote margin. As we shall see, the Volusia recount probably produced an excessive net gain for Gore.

would get 210 more votes and Bush 90 more, increasing Gore's lead by 120 votes. This was doubtless why Gore demanded recounts only in counties in which he had received substantially more votes than Bush in the original count.

The Palm Beach County canvassing board refused to use the Broward criteria, and the Miami-Dade board seemed reluctant to do so. Had Miami-Dade used Palm Beach rather than Broward criteria, Gore would have received fewer than 1,480 votes, though probably enough to overtake Bush's lead, as we shall see.

Many of the disputed ballots could not be objectively read as votes, although the Republicans were on weak ground in arguing that *no* hand count of *any* rejected ballot could be so read. A dangling chad may not be recorded as a vote by the punchcard voting machine, yet it is fairly good evidence of an intent to vote for the candidate whose chad was punched (albeit not all the way through), provided the voter didn't also punch the chad of another candidate for the same office. But inferring a voter's intentions from a merely dimpled chad or, worse, from indentations next to a candidate's chad (rather than indentations on the chads themselves), is highly questionable. A faint dimple or other slight indentation might be created by the handling of the ballot or by its being repeatedly passed through the vote-counting machines. Or the voter may have started to vote for the candidate but then changed his mind, perhaps realizing he had made a mistake. There were many undecided voters in the 2000 Presidential election, some of whom may have gone into the voting booth still undecided and, in the end, "decided" that they could not make up their minds. And no doubt some voters—probably many more than the undecideds—misunderstood or simply neglected to comply with the ballot instructions, even though they were clear and if followed would assure that a vote would be registered. In the counties that used punchcard machines, not only was the voter instructed to punch a clean hole through the ballot (in Broward County, for example, the instruction was to "punch the stylus straight down through the ballot card for the candidates or issues of your choice"), he was also told to turn the ballot over after removing it from the voting machine and make sure there were no bits of paper stuck to it, that is, no dangling chads. But to follow instructions you have to be able to read them, and not all voters are literate. Voters voting on the basis of their recollection of oral instructions received from party activists would be bound often to make mistakes and spoil their ballots.

The punchcard method of voting also requires a minimum of manual dexterity, and some voters lack even that. But emphasis properly falls on "minimum." Since the ballot is softer than an airline boarding pass, the chad is perforated, and there is empty space beneath the ballot, it takes no strength to punch a clean hole, provided the machine is not defective, either because chads of previous voters have filled up the tray or because the holes in the lid (called the "template") of the tray are not aligned with the chads in the ballot.

The undervotes and overvotes were together only a small fraction of the total number of ballots cast in Florida. We are talking about the tail of a distribution of voting competence. The average performance in the tail may have been quite different from that in the rest of the distribution. It would not be surprising if a large fraction of the votes cast by the people in the tail had been cast by undecided, confused, clumsy, illiterate or semiliterate, or inexperienced (first-time) voters. The inference of voter error or indecision in casting punchcard ballots is especially compelling in the case of those undervoted ballots in which the voter punched through the chads of all the other candidates except the Presidential candidates, indicating that the punchcard voting machine itself was not defective. This was the ground on which the Palm Beach County canvassing board eventually decided to exclude such ballots from the recount totals while including those that had several (though apparently the number could be as small as three) dimpled chads. This was also why it would have been wrong for the Miami-Dade County canvassing board, had it decided to count dimpled ballots, to recount only the 10,750 undervotes revealed by the machine count of that county's ballots. Some of the ballots that had been counted for the Presidential candidate whose chad had been punched through may have contained a dangling chad of another Presidential candidate. A hand recount would discover that the voter had voted for two Presidential candidates (had cast, in other words, an overvote), voiding the ballot. We know there were many overvotes, and a ballot in which the voter punched both Presidential chads[11] yet left one dangling is just as persuasive evidence that the voter voted for both candidates as a dangling chad in an undervote is that the voter tried to vote for that candidate. Not that many people intentionally overvote; but when two chads are punched, the fact that one is still dangling is weak evidence that the voter was intending to vote for the other candidate, the one whose chad he punched through. It would not take a large percentage of overvotes by dangling chads, out of the more than 600,000 cast in Miami-Dade County, to offset defective ballots among the 10,750 undervoted ballots.

According to exit polls, which reflect what voters thought they did in the voting booth, at least 1 percent of the voters in Miami-Dade

[11] There were more than two Presidential candidates—in fact there were ten altogether, which was one of the rationales for, and one of the sources of confusion in, the "butterfly ballot" (of which more later). But for the sake of simplicity I will often pretend that there were just Bush and Gore.

County voted for other offices but not the Presidency.[12] If we assume that 6,000 (1 percent of the total vote in Miami-Dade) of the 10,750 undervoted ballots are those in which the voter made a deliberate choice not to vote for President, then fewer than 5,000 remain to be allocated between Bush and Gore. But that is also too many. It must include many ballots that were irrevocably spoiled: the voter wanted to vote for President but failed to do so because he made an error that no recount could dispel.[13]

In sum, unless very conservative criteria of vote recovery are used, a hand recount is bound to introduce new errors. And correct old ones? Surprisingly, this is far from certain. We must ask: what exactly is a voting "error" recoverable by a hand recount. A voting error is not a natural kind, like a star or a penguin or a blade of grass, which are things that exist independently of human cognition. A voting error is a legal category. The belief that it is possible without reference to law to determine who won the popular vote in Florida is the most stubborn fallacy embraced by the critics of the U.S. Supreme Court's intervention to resolve the deadlock.

The legal category "voting error" might be limited to an error in the machine tabulation: the ballot contains a cleanly, completely punched-through vote for Gore and for no other Presidential candidate, yet the counting machine somehow failed to record it as a vote for Gore. There is no evidence that such errors were common or favored either candidate. They make the best fit with the ordinary meaning of an error in tabulating the vote, however, and correcting them is an objective process. You just look for a cleanly, completely punched-through vote for one and only one Presidential candidate. We shall see in the second part of this essay that probably the best reading of the Florida election statute is that a voter's error is not an error in the tabulation of the vote. If that is right, there is very little doubt that Bush was the winner of the popular vote in Florida.

At the other extreme, a recoverable error might also be any improperly marked ballot that a human counter *thinks* (or says he thinks) contains an indication of whom the voter intended to vote for. That was Broward County's concept, and it is dangerously subjective.

In between is the concept of recoverable errors as including (besides ballots in the first category) improperly marked ballots that

---

[12] One estimate is 1.5 to 2 percent; "Election 2000: The Florida Vote," *CNN Live Event/ Special*, Nov. 28, 2000, 10 p.m. E.S.T., Transcript #00112809V54 (remark by Tom Fielder of the *Miami Herald*).

[13] The 1 percent estimate that I am using may be too high; inaccuracy in exit polling was apparently one reason for the erroneous projection on the evening of November 7 that Gore had won Florida; Howard Kurtz, *Errors Plagued Election Night Polling Service*, Washington Post A1 (Dec. 22, 2000).

nevertheless contain objective indicia of the voter's intention to vote for a particular Presidential candidate. This was the concept the Palm Beach County canvassing board eventually settled on when it decided to count as votes in undervoted ballots all dislodged chads plus dimpled chads in ballots that had at least three dimples. The idea was that three dimples composed a pattern suggestive of a deliberate effort to vote for the dimpled candidates. A more conservative method would have been to count dimples only in ballots in which no chads had been punched through, a pattern more clearly consistent with the voter's having tried to punch through and been thwarted, perhaps by a chad buildup or some other defect in the voting machine. Such a buildup would be more likely to hurt Gore than Bush in counties that Gore carried. There would be more chad buildup under Gore's name than Bush's, making dimpled votes more likely to have been intended for Gore than for Bush.

The methods used by the Palm Beach board produced either 176 or 215 extra votes for Gore; the Florida supreme court declined to decide which number was correct, leaving that question to be answered by the trial court in further proceedings that were interrupted before the question could be answered. Assume, favorably to Gore, that the higher number is correct. That number, 215, was 0.08 percent of the votes that the tabulating machinery had counted for Gore in Palm Beach County. Had the Broward and Miami-Dade canvassing boards used the Palm Beach method and produced the same percentage of additional votes for Gore, he would not have overtaken Bush's lead. His total gain in all three counties would have been only 788 votes (215 in Palm Beach as mentioned, 263 in Miami-Dade, and 310 in Broward). In addition, Gore would have had a net gain of only 78, not 98, votes in Volusia County, reducing his overall net gain from hand recounting in the four counties that he selected from 788 to 768, leaving Bush with a lead of 162.[14]

With politically neutral counters (if there are such animals), this number would be even smaller, though probably not much smaller, as the Palm Beach counters appear to have been conscientious. The 168 additional votes that Gore netted in Miami-Dade from the first 20 percent or so of the recounted precincts before the recount was in-

---

[14] Actually more, if the figures are adjusted to reflect the fact that Gore had a larger margin of victory in Broward County than in any of the other three counties. In Broward he won 67 percent of the vote, in Palm Beach 62 percent, and in Miami-Dade and Volusia Counties 53 percent. The figures used in the text are based on Palm Beach County. When they are multiplied by the ratio of Gore's margin in the other counties to his margin in Palm Beach County, he gets the same 215-vote gain in Palm Beach County of course, a 335-vote gain in Broward (67/62 × 310), 225 in Miami-Dade (53/62 × 263), and 67 in Volusia. The result is that Bush retains the lead by a 186-vote margin.

terrupted are a meaningless figure, because these precincts are far more heavily Democratic than the county as a whole. Had Miami-Dade completed a hand recount using Palm Beach rules, Gore could have overtaken Bush only if Broward's 582-vote gain for Gore from counting dimples were allowed to stand. Gore's total gain would then have been 1,060 (263 in Miami-Dade, 582 in Broward, and 215 in Palm Beach), and he would thus have won the election by 130 votes.

Of the disputed votes awarded to either Gore or Bush that yielded Gore's net gain of at most 215 votes in Palm Beach County, 61 percent went to Gore and 39 percent to Bush, compared with a 62/38 percent split of the total machine-counted Palm Beach vote. This suggests that Gore would have received no more than 50 percent of votes recovered in other hand recounts using Palm Beach rules, for that was his total in the machine count; and then of course he would not have overcome Bush's lead. This point also underscores the meaninglessness of the 168-vote gain for Gore from the partial recount in heavily Democratic precincts in Miami-Dade County. He received 70 percent of the additional votes recorded by the recount, though his margin in the county as a whole was only 53 percent. A complete recount might well have reduced the 70 percent margin in the partial count to 53 percent, if the Palm Beach results are representative.

An alternative method of estimating how many recovered votes each candidate might have received in a completed hand recount in the four counties is to compare Gore's vote gain in Palm Beach County with the number of disputed ballots in that county, 14,500. His maximum net gain of 215 votes from the recount of those ballots was only 1.5 percent of the number of ballots. The same percentage of the 10,750 undervoted ballots in Miami-Dade County would have given him a net gain of only 161 votes in that county, compared with 263 by my earlier method of calculation. And even the 161-vote estimate is inflated. Gore received a lower percentage of the total Gore-Bush vote in Miami-Dade County—53 percent, compared with 62 percent in Palm Beach County. If a 24 percent margin (62 – 38) would have yielded Gore 161 extra votes over Bush, a 6 percent margin (53 – 47) would have yielded him only 40.

It might make sense to average the machine-count and hand-recount results, since if their errors are independent, averaging the two results will cause many of the errors to cancel out. But averaging Bush's 930-vote machine lead with a smaller but still positive lead for Bush obviously would not swing the election to Gore.

To summarize the discussion to this point, an analysis of the election statistics indicates that a fair recount of undervotes (remember that Gore did not request and the Florida supreme court did not order that overvotes be recounted) would probably not have altered the result in Florida. This conclusion has since been confirmed by a careful recount, conducted by a media consortium, of all uncounted ballots in the election.[15]

Further insight into the likely consequences of the irregularities in the 2000 election process in Florida can be obtained by means of regression analysis of the spoiled ballots, which enables the effect of individual variables, such as race, literacy, income, and the voting technology employed, to be isolated.[16] We know there are more undervotes in Florida counties that use the punchcard ballot than in those that do not, but we want to know whether other factors besides the type of ballot might influence the number of undervotes, and, relatedly, how big the effect of the type of ballot is when other factors are accounted for. Taking the frequency of undervotes as the dependent variable, then, we want to see how it changes with changes in independent variables that might seem likely to influence it, such as the age or income or race of the voter. We are very interested in the statistical significance of the coefficients of the independent variables, that is, the probability that the sign of the coefficient (positive or negative) would be observed even if the coefficient was actually zero. The size of the coefficients, indicating the magnitude of the relation between the independent and dependent variables, is also very important.

The salient conclusions that emerged from the regression analysis conducted in my book were the following:

1. The choice of voting technology (punchcard versus other, in Florida generally marksense), and the choice to count votes at the precinct level rather than just at the county level, have a substantial influence on the frequency of undervotes and overvotes, respectively, even after correcting for other factors likely to influence these frequencies.
2. The punchcard ballot increases the frequency of undervotes, and counting votes just at the county level increases the frequency of overvotes.[17] The punchcard ballot may actually reduce the frequency of overvotes.
3. The correlated factors of race and literacy influence the frequency of overvotes, and in the predicted direction, suggest-

---

[15] See Joseph L. Gastwirth, *Book Review*, 1 Law, Probability & Risk 53, 65 (2002).

[16] I use the word "spoiled" loosely to include undervotes as well as overvotes, though some undervotes are deliberate nonvotes.

[17] When the vote is counted at the precinct, that is, at the polling place, and the marksense technology is used, the voter has, as explained earlier, a chance to revote if he spoils his first ballot by an overvote. In addition, the precinct election workers are more likely to look at the ballot when it is handed to them by the voter than if they are just putting it into a box for shipment to the county office, and they may notice that the ballot is an undervote or an overvote or otherwise incomplete or improperly completed and let the voter revote. This is an irregular practice that compromises the principle of the secret ballot, but it does occur.

ing that a recount of overvotes, though not sought by Gore, might well have yielded a significant net gain for him.[18]

4. There is no indication that defects in the punchcard voting machines themselves are responsible for many undervotes or overvotes.

5. The punchcard ballot tends to be the choice of more populous counties, and county-level counting the choice of the poorer counties. The latter correlation reinforces (because income and race are correlated) the likely racial effect of a county's decision to count votes at the county level only, although there is no indication that such choices are racially *motivated*.

6. The butterfly ballot used in Palm Beach County appears not to have increased the number of spoiled ballots significantly, although it was confusing, especially to voters with reading problems, and so probably hurt Gore. The distinction that the experience with the butterfly ballot underscores is between a *spoiled* ballot and a clean ballot containing an *unintended* vote.

When I conducted my original regression analysis, however, I did not have access to 2000 Census data for the demographic variables, such as race and income; there were several coding errors; and I had no data on the number of first-time voters, and instead used an imperfect proxy—the number of voters under the age of 25. These errors and omissions are corrected in the tables presented below; I shall focus my analysis on them and at the end ask how many of the conclusions from my original analysis, summarized above, hold up.[19]

As shown in Table 1(a), other things being equal, the punchcard technology actually *reduces* the likelihood of an overvote, though, as

---

[18] A finding confirmed in the media recount, see Gastwirth, 1 Law, Probability & Risk at 65 (cited at note 15), and by M. C. Herron and J. S. Sekhon, *Overvoting and Representation: An Examination of Overvoted Presidential Ballots in Broward and Miami-Dade Counties,* 22 Electoral Studies 21 (2003).

[19] My data source for number of voters, number of voters who hadn't voted in the six years preceding the 2000 election, number of first-time voters, and the percentage of voters who were black came from the Florida Voter File, originally available from the Florida Department of State but now available only to "municipalities or other governmental agencies, candidates, or political committees of continuous existence; and then only for political purposes or for law enforcement." The data on voting systems and ballot spoilage came from the Governor's Select Task Force on Election Procedures, Standards and Technology, conducted by the Collins Center for Public Policy (sporadically available at http://www.collinscenter.org/ingo-url2660/info-url.htm), and the percentage of votes for Gore came from the Florida Elections Division website: (http://election.dos.state.fl.us/elections/resultsarchive/Index.asp(last visited Dec 31, 2003)). Demographic data are from the 2000 Census. All the data are available from me upon request. In the tables showing the results of my regression analysis, one asterisk beside a coefficient indicates statistical significance at the 90 percent level, two at the 95 percent level, and three at the 99 percent level.

Table 1   Explaining the Overvotes and the Undervotes Separately

Independent Variable	(a) Overvotes		(b) Undervotes	
	Coefficient	t-stat.	Coefficient	t-stat.
Punchcard	−3.220***	−4.786	1.552***	5.778
County-counted	4.953***	7.513	−0.388	−1.475
Income	0.014	0.190	−0.017	−0.610
Hispanic	0.026	0.800	−0.020	−1.494
Black	0.129**	2.528	−0.020	−0.967
Literacy	0.027	0.239	−0.057	−1.267
Over 64	−0.025	−0.576	−0.021	−1.205
First-time Voter	−0.051	−1.011	−0.006	−0.297
Constant	−1.897	−0.247	6.386	2.018

$R^2 = .78$	$R^2 = .53$
Adjusted $R^2 = .73$	Adjusted $R^2 = .44$
F = 17.84	F = 5.76
Probability > F = 0.000	Probability > F = 0.001
N = 50	N = 50

expected, counting the ballots at just the county level increases it, and so does the percentage of the county population that is black. (None of the other independent variables is statistically significant.) The correlation between race and overvotes reinforces the inference that Gore would have picked up votes from a recount of overvotes, given the overwhelming black preference for Gore over Bush; exit poll data showing that blacks favored Gore by a margin of 93 percent to 7 percent.[20] Moreover, less literate voters are both more likely to overvote and more likely to vote Democratic, and there is a strong negative correlation in my data between literacy and being black (−.55).

How could the punchcard technology reduce the likelihood of an overvote, and thus help Gore? The answer is that if because a punchcard machine is defective, or because of a failure to follow instructions, lack of manual dexterity, general confusion, or indecision, some voters have difficulty punching through, which they would not have if they were using a marksense machine, there will be fewer overvotes. At the same time, however, the use of punchard machines should, and Table 1(b) indicates that it does, increase the likelihood of an undervote. None of the other independent variables is statistically significant in this equation—including the county-counting variable, the reason being that it is easier for a precinct election worker to spot an

[20] This may be something of an exaggeration, however. Blacks who vote Republican may be reluctant to acknowledge the fact, because of the strong social pressure on blacks in Florida to vote for Gore.

overvote as an error and thus invite the voter to vote again than to spot an undervote as an error. An undervote may be deliberate (the voter did not want to vote for President), whereas an overvote, except in the rare case in which it is intended as a protest vote, must be accidental. More important, many undervotes *are* deliberate, are not errors, and so will not be changed even if the voter has an opportunity to revote.

The opposite effects of the punchcard technology in the two equations in Table 1 complicate an overall assessment; as shown in Table 2, where the dependent variable is the sum of undervotes and overvotes, the punchcard and county-counted variables have opposite effects and the race variable ceases to be significant. Literacy, however (which is correlated with race), is marginally significant and in the expected direction.

The lack of significance of the type of voting machine used (that is,

Table 2   Explaining the Spoiled Ballots

Independent Variable	Coefficient	t-stat.
Punchcard	−1.188*	−2.001
County-counted	4.161***	6.666
Income	0.034	0.528
Hispanic	−0.019	−0.614
Black	0.043	1.055
Literacy	−0.175*	−1.797
Over 64	−0.089**	−2.320
First-time Voter	−0.054	−1.109
Constant	16.123	2.518

$$R^2 = .76$$
$$\text{Adjusted } R^2 = .72$$
$$F = 20.69$$
$$\text{Probability} > F = 0.000$$
$$N = 62$$

whether it is a punchcard machine or a marksense machine) and the significant negative effect of literacy on the percentage of spoiled votes suggest that the undervotes and overvotes are a consequence mainly of voter error rather than of defects in the voting machines. The instructions for voting were clear—if you could read. If you had difficulty reading, you could easily make a mistake that would spoil the ballot. Further evidence in support of this conclusion is provided by the fact that when the Broward, Palm Beach, and Miami-Dade canvassing boards asked for an extension of the deadline for completing the hand recounts and submitting final vote totals to the secretary of state, they did not offer as a reason that any of the punchcard voting machines had been defective—though that would have been the best reason they could have given.

The magnitude of the effects identified by Table 1 given by the size as distinguished from the sign of the coefficients of the independent variables. The coefficients in that table estimate the number of percentage points that each variable adds to the percentages of undervotes and overvotes (the dependent variables[21]). The average percentage of undervotes in counties that do not use the punchcard ballot is only 0.55 percent, and so the effect of the punchcard variable (the coefficient of which is 1.55 percent) is substantial—it almost quadruples the undervote percentage. The average percentage of overvotes in counties that count the votes at the precinct level is 0.28 percent, and the coefficient of the county-counted variable is 4.95 percent, an almost 19-fold increase.

Various transformations are possible to test the robustness of the regression results, such as transforming the variables (other than the dummy variables) into natural logarithms in order to reduce the weight of extreme observations, which may be unrepresentative, or weighting the observations by the population of each county, rather than to give each county equal weight (the rationale being that the smaller a county's population is, the more likely random factors are to influence the number of spoiled ballots—and the population of Florida counties varies from less than 6,000 to almost two million) or to weight the observations by the number of votes cast per county; but none of these observations make a material difference.

The emphasis that I have placed on race is potentially misleading because of the strong negative correlation between race and income and race and literacy. It is surely not because black people in Florida are racially distinct, but because they are poorer and less literate on average, that they would be likely to encounter greater difficulty than whites in coping with user-unfriendly voting systems. One can get at this problem of correlated variables by rerunning some of the regressions with fewer variables, omitting ones that either have little effect in the earlier regressions or are highly correlated with other variables. This is done in Table 3. Notice that despite the omissions (and tending to validate them), the equations continue to provide a good fit between the dependent and independent variables. Notice, too, how similar the results are to those of the earlier regressions. In the spoiled-ballots equation, the punchard, county-counted, and literacy variables are all significant and in the same direction as in Table 2. These ef-

---

[21] These percentages are actually decimals in the regressions, as are the coefficients of the independent variables.

Table 3   Regressions with Omitted Variables

Independent Variable	Spoiled		Overvotes		Undervotes	
	Coefficient	t-stat.	Coefficient	t-stat.	Coefficient	t-stat.
Punchcard	−1.386**	−2.432	−3.228***	−5.132	1.166***	6.296
County-ctd.	4.324***	7.069	5.149***	7.804		
Income					0.036**	−2.318
Literacy	−0.202***	−5.040	−0.112**	−2.402		
Over 64	−0.119***	−0.295	−0.096***	−2.972		
Constant	19.160	6.000	10.861	2.892	1.700	3.340

	Spoiled	Overvotes	Undervotes
	$R^2 = .73$	$R^2 = .73$	$R^2 = .45$
	Adjusted $R^2 = .71$	Adj. $R^2 = .71$	Adj. $R^2 = .43$
	F = 39.53	F = 30.88	F = 20.32
	Prob > F = 0.000	Prob > F = 0.000	Prob > F = 0.000
	N = 63	N = 51	N = 53

fects persist in the separate equation for overvotes, which in addition shows a pronounced effect of age in reducing the incidence of overvotes, probably because older voters are more experienced. Notice that in the undervote equation, an increase in income reduces the incidence of undervotes; this is as expected.

Some voters in Palm Beach County who cast ballots that the machine counted were apparently misled by the "butterfly" punchcard ballot used in that county and mistakenly voted for Buchanan when they meant to vote for Gore.[22] The design of the ballot, in which the candidates were listed on both sides of the ballot rather than all on one side, was the brainchild of the Democratic supervisor of elections for the county. Her aim was to enable the candidates' names to be printed in large type, in consideration of the number of elderly voters in the county, while at the same placing before the voter all the candidates for each office on a pair of facing pages; presumably overvotes would be less likely than if there were candidates for the same office on different pages. Another ballot design might thus have disenfranchised some voters who had poor eyesight, who cast their vote before realizing there were additional candidates for the same office on the next page of the ballot, or who cast two votes for candidates for the same office because they failed to realize that there were candidates for the same office on different pages.

[22] See, for statistical evidence, Kevin Quinn and Mark S. Handcock, *Did Your Vote Count?* http://www.csss.washington.edu/csss-spr01.voting.html (visited March 4, 2001), and studies cited there. The early reports by the media that these were mainly elderly Jewish voters are undermined by my regression results, which suggest that age does not lead to mistakes in voting.

Yet, although well intentioned, the design of the ballot does seem to have been, on balance, confusing. Bush was listed first on the left-hand side of the ballot and Gore second, while Buchanan was listed first on the right-hand side, between Bush and Gore rather than opposite Bush. Since the candidates' chads were in the middle of the ballot, Buchanan's chad was between Bush's and Gore's. A voter who wanted to vote for Gore had to punch the third chad down; if he punched the second, which was almost level with the word "Democratic" above Gore and Lieberman's names, he was voting for Buchanan. This would be an easy mistake to make, especially for an inexperienced voter or one with poor eyesight, even though the butterfly format enables larger type and in that respect helps people with poor eyesight. Some voters probably didn't even realize that the names on the right-hand side of the ballot were names of other Presidential candidates. Looking just at the left-hand side, they saw Bush listed first and Gore second and, if they wanted to vote for Gore, punched the second chad from the top.

The error of the butterfly design was irremediable for purposes of deciding who won the 2000 election, however. Not only would altering the outcome of an election on the basis of the confusing design of the ballot open a Pandora's box of election challenges, but there was no reliable method of determining within any reasonable deadline for selecting Florida's electors the actual intent of these voters. A new ballot would have had to be designed, approved, and printed, and arrangements made for reopening and restaffing the polling places and retabulating the votes in the new election, all within a few weeks. The holding of a second election would also have required congressional action, because federal law designated November 7 as the day for selecting each state's electors in 2000.[23] The butterfly ballot may have exacerbated the problem of spoiled ballots. This is not certain; indeed, the likeliest consequence of its misleading design would have been to produce a "clean" vote for Buchanan, which no hand recount could recover for Gore. But it is possible that its confusing character would increase the rate of spoliation. That possibility is examined in Table 4, a repeat of Table 2 with the addition of a dummy variable that takes a value of 1 if the butterfly ballot was used (or, equivalently, if the vote was cast in Palm Beach County, the only county to use the butterfly ballot) and 0 otherwise.

The results are similar to those in Table 2. Although the butterfly ballot has a positive effect on the percentage of spoiled ballots, the effect is statistically significant only at the 10 percent level and it is not a sufficiently large effect to alter the size or significance of the other variables.

[23] 3 U.S.C. § 1.

Table 4   Regression of Spoiled Ballots with Butterfly Ballot

Independent Variable	Coefficient	t-stat.
Punchcard	−1.266**	−2.177
Butterfly	3.122*	1.666
County-counted	4.112***	6.736
Income	0.019	0.300
Hispanic	−0.018	−0.600
Black	0.043	1.077
Literacy	−0.168*	−1.764
Over 64	−0.096**	−2.528
First-time Voter	−0.055	−1.169
Constant	16.218	2.592

$$R^2 = .77$$
$$\text{Adjusted } R^2 = .73$$
$$F = 19.66$$
$$\text{Probability} > F = 0.000$$
$$N = 62$$

Thus the basic problem that gave rise to well-founded concerns with the adequacy of Florida's electoral processes was nothing to do with machine error as such or even the design of the ballot; it was the use in 40 percent of Florida's counties of a voting technology that, despite the abolition of literacy tests for voting, puts a premium on literacy, and the decision of 65 percent of the counties to count votes at the county election office rather than at the precinct, a procedure that makes it impossible to catch voter errors in time for the voter to revote. The choice by some counties of punchcard technology, and of centralized vote counting, not only hurt Gore but hurt him through disenfranchising a disproportionate percentage of blacks who were eligible to vote. This was bound to arouse the black community because of the long history of denying the suffrage to blacks, particularly in the South. If punchcard technology had been replaced throughout Florida by marksense technology, if all votes had been counted at the precinct level, if the butterfly ballot had not been used in Palm Beach County (a county in which Gore ran very strongly despite the ballot), and if the polling places had been better staffed and party activists had instructed their voters more carefully, it is quite likely that Gore would have won the popular vote in Florida on November 7 and would thus have become President without any recounting or litigation.

Stated differently, if the question is what percentage of the people who voted in the Florida election thought they were voting for Gore, the probable answer is more than 50 percent. He may therefore have won a moral victory, though it does not follow that he should have won a legal one; the winner of the "what if" or the "might have been" election need not be the winner of the actual election. But is "moral victory" quite the right term? To speculate responsibly on who would have won a game conducted under different rules requires considering how the players would have adapted their strategies to the different rules. Suppose the populous Democratic-leaning counties in Florida had switched from the punchcard to the marksense voting method *before* the election. Wouldn't Republicans in Florida have warned Bush that there was likely to be a bigger Democratic vote in those counties than if the punchcard method had been retained? And in response to this warning might not Bush have shifted campaign resources from safe Republican states to those counties? Might not this shift have redressed the balance? Unless these questions can be answered, it is impossible to say whether Gore would actually have won if all Florida counties had used marksense voting technology.

The choice of voting technology and counting site cannot be attributed to deliberate racial discrimination or even to indirect discrimination, as might be inferred if the choice were correlated with literacy. Table 5 regresses the ballot and counting-site variables on population and income.[24] The regressions reveal a positive though only marginally significant correlation between punchcard and population, holding income constant, and a significant negative correlation between county-counted and income, holding population constant.

Table 5   Probit Regression of Ballot and Counting Variables

Independent Variable	(1) Punchcard		(2) County-Counted	
	Coefficient	z-statistic	Coefficient	z-statistic
Population (thou)	0.0015*	1.907	0.010	1.342
Income	−0.0129	−0.410	−0.0814**	2.539
Constant	−0.1773	−0.178	2.7822	2.733
	Pseudo R^2 = 0.07		Pseudo R^2 = 0.09	
	LR = 5.74		LR = 7.48	
	Prob > LR = 0.06		Prob > LR = 0.02	
	N = 65		N = 65	

[24] The probit regression model is used because the dependent variables are dummies. LR (likelihood ratio) corresponds to F in a conventional linear regression. The population and income variables have been rescaled to avoid zero coefficients. Regressions of the dependent variables on additional independent variables did not produce any significant correlations and so are not shown.

Poorer counties are more likely to centralize counting because it is more economical than counting at each precinct and then merging the results; smaller staffs and, especially, fewer tabulating machines are required. Why the more populous counties are drawn to the punch-card ballot is less clear, but inquiry of election officials suggests the following reason. When computerized vote tabulation first became feasible in the 1960s, the more populous counties adopted it first because hand counting is slower the more votes there are to be counted, and the only system of computerized vote tabulation available at the time was the punchcard system.[25] The counties that adopted that system were loath to switch later on, when new and better technology became available on the market, because of the cost of buying new equipment when the old was still serviceable. This is an additional reason for believing that any discriminatory effect of the punchcard system, as of county rather than precinct counting, in the Florida 2000 election was unintentional.

III. THE LITIGATION

Florida's election statute entitles a candidate, after the machine re-count, to demand that a county's election board recount by hand a sample of the ballots cast in the county. If the hand recount reveals an "error in the vote tabulation" that may have affected the outcome of the election, the board is authorized to undertake various remedial measures, including a hand recount of all the ballots cast in the county. Gore as we know demanded the sample recount in four heavily Democratic counties (Miami-Dade, Palm Beach, Broward, and Volusia), and when these recounts revealed numerous instances in which voters, by not punching cleanly through the chad of a Presidential candidate,[26] had failed to cast a vote for the candidate which the tabulating machines would record, Gore requested a full hand recount in each of the four counties. The request was granted by each county's election board and the full hand recounts began.

The election statute requires final submission of the county vote

[25] National Clearinghouse of Election Administration, *Voting System Standards: A Report on the Feasibility of Developing Voluntary Standards for Voting Equipment* 10-11 (Federal Election Commission 1984); Roy G. Saltman, *Effective Use of Computing Technology in Vote-Tallying* 10-12 (U.S. Department of Commerce, National Bureau of Standards, March 1975); Eric A. Fischer, *Voting Technologies in the United States* (Congressional Research Service, Report for Congress, RL 30773, Jan. 11, 2001), http://www.cnie.org/nle/rsk-55.html (last visited Dec 31, 2003). In addition, although this is not mentioned in the literature, more populous counties are likely to have more candidates and offices, and that too would slow down hand counting.

[26] All but Volusia County (the smallest) used the punchcard voting technology.

totals to the state division of elections within seven days of the election (with an exception for overseas ballots). Only Volusia County completed a full hand recount by then and so was able to include the results in the final vote totals that it submitted to the state election division. Katherine Harris, who as Florida's secretary of state was the state's highest election official, refused to extend the statutory deadline to enable the other three counties to submit their totals. She ruled that the deadline could be extended only in exigent circumstances, such as a natural disaster that had interfered with vote counting or recounting, that were not present in the 2000 election.

The election statute neither sets forth grounds for an extension of the statutory deadline nor defines the key statutory phrase "error in the vote tabulation." Nor does it specify the criteria to be used in a hand recount to recover votes from ballots spoiled by voter error, although it does say that in the case of "damaged" or "defective" ballots a vote shall be recorded if there is a "clear indication of the intent of the voter."[27] What the statute does do is authorize the state election officials both to interpret and to apply the statute. The head of the division of elections, Katherine Harris's subordinate Clayton Roberts, used his interpretive authority to rule that voter errors are not errors in the vote *tabulation* (just as Harris herself had used the interpretive authority conferred on her by the statute to limit the grounds for extending the statutory deadline for recounts). As a result, there was no legal basis for a full hand recount in any of the four counties, none of the county election boards having based its request for a waiver of the statutory deadline on a defect in the design, maintenance, or operation of the tabulating machines.

Had these rulings stood, Bush would on November 18, 2000, after the addition of the late-arriving overseas ballots to the total, have been declared the winner of the popular vote in Florida by 930 votes. But before this happened, Gore brought suit to extend the statutory deadline for counting the votes. He lost in the lower court. The judge ruled that Harris had not abused her discretion (the canonical standard for judicial review of administrative action—and a good example of Hans Kelsen's concept of law as a ladder of delegations) by refusing to extend the deadline. But on November 21 the Florida supreme court reversed the trial court and ordered the deadline extended to November 26. The court relied in significant part on a provision of the Florida constitution which states, though without mention of voting, that "all political power is inherent in the people." The court not only extended

---

[27] Citations to these and other statutory (and constitutional) provisions, as well as to the various judicial decisions, may be found in Posner, *Breaking the Deadlock* at ch 3 (cited in note 2).

the deadline to a date of its choosing but ruled that in any recount conducted during the enlarged period voter-spoiled ballots should be counted as valid votes as long as the voter's intended choice of candidate was discernible.

Within the extended deadline Broward County completed a full hand recount that produced many new votes for Gore. After inclusion of Broward's results, and other adjustments, Harris on November 26 proclaimed Bush the winner of the Florida popular vote by a meager 527 votes.

Florida's election statute authorizes the bringing of a suit to contest the election result certified by the secretary of state. One of the grounds for such a suit, and the only one relevant to the 2000 Presidential election, is that not all "legal votes," a term characteristically left undefined by the statute, had been recorded. Gore brought a contest suit, complaining principally about the Miami-Dade election board's having abandoned its hand recount because unable to complete it within even the court-extended deadline of November 26. He also contended that the results of the recount by the Palm Beach election board (which showed a net gain of either 176 or 215 votes for Gore—probably the former, but this has never been determined), which was completed only hours after the extended deadline expired, should have been included in the final vote totals. He further complained that the Palm Beach board had used too stringent a standard for recovering votes from voter-spoiled ballots. It had, we recall, refused to count dimpled ballots as votes unless the ballot showed at least three dimples, a pattern the board thought indicated that the voter had been trying to vote in this fashion, as distinguished from having dimpled a chad inadvertently or having failed to punch it all the way through because of a last-minute change of mind about voting for that candidate.

The trial judge found that the Miami-Dade board had not abused its discretion in deciding to abandon the recount, because there was no reason to think a fair hand recount would produce a large enough gain for Gore to make him the winner of the popular vote in the state. (In hindsight, the judge appears to have been correct.) The Palm Beach board's choice of criteria to use in its recount was not an abuse of discretion either. The trial had confirmed that the spoiled ballots were due to voter errors, or to errors in which the voter was at least complicit (for example, for failing to seek assistance from polling-place personnel if unable to punch through a chad because of chad buildup in the tray of the punchcard voting machine), rather than to errors in the design, maintenance, or operation of the tabulating machinery. The trial had also revealed that there was no agreed-upon standard in Florida law for when to record dimples as votes. Dimples had never previously been recorded as votes in a Florida election.

Meanwhile the Florida supreme court's decision of November 21 extending the deadline for submission of final county vote totals had been appealed to the U.S. Supreme Court. The Court agreed to hear the appeal and on December 4 handed down a unanimous decision vacating the Florida court's decision and sending the case back to that court for further consideration. The Court relied on a provision of Article II of the U.S. Constitution (it is section 1, clause 2) which says that a state shall appoint its Presidential electors in the manner directed by the state's legislature. The Court interpreted this "manner directed" clause to forbid a state court to usurp the legislature's prerogative of determining the criteria of appointment. The Court thought the Florida court might have done this in using the "all political power is inherent in the people" provision of the state constitution to support its decision overriding the judgments of the state election officials. But the Court wasn't sure and so it sent the case back to the Florida court for clarification that was not immediately forthcoming.

Eventually, on December 11, the Florida court issued its "clarifying" opinion. The opinion states that the decision of November 21 had actually been based on the "plain language" of the election statute, but does not explain why, if so, that decision had placed so much weight on the "people power" provision of the state constitution. Moreover, what the court seems to have meant by its reference to "plain language" was not, as in the usual understanding of the plain-meaning standard of statutory interpretation, that the language of the statute unequivocally supported its decision, but rather that the decision did no violence to the statute's language because the language was vague. If it was vague, however—and it *was* vague—the court should have deferred to the interpretation of the state election officials. The fact that they were partisan Republicans did not disentitle them to the usual deference that reviewing courts grant to administrative decisions interpreting vague statutes that the administrative agency is responsible for enforcing. The Florida legislature had decided to make the secretary of state an elected official; elected officials are entitled to at least as much judicial deference as bureaucrats, and probably, because of their greater democratic legitimacy, more. And the election board in Miami-Dade County that had decided to abandon the hand recount was dominated by Democrats, not Republicans.

The trial judge's decision throwing out Gore's contest suit had also been issued on December 4 and on the eighth the Florida supreme court reversed, though this time by a vote of four to three (the November 21 decision had been unanimous). The court (which was rather jumping the gun, since it had not yet responded to the Supreme Court's request for clarification of its position) rejected the central thesis of the trial judge's decision. This was that the determination of whether the certified vote totals had excluded enough "legal votes" to change the outcome of the election was one for the state and local election officials to make, subject to judicial review only for abuse of discretion. The court ruled that the judgments of the election officials were entitled to *no* weight. This meant that the election outcome certified by the secretary of the state, even though it was the outcome produced by the court's own extension of the statutory deadline, had not been entitled to even a presumption of correctness in the contest proceeding. But if so, why had the court bothered to extend the deadline, thereby compressing the period for completion of the contest, including any further recount that a judgment in the contest suit might direct?

Unsatisfied that all "legal votes" had been counted, the state supreme court in its December 8 opinion (1) directed that the Palm Beach recount results, along with the partial results of the interrupted Miami-Dade recount, be added to the candidates' totals, a step that pushed Bush's lead below 200 votes; (2) ordered that all the undervoted ballots in the state, some 60,000, be recounted by hand, including the balance of the Miami-Dade ballots, but (3) directed that the recounting be done by judicial personnel throughout the state rather than by the county election boards or state election officials; (4) refused to establish criteria for recovering votes from spoiled ballots more specific than the intent of the voter; and (5) refused to authorize a recount of overvoted ballots. Those are ballots that contain votes or markings interpreted or interpretable as votes for more than one candidate for the same office. There were about 110,000 overvotes.

This decision the U.S. Supreme Court stayed the next day and reversed on December 12 in *Bush v. Gore.* A five-Justice majority (Rehnquist, O'Connor, Scalia, Kennedy, and Thomas) held that the recount order was a denial of the equal protection of the laws. The decision held that rulings (1), (2), (4), and (5) created arbitrary differences in the treatment of different voters' ballots. The normal remedy in such a case would be a remand to the lower court with instructions to purge its order of the unconstitutional features. Alternatively the Court might have specified the terms of a recount order that would satisfy the requirements of equal protection. Instead it declared that Florida law forbade resumption of the recount because it could not be completed by December 12. Of course not—the U.S. Supreme Court's decision was not issued until the night of December 12. With the recount killed, Bush's lead of 527 votes stood, making him the winner of Florida's electoral votes, and so, when the votes of the Electoral College were counted in January, of the Presidential election.

The significance of December 12 was that it was the "safe harbor" deadline under Title III of the U.S. Code, the Electoral Count Act, which is the statute that specifies the procedures for counting the electoral votes. Each state is to vote on December 18 and the votes are to be counted on January 6.[28] If a state appoints its electors by December 12, they cannot be challenged when Congress meets to count the electoral votes. The Florida supreme court's opinions in the election litigation had seemed to treat December 12 as the deadline for picking the state's electors, lest the pick be rejected by Congress. These intimations were the basis for the five-Justice majority's ruling in *Bush v. Gore* that as a matter of Florida law the recount could not resume.

Two Justices, Souter and Breyer, agreed that the recount order raised problems of equal protection that required a remedy but thought the proper remedy would be to send the case back to the Florida court for the design and conduct of a proper recount. Three of the Justices in the majority (Rehnquist, Scalia, and Thomas) opined that in addition to violating equal protection the recount order violated the "manner directed" clause of Article II of the Constitution. Souter and Breyer disagreed. The remaining Justices, Stevens and Ginsburg, disagreed that the recount order violated any constitutional provision.

What would have happened had the Supreme Court not resolved the election deadlock on December 12, 2000? This was and is unclear; but it has a definite bearing on the evaluation of the decision in *Bush v. Gore*. Here is a worst-case scenario that is by no means fantastic, or even highly improbable:

The recount is resumed on December 13, the Supreme Court having affirmed the Florida supreme court's order, and it results in a determination that Gore is the winner of the Florida popular vote. True, as we saw in the first part of this chapter, it now looks as if the recount would have confirmed Bush's victory. But that is on the assumption that it would have been conducted in as neutral and careful a fashion as the recount conducted by the National Opinion Research Center for a media consortium over a period of nine months. That is a heroic assumption, if only because of the extreme haste with which the real recount would have had to be conducted. That recount might well have given Gore the lead.

Next in the worst-case scenario that I am sketching, the state supreme court holds that Gore has indeed won the election and directs Jeb Bush, the Governor of Florida, to certify that the votes of the electors pledged to Gore are the votes to be submitted to Congress. By now, however, because the statewide recount and judicial review of it could not be completed within a week, December 18 has come and gone. It

---

[28] These dates are not specified in the Act. They happen to be the dates in 2000 picked out by the provisions of the Act that set forth the timetable for the decision stages specified in it.

is unclear whether electoral votes cast after that day can be counted at all, because the Constitution provides that all the electoral votes are to be cast on the same day, which in 2000 was December 18. Meanwhile the Florida legislature, dominated by Republicans, has appointed a slate of electors pledged to Bush. It has done that in reliance on a provision of the Electoral Count Act that authorizes the state legislature to select the electors if the normal state procedure (the popular election held on November 7) has failed to do so.

The Act provides that the newly elected Congress shall on its first day (January 6, in 2001) meet in joint session for the counting of the electoral votes, but that the two houses shall then meet separately to resolve any challenges to any of the electoral votes that the states have cast. (That is the nature of a bicameral legislature; the two houses vote separately.) The House is Republican, but the Senate is divided 50-50 and until January 20 the Democrats control it by virtue of the Vice President's authority to vote to break ties; for Gore retains his office until then. The Electoral Count Act provides that if the two houses cannot agree on the resolution of a dispute involving rival slates of electors—given the split control of Congress, a likely outcome in January 2001 had it not been for the Supreme Court's intervention—the electoral votes certified by the state governor shall be the ones counted. The Florida supreme court has ordered Jeb Bush to certify the Gore slate but he has balked and certified the George W. Bush slate instead. The court has responded by holding him in contempt and declaring his certification a nullity and the Gore slate the one legally certified by the governor. The governor remains defiant, so two slates of electors attempt to cast Florida's electoral votes.

The houses of Congress, being controlled by different parties, cannot agree on which slate to accept. Nor can the houses agree on what happens if *no* electoral votes from Florida are counted because the impasse remains unresolved. Does Gore win because he has a majority of the electoral votes that are counted, or does the fact that neither candidate has an absolute majority of those votes throw the election into the House of Representatives, where Bush would win? The Constitution is unclear, and the Electoral Count Act silent, on the question. The U.S. Supreme Court refuses to intervene, invoking the "political questions" doctrine, pursuant to which courts will refuse to resolve an issue if its resolution has been confided to another branch of government and if it lacks the characteristics of a justiciable controversy.[29] The Constitution puts the counting of electoral votes in

---

[29] See Alexander M. Bickel, *The Least Dangerous Branch: The Supreme Court at the Bar of Politics* 185-186 (Yale, 2d ed 1986); Posner, *Breaking the Deadlock* at 182-184 (cited in note 2).

the hands of Congress with no hint of a judicial role and with no indication of a standard that a court might use to resolve a dispute over those votes.

On January 20, the deadlock still unresolved, an Acting President is appointed, probably Lawrence Summers, the Secretary of the Treasury.[30] The order of appointment is Speaker of the House, President pro Tempore of the Senate, Secretary of State, and Secretary of the Treasury (there is no need to dip further into the list, which goes on and on). But anyone who accepts the appointment must resign his office, including membership in Congress in the case of the Speaker and the President pro Tempore. Neither the Speaker of the House (Hastert) nor the President pro Tempore of the Senate (Thurmond) would be likely to accept the appointment under these conditions, the latter because his resignation from the Senate would give control of the Senate to the Democrats. Madeleine Albright, the Secretary of State, is ineligible for the appointment because foreign born.[31]

It is true that the scenario that leads to the appointment of Summers assumes that a Vice President has not been selected, since, if he has been, he becomes Acting President.[32] But it is unlikely that a Vice President would have been picked by January 20. The Twelfth Amendment provides that if no candidate for Vice President receives a majority of electoral votes, the Senate shall choose the Vice President— but to win, a candidate must receive a majority of the entire Senate, and the 50-50 split in the Senate would prevent this. (The Vice President is not a member of the Senate, and so he could not vote to break this tie.) And this is on the assumption that it has somehow been resolved that neither candidate obtained a majority of the electoral votes, an issue itself likely to be deadlocked.

Who becomes Acting President is actually a detail from the standpoint of deciding who shall become President. No constitutional or statutory provision authorizes the appointment of an Acting Vice President, and so there would be no one to break Senate ties, making it unclear, therefore, how, or when, the deadlock over the Presidency would be resolved.

Had the worst-case scenario that the decision averted come to pass, the forty-third President would have taken office after long delay, with no transition, with greatly impaired authority, perhaps amidst unprecedented partisan bickering and bitterness, leaving a trail of poisonous suspicion of covert deals and corrupt maneuvers, and after an

---

[30] See Posner, *Breaking the Deadlock* at 137-139 (cited in note 2).

[31] In my book I expressed uncertainty over whether her ineligibility for the Presidency would carry over to the position of Acting President, See id at 138 n. 83, but I was wrong to be uncertain. I had overlooked 3 USC § 19(e).

[32] US Const Amend XX, § 3.

interregnum unsettling to the global and the U.S. domestic economy and possibly threatening to world peace. How would the crisis over the Chinese seizure of our surveillance plane have been resolved by Acting President Summers? And would other hostile foreign powers or groups have tried to test us during the interregnum? Imagine if the terrorist attacks on the United States that occurred on September 11, 2001, had occurred on January 11 instead, amidst acrimonious debate in Congress over who would be the next President.

The potential harm to the nation from allowing the 2000 Presidential election deadlock to drag on into and maybe even after January 2001 was not the only arresting feature of *Bush v. Gore.* Another was the conflict of interest that all the Supreme Court Justices had in participating in the decision of the case. Judges are not indifferent to who their colleagues and successors are likely to be, and the identity of the President is bound to make a difference—nowadays, given the dependence of Presidential candidates on the good will of the extremists in their parties, especially in appointments matters, probably a big difference—in the kind of person chosen to fill a vacancy on the Supreme Court. Presidents tend to propose and promulgate centrist policies but to throw a bone to the extreme wing of their party when it comes to appointments. Another arresting (and disturbing) feature of the litigation was the absence of an obvious handle in the Constitution for stopping the recount. These two features turn out to be interrelated and so I shall discuss them together.

If the conservative Justices threw their weight behind Bush, as they did, they would be accused of partisanship, as they were, and the prestige and hence authority of the Supreme Court would suffer, as they have, though the damage seems unlikely to be great in the long run.[33] The damage would have been less had the conservative Justices managed to write a convincing opinion in defense of their position. Neither the per curiam majority opinion nor the concurring opinion of Chief Justice Rehnquist (joined by Scalia and Thomas) is convincing. The majority opinion adopts a ground (the equal protection clause of the Fourteenth Amendment) that is neither persuasive in itself nor consistent with the judicial philosophy of the conservative Justices, particularly the three just named, who joined the majority opinion without stated reservation while writing separately. Neither opinion discusses the pragmatic benefit of ending the deadlock, though without that benefit it is hard to see why the Supreme Court agreed to take the case (the Court's jurisdiction is discretionary), let alone why it de-

---

[33] Perhaps for an adventitious reason—the September 11, 2001, terrorist attacks, which focused the nation away from the 2000 election. But even before then, it was apparent, as I'll point out later, that the Court had not suffered a severe blow to its prestige.

cided it as it did. The Court's self-inflicted wound was deepened by
Justice Scalia's action in writing an unconvincing opinion in support
of the stay of the Florida supreme court's December 8 decision. That
action cast Scalia—the Justice praised by name along with Thomas
during the Presidential campaign by Bush and denounced by name,
again along with Thomas, by Gore as a "code word" for opposition to
abortion rights—in the role of the ringleader of a conservative cabal
determined to elect Bush. The wound was also deepened by the tone
of the dissents, particularly Stevens's. Scalia should have realized
that if there was no explanation accompanying the grant of the stay,
the punches in Stevens's dissent would have landed on air. Observers
would have assumed that the Court had reasons for what it did, and
in time plausible reasons would have been conjectured.

Should the Justices have worried that future controversies over appointments to the Court would be embittered by the perceived partisanship of the decision? Probably not, if only because bitter confir-
mation battles are likely for other reasons—reasons connected to the
inescapably pragmatic character of the Supreme Court's constitutional decisions. Long before *Bush v. Gore*, it was understood that the
law crafted by the Supreme Court, especially but not only when the
Court is interpreting vague provisions of the Constitution, is not sta-
bilized by text or precedent or the other tools of formalist judging.
Supreme Court Justices have and exercise broad discretion, however
much they deny it and pretend to be following the dictates of an-
tecedently established principles traceable back to the constitutional
text. That is why ideology rather than competence is the focus of con-
firmation hearings for nominees to the Supreme Court.

Between purely personal or partisan considerations on the one hand
(which may have played a role in the decision, though this has been
denied by every Justice to address the question) and the pragmatic
concern with a looming national crisis on the other lies something
that may help explain the outcome of *Bush v. Gore* better than either
partisan-political or crisis-avoidance considerations: the choice between rival conceptions of democracy. The invocation by the Florida
supreme court of the declaration in the state's constitution that "all
political power is inherent in the people" in support of a desperate effort to make every vote count was suggestive of populist democracy,
and there is an alternative conception of democracy as not an ideology of popular rule but simply the set of ground rules governing the
competition for votes. The alternative conception invites thinking of
the electoral process on the model of a game or other contest, and
everyone understands the importance of the rules' being set *before*
the game is played. In our political system the rules governing both
federal and state electoral contests are fixed by state legislatures in

advance of the election and administered by state officials. If the particular rules happen not to sort well with the ideological strivings
popular democrats or to actualize the general will, that's too bad, or
rather, to the democratic realist, that's fine; the essential point is that
they be adhered to. One can imagine conservative Justices siding with
the Republicans not because they preferred Bush to Gore as President
(though doubtless they did) but because of an aversion to populism?

But how was that aversion to be translated into grounds of decision
that would be accepted as legal grounds? There were two possible approaches the majority could take. The first, which was the one it embraced, was to reason that the recount ordered by the Florida supreme
court would if carried out deny the equal protection of the laws, in violation of the Fourteenth Amendment, by making arbitrary distinctions among voters in the Florida Presidential election. Undervoted
ballots would be recounted but not overvoted ones—the Florida court
did not even try to give a reason for *that* distinction among voters.
And undervoters in Broward County (and perhaps other counties)
would be treated more favorably than undervoters in Palm Beach
County (and perhaps other counties), because the election board in
Broward County had used a more liberal standard for recovering votes
from undervoted ballots than the Palm Beach board had used. The recounts in those two counties had at least been completed. But the
Florida supreme court declined to specify a uniform standard for the
recount of the other 60,000 undervotes throughout the state that it
was ordering, except the "voter's intent" standard, which is hopelessly vague when it comes to counting dimpled chads. The court
made additional disparities inevitable by assigning the recounting to
inexperienced judicial personnel, by truncating the right of the candidates to make objections to the counters' decisions, and by imposing unrealistic deadlines, though understandably so in light of the
looming December 12 safe-harbor deadline.

The recount order was farcical. But did it violate equal protection?
The objection to supposing that it did is that while the recount would
have been a farce, the election itself had been a farce in the same
sense. It had been administered in an arbitrary manner that had produced large differences across and probably within counties in the
percentage of ballots actually recorded as votes. The recount would
probably not have produced a result closer to what a well administered election would have produced; but it is difficult to say that it
would have produced a worse result than the actual election produced. The underlying problem is the decentralization of election administration to the county and even the precinct level, which, along
with a generally insouciant attitude on the part of election officials
toward the details of election administration, causes arbitrary dispar-

ities in the likelihood that a person's vote will actually count. This problem had not previously been thought to rise to the level of a denial of equal protection, and, as I have said, the recount would not have aggravated the problem though it probably would not have ameliorated it either.

So if the recount was a denial of equal protection, the implication is that our system of decentralized election administration is a denial of equal protection too. Unwilling to embrace this far-reaching implication of its decision, the majority as much as said that the decision would have no precedential significance in future election litigation.[34] This made the opinion seem thoroughly unprincipled—and remember that pragmatists, too, believe in the value of the rule of law, one element of which is that rules, including rules laid down by courts in the course of deciding cases, should be general in application in order to minimize subjectivity, bias, and oppression. Likewise unprincipled was the remedy of stopping the recount. If the vice of the recount order was that its terms denied equal protection, the natural remedy would have been to direct the Florida supreme court to redo the order. To rule that Florida law, implicitly Florida case law (for there was nothing in the election statute on this point), forbade a recount after safe-harbor day was unprincipled too, because there was no relevant case law. There were, it is true, hints by the Florida supreme court that December 12 was indeed the deadline for any recounting, but these hints alluded not to any rule of Florida law but merely to judicial discretion to formulate an appropriate, and therefore a timely, remedy for the botched election.

The majority opinion must have been a particular embarrassment to the three most conservative Justices (Rehnquist, Scalia, and Thomas). For while it is not true that these Justices *never* support claims of denial of equal protection, they could not be expected to be sympathetic to a ground of decision that implied that the nation's traditionally decentralized election administration is unconstitutional. But here pragmatic considerations, though of a distinctly unedifying character, come into play again. Had these Justices refused to join the majority opinion, there would still have been a majority to stop the re-

---

[34] "Our consideration is limited to the present circumstances, for the problem of equal protection in election processes generally presents many complexities." *Bush v Gore*, 531 US 98, 109 (2000) (per curiam). It would be more precise to say that the particular Justices who joined the majority opinion do not intend to treat it as a precedent; they cannot prevent other Justices, including their successors, from doing so. And indeed, in litigation challenging the California recall election in October 2003, a three-judge panel of the Ninth Circuit enjoined the election precisely on the ground that the decentralized California election system denied equal protection. The panel was, however, quickly reversed by an en banc panel of the court. See *Southwest Voter Registration Education Project v Shelley*, 344 F3d 914 (9th Cir 2003) (en banc).

count, because these three Justices in their concurring opinion stated that the recount would violate Article II. But now there would have been majorities to reject both grounds for stopping the recount. The three most conservative Justices plus Stevens and Ginsburg would have been voting to reject the equal protection ground, and all but the three most conservative Justices would have been voting to reject the Article II ground. The moral authority of the decision, at best limited because of the Justices' conflict of interest, would have been further weakened by the fact that a majority of the Justices had rejected the only available grounds for the decision.

So did those three conservative Justices join an opinion they actually disagreed with? If the only things that matter to a decision are its consequences, then dishonesty—which might seem the right word for subscribing to a judicial opinion that one thinks all wrong—while no doubt regrettable, becomes just another factor in the decision calculus. But maybe this *is* the right way to think about judicial honesty, or more precisely candor (for "honesty" has irrelevant financial connotations). A judge will often join an opinion with which he doesn't actually agree. He will do so because he doesn't think a dissent (or, what is functionally the same, a concurrence in the result but not in the majority opinion) will have any effect, or because he thinks a dissent would merely draw attention to a majority opinion otherwise likely to be ignored, or because, recognizing law's frequent indeterminacy, he lacks confidence that his view is sounder than that of his colleagues, or because he does not think the issue important enough to warrant the bother of writing a dissent and doesn't want to encourage other judges to dissent at the drop of a hat, or because he used the threat of dissent to obtain changes that made the majority opinion more palatable to him. These are pragmatic judgments, ones that I have made unapologetically a number of times in my own judicial career, and such judgments suffuse the writing of a judicial opinion as well, where tact and candor are frequent opponents. Are these bows to the practical to be regarded as tokens of a subtle form of corruption brought about by yielding to the pragmatic Sirens? If not, maybe the decision of the conservative Justices to join the majority opinion in *Bush v. Gore* is defensible even if they had to hold their noses to do so.

The Article II ground for stopping the recount was far stronger than the equal protection ground, and the refusal of Justices O'Connor and Kennedy to adopt it strikes me as a failure of judicial statesmanship. Article II is explicit that the setting of the ground rules for the selection of a state's Presidential electors is the prerogative of the state's *legislature*. Granted, there is no indication that the choice of this word in lieu of "state" was deliberate or that the framers of the Constitution foresaw the use of Article II to limit the scope of state judicial intervention in the selection of a state's electors. But ever since the time of John Marshall, constitutional provisions have been treated more as resources than as commands, resources that judges use to craft solutions to problems the framers did not foresee. The problem at hand was a state court's intervening to (possibly) change the result of an election of the state's Presidential electors by changing the ground rules under which the election had been held. The intervention set the stage for an interbranch struggle within the state over the choice of the electors, and such a struggle would be likely to lead to the appointment of rival slates and hence to the kind of crisis that *Bush v. Gore* headed off. Article II interpreted as confirming the state legislature's prerogative in the determination of the ground rules for selecting a state's Presidential electors establishes a clear line of demarcation between the judicial and the legislative roles. By doing so it prevents state courts from hijacking an election by changing the rules after the outcome of the election is known.

The Article II ground has been criticized as implying that state courts have no power to interpret their state's election statute so far as bears on Presidential elections no matter how ambiguous or riddled with gaps the statute is, and no power to declare it unconstitutional no matter how blatantly its terms violate settled constitutional principles, whether federal or state. But that is not what the ground implies. The state courts retain their ordinary powers but the U.S. Supreme Court is authorized to intervene if, in the guise of interpretation, the state courts rewrite the state election law, usurping the legislature's authority. The difference between interpretive and usurpative judicial "work" on statutes is subtle, but is illuminated by comparison to the settled distinction in the law of labor arbitration between an arbitrator's interpreting a collective bargaining agreement, on the one hand, and, on the other, importing his own views of industrial justice in disregard of the agreement. The former is legitimate interpretation and is insulated from judicial review; the latter is usurpative and is forbidden. The distinction is not between interpretation and invention. Interpretation in the law is a spectrum running from narrow, literal, or strict at one end to broad, loose, or free-wheeling at the other. Contracts are interpreted narrowly, vague constitutional provisions broadly. An arbitrator is constrained to narrow interpretation. He is not allowed to bring to bear his notions of industrial justice. Not because such background notions are foreign to interpretation, but because the scope of *his* interpretive authority is limited. Article II, section 1, clause 2 can reasonably be understood to constrain state courts similarly.

The interpretation that I have just sketched seemed to command the support of all nine Justices in the first opinion in the election litigation, that of December 4.[35] A unanimous decision by the Supreme Court may well be wrong, but it is unlikely to be so far wrong as to impair the Court's authority by making the Court a laughingstock. The issue that later divided the Justices was whether the Florida supreme court had stepped so far out of the line of the statute as to bring down the bar of Article II. That is a difficult issue, but, as I have argued elsewhere,[36] resolving it in favor of invalidating the Florida court's rulings and hence stopping the recount would have been a plausible application of Article II. A majority opinion so finding with emphasis on pragmatic factors would have been a defensible specimen of pragmatic adjudication.[37] Such an opinion could have been structured as follows: (1) a full description of the danger of a Presidential succession crisis, a danger inherent in the fact that neither the Constitution nor federal statutory or common law provides a mechanism for resolving a dispute over Presidential electors when the House and the Senate are controlled by different parties; (2) an explanation that the danger is particularly likely to materialize when a branch of state government, such as the judicial, changes the ground rules of the election after the election has been conducted, thus inciting another branch (the Florida legislature) to appoint its own slate of electors; (3) a conclusion that Article II, section 1, clause 2 is a resource available to avert the succession crisis by preventing state courts (or, for that matter, other branches of state government) from revising the state's electoral code, whether in the guise of "interpretation" or otherwise, after the election.[38]

Such an opinion would have deprived critics of the Court of much of their ammunition. The Justices could not have been accused of betraying their settled convictions, because none of them had ever written or joined an opinion dealing with the "manner directed" clause of Article II, which was last (and first) before the Supreme Court in 1892,[39] and because views of the clause do not divide along "liberal" and "conservative" lines, as views of equal protection do. The Justices would have eluded other criticisms as well: The majority opinion would not have had to say that the decision had no precedential

---

[35] See *Bush v Palm Beach County Canvassing Board*, 531 US 70, 76-78 (2000) (per curiam).

[36] Posner, *Breaking the Deadlock* at chs 2-3 (cited in note 2). For further elaboration of my views, see Richard A. Posner, Bush v Gore—*Reply to Friedman*, 29 Fla St U L Rev 871 (2001).

[37] Posner, *Breaking the Deadlock* at 156-161 (cited in note 2).

[38] The due process clause of the Fourteenth Amendment would provide an alternative constitutional grounding for this argument. "Stealing" an election by revising the rules after the election has taken place would be the equivalent of stuffing the ballot box and of other election frauds that deprive people of their right to vote.

[39] *McPherson v Blacker*, 146 US 1 (1892).

effect, because the ground of the decision would have had no implications for election administration generally. The Article II ground,
being esoteric, would not have provided a handle for criticisms that
the general public could understand. Formalists would have had to
acknowledge that the ground had a textual basis in the word "legislature" in Article II. The ground could be persuasively related to the
avoidance of the looming crisis. Overriding the Florida supreme court
on the basis of Article II would not have been an affront to states'
rights (which conservative Supreme Court Justices have tended to favor in recent years), since it would have been vindicating the authority of state legislatures. And there would have been no awkwardness
in the remedy of stopping the recount, because if the recount order
should never have been issued, rather than merely should have been
configured differently, there would have been no occasion for a remand of the case to the Florida court rather than an outright reversal.

A decision based on Article II would have had the further advantage of being unlikely to generate many consequences beyond the
specific case. This is not only because Article II, section 1, clause 2
has a limited scope, but also because the problem to which it is addressed occurs so rarely; before *Bush v. Gore,* it had not figured in a
Supreme Court case for more than a century. Virtually the only consequence of a decision based on that clause would have been to head
off a looming national crisis.

The failure of the majority in *Bush v. Gore* to adopt the Article II
ground was a particular embarrassment for the Court's two most conservative Justices, Scalia and Thomas. For they had gone out of their
way in opinions and (in Scalia's case) in speeches and articles to urge
a concept of adjudication that is inconsistent with the majority opinion that they joined. *Bush v. Gore's* severest critic, Alan Dershowitz,
revels in being able to quote Scalia's statement that when he writes a
majority opinion, he limits his freedom of action:

> If the next case should have such different facts that my politi-
> cal or policy preferences regarding the outcomes are quite the
> opposite, I will be unable to indulge those preferences; I have
> committed myself to the governing principle. In the real world
> of appellate judging, it displays more judicial restraint to adopt
> such a course than to announce that, "on balance," we think the
> law was violated here—leaving ourselves free to say in the next
> case that, "on balance," it was not . . . Only by announcing rules
> do we hedge ourselves in.[40]

[40] Antonin Scalia, *The Rule of Law as a Law of Rules,* 56 U Chi L Rev 1175, 1179-
1180 (1989), in Dershowitz, *Supreme Injustice: How the High Court Hijacked Election 2000* at 123-124 (cited in note 1).

How does this square with the statement in the majority opinion in *Bush v. Gore*, which Scalia joined however reluctantly, that "our consideration is limited to the present circumstances, for the problem of equal protection in election processes generally presents many complexities"? It does not, thus inviting charges of hypocrisy, or worse— the charge of rank partisanship leveled against Scalia by Dershowitz on insufficient evidence but plausible enough to resonate with those Americans who already distrust the good faith of government officials.

The trouble Scalia got into with the passage I have just quoted illustrates the perils of formalism. Few American judges, especially at the higher levels of the judiciary, where indeterminacy characterizes so many of the important cases, are practicing formalists; and Scalia is not one of them. A judge who is not a formalist yet describes himself as one, who commits himself to principled adjudication and then joins an unprincipled opinion, opens himself to charges of hypocrisy. And if one thinks about it, the passage I quoted from Scalia shows formalism at its worst. He seems to be saying that a court should always adopt an inflexible rule in the first case to present an issue, refusing to modify the rule in the light of subsequent cases that involve new facts that may show that the rule was unsound, overbroad, too narrow, or premature. That doesn't sound like a sensible procedure, or one remotely descriptive of any actual Supreme Court Justice's practice.

One reason *Bush v. Gore* has proved so controversial in legal academic circles is that it suggests that at bottom *all* the Justices of the Supreme Court are pragmatists, albeit closeted ones. Pragmatism, especially of the everyday variety, the sense in which I am using the word to describe the Justices—not one of whom, I am pretty certain, has the slightest interest in philosophical pragmatism—is unpopular among legal academics because it implies that there is really nothing very special about legal reasoning. It is just practical reasoning applied to a particular class of disputes and dressed up in a special jargon. Law professors have to know the cases and statutes and other canonical materials that lawyers and judges refer to, have to know in other words how to talk the talk and walk the walk. But their knowledge and their rhetoric do not yield an understanding of how novel cases should be decided; for that, a pragmatic enterprise, the law professors would have to know a lot about the facts and politics of the particular case. They resist this conclusion, of course. Whether the majority and dissenting Justices in *Bush v. Gore* were motivated by partisan concerns, rival conceptions of democracy, or practical concerns about the consequences either of a botched Presidential succession or of the Supreme Court's deciding the election, none of their opinions can be explained by reference to "the law" in a sense that a conventional legal academic would recognize.

To summarize, *Bush v. Gore* is at best a questionable decision and at worst, especially if one focuses on the actual opinions and not on the best possible rationale for the decision, a very bad one. But so what? Can't a bad decision be good? If these rhetorical questions sound paradoxical to the point of absurdity, consider Professor Sanford Levinson's recent avowal that "Marshall's opinion in *Marbury* [v. *Madison*] is not more defensible than is the per curiam (or the concurrence) in *Bush v. Gore*," and he goes on to note very pertinently the elements of conflict of interest in Marshall's participation in *Marbury*.[41] But *Marbury* is a great decision, and Marshall the greatest Chief Justice in our history. As Levinson's deliberately provocative comparison brings out, the legal professoriat's criteria for good and bad decisions do not fit novel decisions, yet American law is to a great extent the residue of such decisions.

Could it be that constitutional law (and much other law as well) exists beyond right or wrong? Here is Professor Levinson again:

> Constitutional lawyers, whether judges or academics, seem to feel relatively few genuine constraints in [*sic*—he means on] the kinds of arguments they are willing to make or endorse. It is, I am confident, harder to recognize a "frivolous argument" in constitutional law than in any other area of legal analysis. Almost all constitutional analysts, as a matter of brute fact, seem committed to a de-facto theory of "happy endings," whereby one's skills as a rhetorical manipulator of . . . the "modalities" of legal argument are devoted to achieving satisfying results.[42]

The Constitution's vagueness and age (now, not when *Marbury v. Madison* was decided), and the political and social consequences and controversies that constitutional disputes produce, exert a pressure on judges that overwhelms their commitment to the mandarin values that shape professional as distinct from political critique of judicial behavior. It seems that a bad judge can be a great Justice of the Supreme Court, and a good judge an indifferent Justice.

One might have supposed that the botch that the Supreme Court made of the election litigation—the choice of the wrong ground of decision, Scalia's defense of the stay, and the shrill tone of some of the

[41] Sanford Levinson, Bush v Gore *and the French Revolution: A Tentative List of Some Early Lessons* 19-20 (U of Texas School of Law, 2001). Levinson notes "the absolutely remarkable conflict of interest presented by the spectacle of Marshall deciding on the legal status of a commission that he himself had signed, but failed to deliver to Marbury, while serving as John Adams' Secretary of State, the very office now occupied by James Madison." Id at 20.

[42] Id at 6 (footnote omitted).

dissents[43]—the botch that armed Dershowitz and other critics—would have lowered the Court in the eyes of the people. Not so. In June of 2000 only 47 percent of the population had "a great deal" or "quite a lot" of confidence in the Supreme Court. A year later, six months after *Bush v. Gore*, that figure had risen to 50 percent, putting the Court behind only the military, organized religion, and the police in the list of institutions that the respondents were asked about in the survey, and ahead of the Presidency (47 percent), the medical system, the media, business, labor, and Congress (26 percent).[44] The Court averted a possible Presidential succession crisis. The fact that it did so with a notable lack of juristic finesse, arousing the rage of the keepers of the legal flame, bothered few real people.

[43] A strong critic of the decision nevertheless aptly characterizes the dissents by Stevens and Ginsburg as "choleric" and a failure of self-restraint. Larry D. Kramer, *The Supreme Court in Politics*, in Jack N. Rakove ed, *The Unfinished Election of 2000* 105, 146 (Basic Books, 2001).

[44] Gallup Organization, *Confidence in Institutions* (June 8-10, 2001).

Electoral College Alternatives and US Presidential Elections

*Vincy Fon**

The President of the United States is chosen directly by the Electoral College, although indirectly the citizens select the President. Different states currently employ two systems of electoral-vote allocation under the Electoral College framework: the widely adopted winner-take-all system and the system adopted by Maine and Nebraska. The properties of these two systems are analyzed against the backdrop of majority rule and the notion that every vote counts. Two variants of the existing systems are then introduced, using intuitive proportional rules to allocate electoral votes under the Electoral College. These proposed systems are compared to the existing winner-take-all system and to the Maine-Nebraska system. Further, the outcomes of three historical Presidential Elections are considered under different electoral allocation systems. This study highlights basic properties of the Electoral College and possible variants of the current system so that better judgments can be made in future debates.

I. INTRODUCTION

The beliefs of many Americans in majority rule and in every-vote-counts were severely challenged by the 2000 Presidential election. As vote counting and recounting in Florida dragged on, many citizens re-

* Department of Economics, The George Washington University. I owe huge debts to Dan Milkove and Bob Goldfarb for their insightful and extensive comments. Thanks are also due Mary Holman for her useful comments and Francesco Parisi for his encouragement. All opinions, conclusions and errors are my sole responsibility.

newed their acquaintance with the Electoral College and confronted the reality that the country does not directly vote for the President.[1]

Understandably, alternatives to the existing winner-take-all system were discussed and reforms were proposed almost immediately after the election. The two usual proposals are election by direct popular vote and choosing electors by district, but other options exist. This paper points out weaknesses of the two familiar proposals and introduces two alternatives under the Electoral College framework: the Perfect Proportion system and the Integral Proportion system. While studying the strengths of these systems, it is stressed that a candidate can win the popular vote but lose the election under any electoral allocation system.

The framers of the Constitution established the Electoral College. Each state has a number of electors equal to the number of senators plus the number of districts or congressmen in that state.[2, 3] The electors vote for the President and the Vice President through majority rule.[4, 5] How electors are selected in each state is not specified in the Constitution. From the beginning, a few states allowed direct election by the voters, and the idea that the winner of the popular vote should take all the electoral votes in a state was adopted.[6] Meanwhile, a few other states did not allow their voters to cast ballots for the President, and the electors were chosen by their respective legislatures.[7] However, by 1836 the roots of the present "winner takes all"

---

[1] In the US Presidential Election, voters officially vote for a slate of electors in their state that is associated with a political party and its candidates. Once elected, the slate of electors cast their vote for the candidate in the Electoral College meetings. Hence voters only vote for the president indirectly. Details follow in the text.

[2] Although the District of Columbia is not a state, the 23rd Amendment assigned 3 electoral votes to the District. In this paper any mention of all states is meant to include Washington DC.

[3] At the time of the 2000 election, there were 538 electoral votes in the US Electoral College, since there were 100 senators, 435 congressmen, and 3 electoral votes associated with the District of Columbia. Following the 2000 Census, the total number of electoral votes would be fixed, but the number of districts and hence the number of electoral votes in each state would be reapportioned according to population changes since the 1990 census.

[4] Each state's electors gather together and vote in their individual states instead of all electors from all states getting together in one place to cast their ballots. This is designed to avoid collusion among electors from different states.

[5] If no majority is reached among the votes cast by all electors, then Congress decides which candidate will become President or Vice President. The House votes for President and the Senate for Vice President.

[6] In the first Presidential Election after the establishment of the Electoral College in 1789, of the 10 states choosing presidential electors, only Delaware, Maryland, Pennsylvania and Virginia allowed direct election by the voters.

[7] In the 1789 election, Connecticut, Georgia, New Jersey, and South Carolina chose their electors without a direct popular vote.

system, where the winner of a statewide popular plurality vote gets all the electoral votes from that state, was firmly in place.[8]

The US Presidential Election has been run mainly under this winner-take-all Electoral College system at the state level. Called the E system in this paper, it is currently adopted by all states except Maine and Nebraska. The Electoral College is generally considered a success, though detractors frequently attempt to alter or abolish the system in Congress. While it is not the intention to defend the merits of the Electoral College, this paper does mention some of its strengths and weaknesses. The paper also endorses and investigates the possibility of keeping the institutional structure of the Electoral College while changing how each state allocates its electoral votes. In particular, to allocate electoral votes within a state, consider replacing the winner-take-all system by a proportional system. Two variants of a proportional system are a perfect proportional system using fractions and an integral proportional system using whole numbers. These intuitive electoral-vote allocation rules endorse the notion of every-vote-counts more strongly while preserving the important properties of the Electoral College. Further, the integral proportional system could also help minimize potential vote counting difficulties in elections.

Why have there been so many attempts to change the system? The main reason is that a president can be elected without winning a majority of the popular vote.[9] Worse, a president can be elected without winning a plurality of the popular vote.[10] These possibilities seem to violate the ideas of one-person-one-vote and of every-vote-counts: if every vote counts, how could the winner of the majority vote not gain the presidency? If the Electoral College is capable of producing these outcomes, and these possibilities become realities often enough to make us uncomfortable, shouldn't the system be changed so that every vote counts equally? Or if that is not possible, could the system be improved to strengthen the notion of equal votes without violating the Constitution? Can the election process be revised to minimize the likelihood that a candidate becomes President without winning a majority or a plurality of the popular vote? If the current Presiden-

[8] This was true for 25 out of 26 states by 1836, South Carolina being the exception.

[9] In fact, a president with a minority of the popular vote has won the Electoral College vote 16 times in U.S. history. In 1992 and 1996, Clinton won only 43 percent and 49 percent of the popular vote, respectively. Most recently in 2000, Bush won 48.26 percent of the popular vote.

[10] In 1876, Rutherford B. Hayes was elected president, beating Samuel J. Tilden without winning a plurality of popular votes. Likewise, in 1888, Benjamin Harrison, defeating Grover Cleveland, was elected President. In the most notorious case of all, in 1824, John Quincy Adams beat Andrew Jackson although Jackson received a plurality of the popular votes and electoral votes initially. Most recently in 2000, George W. Bush defeated Al Gore even though Gore won the plurality contest.

tial Election process is to be changed, some natural alternatives present themselves.

The first alternative is to allow a direct popular vote for a President. Though it means that every vote counts as much as any other, this approach clearly was not what the framers of the Constitution had in mind. The Constitution did not specify popular voting in each state, let alone the whole country. Through the electors of the various states, the Constitution leaves the election of the President in the hands of the state legislatures. This means that the founding fathers emphasized the interests of the states, not of individual citizens, in the election of the President. Moreover, the Electoral College arrangement can minimize the problem of vote counting, as only a few states with close votes may have to do any recounting.[11]

The next alternative preserves the Electoral College framework, but replaces the winner-take-all allocation system by an allocation method that allows the splitting of the slate of electors to reflect the popular vote in the state. This has been done occasionally throughout US history.[12] One method is to allocate electors by popular vote per district.[13] Most recently, in 1969 Maine authorized each district's electoral vote to be decided by the popular vote, with the two remaining electoral votes going to the state's majority or plurality winner.[14] Nebraska also adopted this electoral allocation system in 1996.[15] Currently, these are the only states adopting the elector-by-districts system, although historically many states experimented with it. This paper will refer to the latter system as the Maine-Nebraska model, or the E^{mn} system, and will expand on its properties.

The goal of this paper is to consider alternatives to the direct popular vote and the existing widely adopted winner-take-all E system, and to gain a deeper understanding of different alternatives within the Electoral College framework established by the founding fathers. To this end, the properties of the E system are discussed first. Many of these properties are familiar. Next the properties of the E^{mn} system are investigated. Among its undesirable characteristics, a candidate in a state could lose the electoral vote even though he wins the pop-

[11] Imagine a scenario in which every popular vote counts, many counties, or districts bicker over vote-counts, and every high court in the Land participates in the vote counting debate in the weeks following Election Day.

[12] For example, in 1789 Massachusetts and New Hampshire combined direct election by the voters with choice by the legislature.

[13] For example, in 1824, Illinois, Kentucky, Maine, Maryland, Missouri and Tennessee elected their respective electors by popular vote per district. However, shortly thereafter, most states abandoned the popular vote per district. See note 8.

[14] Maine was the first state in 80 years to do so.

[15] Because Maine and Nebraska allow each district to choose its own candidate, a splitting of the slate of electors is possible, but this has not yet occurred.

ular vote. This can happen if the E^{mn} system is adopted by states larger than Maine and Nebraska: those with at least 7 electors.[16] I consider this a defect and hence consider alternative proportional allocation systems for electoral votes.

The most intuitive proportional electoral-vote allocation system would be to perfectly apportion the number of electoral votes by the popular vote in the state.[17] For example, if 51.29 percent of the state's votes go to a candidate, and if the state has 8 electors, then the state should allocate 4.1032 (= 0.5129*8) electoral votes to the candidate in question. This system will be designated the perfect proportional allocation system E'. A couple of problems with this system present themselves. A minor one is the need to use many decimal places. Imagine one day when the media has to read off and newspapers need to print the many decimals associated with the electoral votes for each state. Does anyone want to contemplate and to compare such numbers?[18] The second issue is more problematic: under the perfect allocation system, a precise count of the votes is important and hence much effort has to be spent by all states after the election. In other words, problems similar to the nationwide popular vote will manifest themselves again. It is true that the voting controversy in Florida and elsewhere may (hopefully) lead to reforms and better use of technology that take counting problems out of the equation. But the fraud issue in voting may become more problematic. In light of these issues, consider yet another proportional system of allocating electoral votes.[19]

The next alternative is intuitive and makes use of natural numbers. It is proposed that the slate of electors in a state is split roughly in proportion to the state's popular vote, with the modification that the plurality winner receives a favorable marginal adjustment. For example, take the earlier example where 51.29 percent of the votes in the state go to candidate A, and the state has 8 electors. As a perfect reflection of the popular vote requires giving 0.5129*8 = 4.1032 votes to A, it seems reasonable to allocate 5 electoral votes to A. This way, while receiving the most electoral votes, the plurality winner gets a small favorable adjustment, unlike the existing E system under which the plurality winner garners all the electoral votes. After awarding

[16] As of the 2000 election, Maine has 4 electors and Nebraska has 5 electors.

[17] This means that the human electors would have to be abolished.

[18] With the current technology, the calculation can easily be done. But the point here is that it is not as easily remembered or understood by voters. On the other hand, rounding off to 1 or 2 decimals will probably work fine most of the time.

[19] Still, the investigation of the properties of the perfect allocation system E' is important because it shows us what outcome, no matter how undesirable, might be possible as long as the Electoral College framework is retained.

some electoral votes to the plurality winner, the process continues in a similar fashion to allocate the remaining electoral votes to the rest of the candidates. In particular, most of the remaining electoral votes are given to the next plurality winner. The allocation process stops when no more electoral vote is left. Note that this allocation system, to be referred to as the integral proportional system, or the E^* system, preserves partially the preferences of popular voters. The plurality winner gets the most votes, but the minority winner (the candidate with the second most votes) may get some electoral votes as well. Even a third place finisher in the popular vote might win an electoral vote or two.

Since there is a range in which the plurality winner gets a certain number of electoral votes, this system has the virtue that close votes in some states may not matter as much as it does under the winner-take-all system. For example, in a state with 7 electoral votes, as long as A, the plurality winner, has a margin of victory of between 43 percent and 57 percent, he will receive 4 out of the 7 electoral votes. This is true because $0.43^*7 = 3.01$ and $0.57^*7 = 3.99$; with the favorable marginal adjustment, the candidate receives 4 electoral votes either way. If candidate A were to lose the popular battle to candidate B with 42% of the popular vote, he would have garnered 3 electoral votes instead. In this example, whether candidate A wins 42 percent or 43 percent of the popular vote translates to a difference of 1 electoral vote. Under the winner-take-all system E, it is a matter of 7 electoral votes. With this distinguishing feature and the simplicity of natural numbers, the integral proportional system presents itself as a serious contender as an alternative to the existing winner-take-all system.

If adopted by all states, the perfect allocation system E' and the integral allocation system E^* under the Electoral College framework retain the goals set forth in the Constitution by respecting the interests of the states. Further, both systems pay more respect to the will of the people, both majority and minority alike. The paper hence turns to investigating properties of the E' and the E^* systems, as compared to the E^{mn} system, and more importantly, as compared to the E system. It will be pointed out that as long as the Electoral College is retained, there is no guarantee that the nationwide popular vote winner will become President. This is true because the nationwide popular vote may not be consistent with the interests of the states.

After discussing the properties of all the systems, the incentive for different states to change the status quo are discussed. Presidential Election votes from 2000, 1968, and 1960 are also computed according to the proposed E' and E^* systems. The 2000 election inspired the research of this paper because of the tight popular vote and the unprecedented controversial vote count involving many court battles.[20] The 1968 election was chosen because of the major third party effect: Nixon won the presidency with only 43.4 percent of the popular vote to Hubert Humphrey's 42.7 percent and George Wallace's 13.5 percent. The 1960 election left many with the suspicion that fraud in several states allowed Kennedy to defeat Nixon. The paper then concludes with the findings and reiterates the lessons learned.

The main text of the paper uses simple examples in table form to illustrate properties of the different systems. These properties are listed as observations, and will be analyzed assuming that all states adopt the same system. Often these observations are examples counter to properties desired by many people. Most historical examples are relegated to footnotes or appendixes.

II. THE CURRENT SYSTEMS

A. Properties of the Winner-take-all or E System

This paper abstracts from the voters participation problem and creates simplified examples to help illustrate the issues at hand.[21, 22] To this end, assume that for approximately every 25 voters in a state, there is one district assigned to the state.[23] Hence, a state with 75 voters has 3 districts. Adding the two senators gives the state a total of 5 electoral votes.

Further, all examples have only a few states, and these states together will be referred to as the nation or all the states.[24] Given that

[20] For more detailed analysis on the legal battles concerning the Florida vote counts, see Richard A. Posner, *The 2000 Presidential Election: A Statistical and Legal Analysis,* 12 S Ct Econ Rev 1 (2004).

[21] In reality, not all citizens vote, and voter participation rates change from jurisdiction to jurisdiction.

[22] The paper also abstracts from the so-called "faithless electors" problem. Faithless electors are people elected to cast their ballots in the Electoral College on behalf of a particular Presidential candidate but who cast their votes for someone else. No Constitutional provision or Federal law requires electors to vote in accordance with the popular vote in their States, hence the possibility of a faithless elector. Some states do have laws that faithless electors may be subject to fines or may be disqualified for casting an invalid vote and be replaced by substitute electors. This paper assumes that all electors cast votes consistent with the popular vote in the state.

[23] Since the congressional districts are only reassigned once every decade and since voter participation can change from election to election, the examples mostly assume 25 voters in a district, but sometimes due to the nature of the example, more voters are assumed.

[24] Attention is mainly focused on races between two candidates, but occasionally cases with more than two candidates are discussed.

the concern is to see how popular votes are translated into electoral votes, and how the interaction among popular votes differs from the interaction among electoral votes, the examples serve to demonstrate the underlying competing or augmenting forces at work across all states under the Electoral College system. In the examples, Si denotes State i. Pa and Pb denote the numbers of popular votes cast for candidates A and B in an individual state. Likewise, Ea and Eb denote the numbers of electoral votes cast for candidates A and B in a state. The notation P:A and E:A represent the fact that the popular vote winner or the electoral vote winner is A.

1. Observation 1

Under E, a close popular vote can *generate either an electoral landslide or a close electoral vote. A landslide in the popular vote can generate either a close electoral vote or an electoral landslide.*

Table 1 and Table 2 show a simplified nation with two small states and one large state, with three times as many voters in the large state as in each of the small states. The tables present two different scenarios under which close popular votes leave a majority in the nation favoring candidate A, yet either a landslide or a close outcome can occur in the Electoral College vote. In Table 1 slight majorities in S1 and S2 favor candidate A and this creates a landslide in electoral votes for A. However, in Table 2 the slight majorities in S2 and S3 favor A and this leads to a close majority win in the Electoral College for A.

Table 1

	Pa	Pb	Pa+Pb	Ea	Eb
S1	38	37	75	5	
S2	13	12	25	3	
S3	12	13	25		3
Sum	63	62	125	8	3
	P : A			E : A	
	close vote			landslide	

Table 3 and Table 4 show two scenarios under which the landslide popular votes across states are the same, while the electoral outcome can be close or a landslide.

Consider next a comparison of Table 1 and Table 4. In both tables the popular votes in the small states S2 and S3 are close and the ma-

Table 2

	Pa	Pb	Pa+Pb	Ea	Eb
S1	37	38	75		5
S2	13	12	25	3	
S3	13	12	25	3	
Sum	63	62	125	6	5
	P : A close vote			E : A close vote	

Table 3

	Pa	Pb	Pa+Pb	Ea	Eb
S1	37	38	75		5
S2	20	5	25	3	
S3	17	8	25	3	
Sum	74	51	125	6	5
	P : A landslide			E : A close vote	

Table 4

	Pa	Pb	Pa+Pb	Ea	Eb
S1	49	26	75	5	
S2	13	12	25	3	
S3	12	13	25		3
Sum	74	51	125	8	3
	P : A landslide			E : A landslide	

jorities go in the opposite direction. So the electoral votes from the two small states "cancel" each other, and the large state becomes the sway vote. The many electors from the large state, with the help of the electors from the small state, create a landslide in electoral votes. Meanwhile, depending on the popular vote margin in the large state, the margin for the nationwide popular vote can either be small or large.

Now compare Table 2 and Table 3. In these tables, the popular vote in each small state favors one candidate, while the large state favors the other candidate. This can lead to a close vote in the Electoral College if the sum of the electors from the small states is close to the number of electors in the large state. Since a winner takes all electoral votes in each state, a slight or a large majority in the state's popular vote garners the same electoral votes. The strength of these majorities from all the states then determines whether the nationwide popular vote is a close vote or a landslide.

The above comparisons illustrate that, under the E system, *there is no consistent relationship between the popular vote margin and the electoral vote margin.* But this suggests the more troubling possibility that there may be no relationship between the outcome of the E system and the result of the nationwide popular vote. This is indeed the case as the next two observations indicate.

2. Observation 2

The winner of the E system does not necessarily win the simple popular vote for the nation.[25] *That is, a candidate can become the winner of the E system and hence the President with a minority of the popular vote. This possibility is called the nationwide inconsistency problem because the E outcome does not reflect the P outcome for all states.*

Table 5 illustrates a case under which all states are identical in size and have the same number of electors. There is a slight majority for candidate A across all states. However, because two out of three states prefer candidate B, the Electoral College selects B as the President, despite the nationwide popular majority vote for A.

This example clearly demonstrates an important property of the

Table 5

	Pa	Pb	Pa+Pb	Ea	Eb
S1	14	11	25	3	
S2	12	13	25		3
S3	12	13	25		3
Sum	38	37	75	3	6
	P : A				E : B

Electoral College system: the candidate with the most popular votes does not necessarily become President, as winning the popular vote does not guarantee winning the electoral vote. More importantly, the

[25] See note 10.

example shows that *even if* all states had the same number of residents and voters, there is still no guarantee that the winner of the nation's popular vote will win the Electoral College vote. In practice, with different states having different numbers of electors, the problem is further compounded. This problem—that the electoral outcome can differ from the simple popular vote outcome across all states—will be referred to as the nationwide inconsistency problem.

So far, overall features of the E system *across all states* have been discussed. Next consider two straightforward limited features of the E system *within a state*. These are important for comparisons with alternative systems within the Electoral College setting.

3. Observation 3

The winner-take-all Electoral College outcome is consistent with the statewide popular vote, or, is "statewide popular-vote consistent." However, the E outcome does not measure the extent of voter-preference. That is, under the E system, the winner of the electoral vote also wins the popular vote in the state; but the number of electoral votes obtained by a presidential candidate does not reflect the popular margin by which this candidate won in that state.

The statewide consistency property is trivial because the winner of the popular vote takes all the electoral votes in a state under the E system. However, as observations show, the E outcome does not indicate or reflect the margin of victory in the state, since both slight and large margins of victory produce the same number of electoral votes in a state.

As long as a candidate receives one more vote than any other candidate in the state, he wins the popular vote and garners all electoral votes under E. This is a "single threshold" property; once the number of votes reaches this threshold, any additional votes for this candidate do not matter. However, when popular votes across all states are tabulated to form electoral votes, a single threshold will not reflect votes in a state as well as using multiple thresholds, which involves splitting the slate of electors in a state. This alternative will be analyzed after briefly discussing the Maine-Nebraska system.

4. Concluding Remarks on the E System

Recapping the main properties of the E system, the E outcome reflects voter preferences within a state, but the electoral vote does not indicate whether the popular vote was close or a landslide. Across all states, the winner under the E system does not have to win the nationwide popular vote and the winning electoral vote margin bears no relationship to the popular vote's winning margin.

B. Properties of the Maine-Nebraska Model or the E^{mn} System

As noted, the elector-by-district model, currently used by Maine and Nebraska, was adopted by many other states at various times in the past. It is intuitively appealing because it respects the preferences of different congressional districts and presumably should reflect the preferences of all voters. Unfortunately, it may not adequately reflect the popular vote in the entire state. The question then is how fine a unit should be used to partition votes in determining our national leader? This issue will be addressed later. The next two observations point out a desirable feature of the E^{mn} system, then a problematic aspect. Examples in this section refer to different districts of *one state*, unlike the previous examples dealing with different states. To facilitate the discussion, assume that each district has about 25 voters.

1. Observation 4

The E^{mn} outcome may *reflect statewide voter preferences better than the E outcome.*

In general, the E^{mn} system is expected to produce a better representation of the voter sentiment than the winner-take-all system E. This is illustrated in Table 6. The state in question has 3 districts and 5 electors. Since candidate A wins the popular vote, he receives all the electoral votes under E, 5 to 0 against his opponent. If each district assigns its electoral vote, then candidate B receives 2 electoral votes because D1 and D2 vote for him. As candidate A wins the majority vote in district D3 as well as the state, he garners 3 electoral votes (one for winning the district, and two for winning the state majority). Candidate A is ahead in this state when the votes are split. It is clear that in this case the E^{mn} votes reflect the popular votes in the state better than the E system.

Table 6

	Pa	Pb	Ea	Eb	$E^{mn}a$	$E^{mn}b$
D1	12	13				1
D2	12	13				1
D3	20	5			1	
State	44	31	5	0	3	2
	P : A		E : A		E^{mn} : A	

2. Observation 5

The E^{mn} system has a statewide inconsistency problem: it can provide an electoral winner that is inconsistent with the popular vote in the state. In particular, the E^{mn} outcome can be inconsistent with the statewide popular vote if the state has at least 5 districts and 7 electoral votes.

Table 7 shows that voters in two districts (D1 and D2) give majorities to candidate A, hence two electoral votes go to A. Furthermore, because the state's majority voters prefer A, 2 more electoral votes are assigned to A. That is, $E^{mn}a = 2 + 2 = 4$. Given that B did not win the majority vote, his electoral vote equals the number of districts voting for him. That is, $E^{mn}b = 1$. Note that in Table 7, the majority of the electoral votes go to candidate A, and this outcome matches the majority preference of the state's population. One might argue that the E^{mn} margin of 4 to 1 for candidate A does not reflect the popular margin well. But at least the outcome is consistent.

Table 7

	Pa	Pb	$E^{mn}a$	$E^{mn}b$
D1	13	12	1	
D2	13	12	1	
D3	12	13		1
State	38	37	4	1
	P : A		E^{mn} : A	

Table 8

	Pa	Pb	$E^{mn}a$	$E^{mn}b$
D1	20	5	1	
D2	12	13		1
D3	12	13		1
D4	12	13		1
D5	12	13		1
State	68	57	3	4
	P : A			E^{mn} : B

In Table 8, even a landslide in the popular vote in a different state leaves candidate A a loser to candidate B in terms of electoral votes. That is, although candidate A is heavily favored by the voters in the state, he is behind in the electoral votes under the elector-by-district system. Therefore, the E^{mn} outcome does not necessarily match the popular outcome in choosing the winner.

This E^{mn} reversal in outcome is considered an undesirable property of an electoral vote system. The majority vote in a state ought to be respected by allocating a majority of the electoral votes to the candidate who collects the most popular votes. Readers may have noted the differing number of districts in Table 7 versus Table 8. This statewide inconsistency can only appear if the state has a sufficient number of districts.

If the same candidate wins the popular vote in every district in a state, then the E^{mn} outcome will always be consistent with the popular outcome. Otherwise, this may not be the case. Assume that candidate A wins 1 district with a large margin, whereas candidate B wins the remaining N districts with only 1 vote to spare in each district. Further assume that candidate A wins the statewide popular vote. For the E^{mn} outcome to reverse the popular outcome, the N electoral votes garnered by candidate B (from the N districts) must exceed the 3 electoral votes collected by candidate A (1 district and 2 for winning the state's popular vote). As N must exceed 3, the total number of districts in the state (N + 1) must be greater than or equal to 5. Alternatively, the number of electors in the state must be at least 7.

Since currently Maine has 4 electors and Nebraska has 5, neither state could produce an electoral majority opposite to the popular majority. But if a state with at least 7 electoral votes adopts E^{mn}, it would be possible for its electoral vote to go against its popular vote.

3. Observation 6

The E^{mn} system can be unstable: given a change in the residency distribution of the voters, the consistency of the E^{mn} outcome can change even with no change in overall voter preference in the state.

A change in the residency distribution of the majority voters within the state can affect the E^{mn} outcome. Table 9 and Table 10 show voter preferences in a state with 5 districts, and with identical popular votes favoring candidate A by a slight margin of victory. In Table 9, only D1 produces a majority vote for A, and A loses the electoral vote despite a win of the popular vote. Now consider the case in which two candidate-A supporters move from D1 to D2 (Table 10). These moves produce a popular majority vote within D2, without losing the ma-

Table 9

	Pa	Pb	$E^{mn}a$	$E^{mn}b$
D1	16	11	1	
D2	12	13		1
D3	12	13		1
D4	12	13		1
D5	12	13		1
State	64	63	3	4
	P : A			E^{mn} : B

Table 10

	Pa	Pb	$E^{mn}a$	$E^{mn}b$
D1	14	11	1	
D2	14	13	1	
D3	12	13		1
D4	12	13		1
D5	12	13		1
State	64	63	4	3
	P : A		E^{mn} : A	

jority vote in D1. The additional electoral vote from D2 then gives the electoral victory to candidate A, which happens to match the sentiment of the majority of state voters.

These two scenarios illustrate the second unsettling property of the E^{mn} model. The outcome of the electoral vote should not depend on the residency distribution of the voters. The example suggests that the E^{mn} system might provide a greater impetus to state legislatures to engage in gerrymandering, the practice of creatively carving out the boundaries of congressional districts when they are modified following a decennial census. For example, a state where the Republicans have a majority in the state legislature might concentrate Democratic neighborhoods in one or two districts, ceding control there in return for a higher probability of maintaining dominance in other districts. Under E^{mn} this also would tend to maximize electoral votes for the party in power. Also, citizens frequently move from one district to another within the same state. Should the selection of our national leader depend on which district someone happens to reside during the election? To raise the question suggests that the answer should be negative.

4. Observation 7

The winner of the E^{mn} system does not necessarily win the simple popular vote for the nation. That is, the E^{mn} outcome may be inconsistent with the nationwide popular vote.

The nationwide inconsistency property of the E^{mn} system originates from the structure of the Electoral College. Given that all allocation systems discussed are under the Electoral College framework, they all share this undesirable nationwide inconsistency property. Under E^{mn}, as each state's electoral votes may not be consistent with its popular vote, the nationwide electoral outcome need not be consistent with the nationwide popular outcome after aggregating all the states.

5. Concluding Remarks on the E^{mn} System

To recap the properties of the E^{mn} system, the system seems intuitively appealing and its outcome is expected to reflect the statewide popular vote better than the E system. Unfortunately, sometimes it doesn't. Under the E^{mn} system, the state popular vote may not win the electoral vote, if the state has at least 7 electors. Further, the outcome is sensitive to the residency distribution of voters in a state. Lastly, if adopted by all states, the E^{mn} outcome may not be consistent with the nationwide popular vote.

Counter to intuition, the E^{mn} system does not always fare much better than the E system.[26] Like the E system, the E^{mn} system may not be nationwide consistent with the popular vote. Unlike the E system where the electoral vote is always consistent with the statewide popular vote, the E^{mn} system cannot assure this. The force that gives the district-residency distribution the power to impact the state's electoral vote is similar to the force that gives the state-residency distribution the power to impact the nation's electoral vote. Some may argue that to select a national leader in a manner that respects the principle of federalism, it may be logical to accept the nationwide inconsistency property of the Electoral College framework. But the statewide inconsistency issue is a different matter. It may not be logical to take the district as a unit and build in the interest of the district to determine the electoral vote for a president. If the interests of different districts vary, then the electoral vote that supposedly represents the state's interest may easily flip-flop (as was shown in Table 9

---

[26] The Economist magazine wrote an editorial suggesting that the Maine-Nebraska system should be widely adopted. See The Economist at 42 (November 18, 2000).

and Table 10). And the electoral vote may not be consistent with the preference of the majority of the state's population (as was shown in Table 8 or Table 9).

All this suggests considering alternative proportional systems that incorporate a state's popular vote under the Electoral College framework. Two intuitive alternatives are the perfect proportional system E′ and the integral proportional system E*. The E′ system would accept fractional numbers of electoral votes that perfectly reflect the proportion of the popular vote for each candidate. The E* system would only take integral numbers of electoral votes and allocate them in a way that approximately reflects the popular vote in a state with a tilt towards the plurality winner. In these proposed systems, individual districts play no role. Like the existing E system, the state is the unit under which the popular vote is tabulated and included in the electoral votes.

III. POSSIBLE VARIANTS TO THE CURRENT SYSTEMS

A. The Perfect Proportional System E′ and the Integral Proportional System E*

Under the perfect proportional system E′, if a state has N electors and candidate A receives α% of the popular vote, then the number of electoral votes assigned to candidate A is α% times N. The slate of electors in a state is split in as many ways as there are candidates.

Under the integral proportional system E*, the electoral vote received by a candidate is always a whole number. Assume that there are N electors in the state and three candidates, A, B, and C receive α%, β% and γ% of the popular vote, respectively. Assume further that $\alpha > \beta > \gamma$ and hence candidate A is the plurality winner. Then the number of electoral votes assigned to candidate A is the larger of the following two quantities: (1) the largest integer greater than α% times N; or (2) the largest integer greater than or equal to half of the electoral votes.[27, 28] If there are any residual electoral votes, the number of electoral votes will be similarly assigned to B. That is, the number of electoral votes assigned to B is the larger of the following two quanti-

---

[27] To guarantee that the popular vote winner garners the most electoral votes, it is important to assign him at least half the electoral votes.

[28] There is still the issue of a tie vote. Currently some states resolve a tie by chance. For example, Florida state law stipulates that candidates should draw lots to determine who shall be elected to the office. Likewise, New Mexico state constitution calls for a game of chance, the type of game to be determined by a judge, to resolve a tie.

ties: (1) the largest integer greater than β% times N and less than or equal to the number of remaining electoral votes; or (2) the largest integer greater than or equal to half of the remaining electoral votes. If any votes are left, assign them to candidate C. In this way, the E^* system splits the slate of electors in favor of the majority winner by assuring that his proportion of electoral votes is close to but greater than his proportion of popular votes.

The two proportional allocation systems investigated split the slate of electors in a state. Given that more than two candidates can garner substantial popular votes, more than two candidates can receive electoral votes under E' and E^*.[29] Hence, if either of the two proposed allocation systems were to be adopted, one might want to change the constitution to allow the winner of a plurality of electoral votes to win the Presidency of the United States.[30]

Some supporters of the Electoral College argue that the existing winner-take-all system tends to magnify the victory margin of the winner, and that this is desirable. The perfect proportional system does not keep this property. The integral proportional system does retain some magnification of the margin of the winner.[31, 32]

Next turn to the properties of the E' and the E^* systems, and compare them to the E^{mn} and the E systems.

---

[29] A proportional allocation system might therefore encourage more candidates, which some people would not consider a good feature. For example, a one-issue candidate might hope to promise his electoral votes to a candidate who promises to support his issue. The E^* system should minimize this impact since some threshold must be achieved before gaining any electoral votes.

[30] If no candidate receives a majority of electoral votes, the constitution states that the House of Representatives determines who becomes President. Since a lack of a majority becomes more likely under E' or E^*, widespread adoption of either system should probably be accompanied by a constitutional amendment that a candidate need only win a plurality of electoral votes to become President.

[31] Strictly speaking, the degree of magnification under the E system is not uniform across all states either. This is due to the different number of electors assigned to the states. For example, in California, a 51% win in the popular vote can be parlayed into 54 electoral votes while in Delaware, a 51% win can only be turned into 3 electoral votes. Alternatively, from the 2000 Presidential Election, the extra 79,382 votes in Arizona that went to Bush turned into 8 electoral votes for him. The extra 79,474 votes cast for Bush in North Dakota only generated 3 electoral votes. (The votes in Arizona were: Bush 715,112 and Gore 635,730. The votes in North Dakota were: Bush 175,572 and Gore 96,098.) Likewise, the degree of magnification under the E^* system is not uniform across all states, because it depends on the margin of victory and because different numbers of electors are assigned to the states.

[32] Under E the electoral vote magnification is insensitive to the margin of victory once the threshold of victory is crossed. Under E^*, the electoral vote magnification may depend on the margin of victory to some extent. Also, under E^* the minority popular vote may not be totally de-magnified to zero, as is the case under E.

1. Observation 8

The E' and the E* outcomes are consistent with the statewide popular vote while the E^{mn} outcome may not be. In general, the E' and the E* electoral vote assignments reflect statewide voter preferences better than the E^{mn} electoral vote.

Table 11 takes the voter preference presented in Table 8, where the E^{mn} winner does not win the popular vote, and shows the electoral votes assigned to each candidate under the proposed E' and the E* systems. The state in question has 7 electoral votes and candidate A receives $68/(68 + 57) = 0.544$ of the popular votes cast. As 3.808 equals 0.544×7, this is the number of electoral votes received by candidate A under E'. Given that $57/(68 + 57) = 0.456$, $3.192 (= 0.456 \times 7)$ is the number of electoral votes assigned to candidate B. Under E' candidate A receives more electoral votes than candidate B because electoral votes perfectly reflect fractions of the popular vote going to either candidate. In particular, the ratio of the number of popular votes for A and that for B (the ratio of 68 to 57) and the ratio of the number of E' votes for A and that for B (the ratio of 3.808 to 3.192) are equal: they are both 1.193.

Since candidate A receives the most popular votes and since the perfect proportional number is 3.808, rounding up to a whole number means that 4 electoral votes are assigned to candidate A under E*. The remaining 3 electoral votes are assigned to candidate B. Again, under E* candidate A receives more electoral votes than candidate B, although under E^{mn} candidate A receives fewer electoral votes.

Table 11

	Pa	Pb	$E^{mn}a$	$E^{mn}b$	E'a	E'b	E*a	E*b
D1	20	5	1					
D2	12	13		1				
D3	12	13		1				
D4	12	13		1				
D5	12	13		1				
State	68	57	3	4	3.808	3.192	4	3
	P : A			E^{mn} : B	E' : A		E* : A	

In general, because both the E' and the E* systems always assign the largest number of electoral votes to the popular winner in the state, and the next largest number of electoral votes to the next popular winner, etc, these numbers are superior to the E^{mn} assignment of electoral votes. The E' and the E* votes reflect the state's popular vote in two ways. First, the E′ and the E* outcomes are always statewide popular-vote consistent, since they count each voter in the state equally, disregarding the district a voter resides in. Second, in the case where even the E^{mn} outcome is statewide popular-vote consistent, the E′ and the E* electoral votes reflect the popular majority vote, but the E^{mn} electoral vote bears little relationship to the statewide popular vote.

2. Observation 9

Like the winner-take-all system E, the E′ and the E outcomes are always* statewide popular-vote consistent *with the popular vote in producing a winner. Further, the E′ and E* electoral votes reflect statewide popular votes better than the E electoral votes.*

As indicated in the previous observation, the statewide popular vote winner always wins the largest proportion of electoral votes under E′ or E* because winning the popular vote means that he gets the most electoral votes in the state under either proportional system. That the electoral votes under E′ and under E* reflect the statewide voter preference better than that under E is also intuitive. The E′ and the E* systems allow the possibility of assigning some electoral votes to other candidates, while under the E system, the second place winner does not garner any votes.[33] For example, in a state with 3 electors, under E′ any winner garners some votes so that the E′ system reflects the popular vote sentiment much better than the winner-take-all system E. Likewise, under E*, a popular winner who collects less than 2/3 of the popular votes gets only 2 electoral votes. A second candidate who garners most of the remaining popular votes receives 1 electoral vote. This 2-1 allocation of electoral votes under E* is also a better reflection than the 3-0 allocation of electoral votes under E.

3. Observation 10

Like the winner-take-all system E, the E′ and the E outcomes may be* nationwide inconsistent *with the popular vote. That is, under E′ or E*, it is possible for a minority popular winner to garner a majority of the electoral votes and become president.*[34]

Table 12 uses the voter preference from Table 5 to show how the E′ and the E* electoral vote allocations differ from that of the E system. In this example, across all states candidate A wins the popular vote

[33] This is true as long as the proportion of popular votes garnered by the minority winner is fairly large under E*.

[34] Like the E system, there is still no relationship between the popular vote and the nationwide electoral vote under the E* system. That is, Observation 1 still applies to the E* system.

with a slight majority. However, because the majorities in two states vote for candidate B, the winner-take-all system declares candidate B the winner. Similarly, since being a majority winner in a state means that a premium of electoral votes is awarded to the candidate, B also wins the integral proportional system E^*. However, candidate A is the winner under the perfect proportional system E' because the winning margins in states S2 and S3 for candidate B are not large enough to overwhelm the winning margin in S1 for candidate A.

Table 12

	Pa	Pb	Ea	Eb	E'a	E'b	E*a	E*b
S1	14	11	3		1.68	1.32	2	1
S2	12	13		3	1.44	1.56	1	2
S3	12	13		3	1.44	1.56	1	2
Sum	38	37	3	6	4.56	4.44	4	5
Winner	A			B	A			B
Consistency with P				No	Yes			No

B. The Proportional Systems and the Existing Systems

The outcomes illustrated in Table 12 seem comforting. After all, the political authority did its best to give the right proportions of electoral votes to different candidates according to voter preferences in the state. Hence the perfect proportional allocation system E' is expected to provide the best representation in terms of electoral votes. Unfortunately, this example may generate a false sense of security that the outcome under E' is always consistent with the popular vote across all states. In fact this is not the case, as examples in Appendix 1 show.

Examples in Appendix 1 show that it is plausible under any Electoral College system to have a Presidential Candidate losing the election while winning the popular vote. The examples illustrate the unstable properties of any allocation system under an Electoral College. If the number of districts, voter participation, or margins of victory change slightly, the popular winner and the winners of different electoral allocation systems can change. Indeed, this lack of a fixed relationship between outcomes of different electoral allocation systems and the popular vote is the price that must be paid to preserve the Electoral College.

IV. HISTORICAL EXAMPLES

To ease any doubt that the previous examples are artificial, three more historical examples are presented. First, Appendix 2 reworks the

2000 Presidential Election using data from cbsnews.com downloaded on Dec 16, 2000. As the source only provided votes for the top four candidates, sum the votes for Gore, Bush, Nader, and Buchanan in each state and assume that that is the total number of votes in this state.[35] Although Gore won the nationwide popular vote, Bush ended up winning the Presidency by garnering 271 electoral votes to Gore's 267. When computed under the perfect allocation system, Bush wins with 261.01 to Gore's 259.89 electoral votes.[36] Under the integral allocation system, Bush still wins with 272 to Gore's 263 electoral votes. (In this case, Nader receives 3 electoral votes.) Note that in this election, all allocation systems under the Electoral College framework provide outcomes that are inconsistent with the popular vote.

Table 13 further sorts pairs of states from the 2000 Presidential Election to see the consistency issue between different electoral college allocation systems and the popular vote across states. The criterion is to choose pairs of states that produce an E outcome that is inconsistent with the popular outcome across the two states.[37] In the case of Hawaii and South Dakota, the E, E′, and E* outcomes are all opposite from the popular outcome across states. In the remaining three comparisons, the perfect proportional system and the integral proportional system both generate results consistent with the popular vote although the winner-take-all system does not.

Finally, Table 14 presents hypothetical outcomes under E′ and E* along with the historical popular and electoral votes garnered by each candidate under E for three elections. In 1960, Nixon would have won the election if the integral proportional system E* was used, but Kennedy would have still won the election if E′ was used.[38] In 1968, the third candidate in terms of popular votes, George C. Wallace, garnered 46 electoral votes under E. Computations show that all allocation systems would have declared Nixon the winner.[39]

[35] Details of the electoral votes assigned in each state are found in the Appendix.

[36] With only 261.01 electoral votes, election of the President would actually fall to the House of Representatives unless the constitution was amended to let a plurality of electoral votes determine the winner.

[37] Since only votes for Gore and Bush are examined and votes going to the other candidates are ignored, the sum of electoral votes going to Gore and Bush need not equal the number of electors for each state. However, for the pairs of states chosen, neither Nader nor Buchanan won any electoral vote under E*. Hence the sum of the electoral votes going to Gore and Bush always equal the number of electors for the state in question.

[38] Because the District of Columbia did not have any electors in 1960, the total number of states is 50.

[39] Recall that under E′ and E*, it is necessary to declare an electoral vote plurality winner to be the President to avoid the current requirement under which the House of Representatives determines the winner.

Table 13

	Pg/T	Pb/T	Pg	Pb	Eg	Eb	E'g	E'b	$E*g_1$	$E*g_2$	$E*b_1$	$E*b_2$
Hawaii 4	**0.561**	0.377	205,209	137,785	4		2.245	1.507	3			1
South Dakota 3	0.380	**0.609**	118,750	190,515		3	1.14	1.828		1	2	
Total			323,959	**328,300**	**4**	**3**	**3.384**	3.336				
Total of E*										**4**		3
Winner				Bush	Gore		Gore			Gore		
Consistent w/ P					No		No			No		
Vermont 3	**0.512**	0.412	148,166	119,273	3		1.536	1.236	2			1
Wyoming 3	0.287	**0.700**	60,421	147,674		3	0.86	2.101		0	3	
Total			208,587	**266,947**	**3**	**3**	2.396	**3.338**				
Total of E*										2		**4**
Winner				Bush	Tie			Bush				Bush
Consistent w/ P					No			Yes				Yes

continued

Table 13 *continued*

	Pg/T	Pb/T	Pg	Pb	Eg	Eb	$E'g$	$E'b$	E^*g_1	E^*g_2	E^*b_1	E^*b_2
Oregon 7	**0.474**	0.470	719,165	712,705	7		3.32	3.291	4			3
New Hampshire 4	0.472	**0.484**	265,853	273,135		4	1.886	1.938		1	3	
Total			985,018	**985,840**								
Total of E*					7	4	5.207	**5.229**		5		**6**
Winner				Bush	Gore			Bush				Bush
Consistent w/ P					No			Yes				Yes
Massachusetts 12	**0.603**	0.328	1,610,175	876,906	12		7.232	3.938	8		8	
Georgia 13	0.438	**0.558**	1,110,755	1,416,085		13	5.69	7.254		5		4
Total			**2,720,930**	2,292,991								
Total of E*					12	13	**12.92**	11.19		**13**		12
Winner			Gore			Bush	Gore			Gore		
Consistent w/ P						No	Yes			Yes		

Pg/T & Pb/T are the percentages of popular votes gained by Gore and by Bush, respectively.
Pg and Pb are the actual numbers of popular vote received by Gore and Bush.
Eg and Eb are votes garnered by Gore and Bush under the E system.
$E'g$ and $E'b$ are votes collected by Gore and Bush under the E' system.
E^*g_1 and E^*g_2 are votes allocated to Gore as the first place and the second place popular vote winner, respectively.

Table 14

1960	States	P	E	E'	E*
Kennedy (D)	23	34,221,344	303	266.13	265
Nixon (R)	26	34,106,671	219	263.71	267
Byrd	1		15	7.17	5
Total	50	68,328,015	537	537.01	537
Winner		Kennedy	Kennedy	Kennedy	Nixon
Consistency with P winner			Yes	Yes	No

1968	States	P	E	E'	E*
Humphrey (D)	14	31,274,503	191	225.91	220
Nixon (R)	32	31,785,148	301	232.67	257
Wallace	5	9,901,151	46	79.42	61
Total	51	72,960,802	538	538.00	538
Winner		Nixon	Nixon	Nixon	Nixon
Consistency with P winner			Yes	Yes	Yes

2000	States	P	E	E'	E*
Gore (D)	21	50,148,801	267	259.89	263
Bush (R)	30	49,790,449	271	261.01	272
Nader	0	2,772,967	0	14.61	3
Buchanan	0	449,095	0	2.49	0
Total	51	103,161,312	538	538.00	538
Winner		Gore	Bush	Bush	Bush
Consistency with P winner			No	No	No

Under E, the 267 electoral votes for Gore included the vote that a Faithless elector from DC should have cast for him.

In 2000, the popular vote in Florida was very close and Florida's 25 electoral votes meant that whoever won Florida would win the Presidency under the winner-take-all system. Hence there were many debates on how to count pregnant chads and various legal battles. The E* outcome has Bush winning 272 electoral votes to Gore's 263 votes, with 3 votes going to Nader. If the election were held under the E* system, Bush would have garnered 13 electoral votes as opposed to Gore's 12 electoral votes. But even if Gore had won Florida, Bush would have garnered 12 votes and Gore 13 votes. Then under E*, the grand totals of electoral votes for Bush and Gore would have been 271 and 264 respectively; and Bush would still have won. Hence, the unprecedented battle in the Florida vote count would not have mattered if the integral proportional system had been adopted.

V. LESSONS AND CONCLUSION

The 2000 election led to much talk in Congress about reforming the election process. Numerous failed reform attempts made over the course of US history cast serious doubt whether any reform can ever be enacted. On the other hand, reform is impossible if no attempt is ever made. In order for any possible reform to occur, all must fully understand the properties of the existing systems adopted by states under the umbrella of the Electoral College.

Dissatisfaction with the status quo results from recognizing that the popular vote outcome need not jibe with the Electoral College outcome. Thus, there is a demand for a system that better reflects actual popular voting outcomes. Naturally, a direct popular vote for the President would accomplish this. However, this practice clashes directly with the intention of the constitution's framers who focused on representation by states, using the Electoral College mechanism. Although the number of electors assigned to each state is determined by population, the manner of selecting electors is left to each state, and the practice of a popular vote (even within a state) was not endorsed in the Constitution.

The principles of federalism and the interests of the states underlie the Constitution. If these principles are to be sustained, the Electoral College should be maintained. If the principle of equality of voters is to be enhanced, a fundamental question is the following. *How should the interest of the state be determined by its citizens?* Two models are used at present: winner-take-all and Maine-Nebraska. For all practical purposes, the winner-take-all model currently decides the Presidential Election; it is precisely this model that many people believe needs improvements.

One frequently proposed alternative is the Maine-Nebraska model. Should the interest of a state be determined by the interests of its districts? If so, then the Maine-Nebraska system has some attractions. After all, voters from each district decide on the interest of the district and different districts together decide the interest of the state and therefore the allocation of electors for different candidates. Unfortunately, because the winner of the popular vote in a large state may not garner the most electoral votes from the state, this could generate inconsistent outcomes between the popular and electoral votes.[40] Further, if the principle of voter equality is to complement the interests of the states in selecting a President, why go through an

---

[40] Recall that the outcome under the Maine-Nebraska model may be inconsistent with a state's popular vote provided that the state has at least 7 electors.

unnecessary layer of districts? Although the Maine-Nebraska model has intuitive appeal at first blush, it is not satisfactory.

However, there are some attractive alternatives available. Other than the winner-take-all system, the most intuitive system is the perfect proportional system. This system has the virtue of keeping the principles of federalism and of "every vote counts equally" in the state, as the fraction of electoral votes assigned to any candidate reflects precisely his fraction of popular votes in the state. Minor problems with this system are that vote counting becomes important and that fractional numbers of electoral votes must be accepted. However, a worthwhile feature of this system is that it captures the principles set forth in the constitution and the newer concept of equality of all voters (as close as possible).

Another alternative that maintains the compromise between federalism and respect for voter preference is the integral proportional system. This system gives an imperfect proportion of electoral votes to the plurality winner in a state. The number assigned to the winner always favors him by apportioning the next integer that is larger than the fraction of the popular vote garnered by him. It is always greater than half the total electoral votes in the state to ensure the principle of plurality. A major virtue of the integral proportional system is that the margin of victory is magnified whereas the minority voter preferences are not forgotten. Given that the winner-take-all system magnifies the margin of victory of the plurality winner to the extreme and completely ignores other votes, the integral system is an improvement in preserving voter preference from a state. It has two additional virtues. It is elegant because it deals with whole numbers and close votes in some states do not matter.[41] This means that the vote counting and recounting problem is minimized.[42] The likelihood of fraud may also be minimized since results are less sensitive to small changes in vote counts.

However, as the Electoral College framework is retained, *no allocation system of electoral votes* can assure that the nationwide popular vote winner becomes President. The outcome of the electoral vote in a state, and hence the outcome of the Electoral College vote,

[41] For example, in a state with 3 electors, as long as a plurality winner wins somewhat less than 2/3 of the popular vote, the margin of victory is not very important as he collects 2 electoral votes from the state. Similarly, in a state with 9 electors, as long as the margin of victory of a majority winner falls safely in between 55.6% (5/9) and 66.7% (6/9), the precise margin does not matter and he receives 6 votes.

[42] If the integral proportional system had been adopted, the 2000 vote count fiasco in Florida could have been avoided. Presumably, similar vote count issues can be minimized in the future as well.

depends on the margin of victory but not on voter participation rates in that state. The outcome of the nationwide popular vote depends on voter participation in every state but not on the margin of victory in each state. Therefore, as long as the nation accepts the principles set forth in the Constitution and wants to retain the Electoral College framework, there can be no expectation that the popular vote winner will necessarily win the Presidency.

How likely is it that a state will be willing to change its system? The state legislature of a fairly strong Democratic state or a fairly strong Republican state would not be willing to split its electoral votes. After all, why not keep all the electoral votes for their party? However, election results from 1960, 1968, 1992, and 2000 show that 29 states changed their party line in choosing a presidential candidate. Almost sixty percent of the states switch the party line in choosing their presidential candidate—this is not a small figure. Hence there is no comfort in maintaining the status quo of the winner-take-all system as far as presidential election goes.

Currently the media reports that some members of Congress and state legislatures are proposing changes in the presidential election process. The Maine-Nebraska model is often mentioned. As observed, the compatibility of outcomes between any Electoral College system and the popular vote is tenuous. If only a few states are convinced to switch from the status quo, then more unpleasant and seemingly unfair results are sure to follow. It would seem preferable to have a reform adopted by all states, not just a few.

Appendix I. Under any Electoral College System One Can Win the Popular Vote but Lose the Election

The following example shows how easy it is under any Electoral College system to have someone losing the election and winning the popular vote. Table 15 examines the case of two states and compares popular vote outcomes across the two states with the different electoral vote outcomes. The idea is that the interaction between two states can lead to an understanding in the case of many states. In particular, the table gives the number of districts (#D), the average number of voters in each district (V per D), and the percentages of voters selecting candidates A and B (% for A and % for B, respectively).[43] Section A provides the basic setting in which the outcomes are similar to those in Table 12: the E′ outcome is consistent with the popular vote across states while the E and the E* outcomes are inconsistent. Sec-

---

[43] The numbers appearing under the columns V per D, Pa, and Pb should be measured in units of 100,000.

Table 15

		(1)	(2)	(3)	(4)	(5)	(6)	(7)	(8)	(9)	(10)	(11)	(12)
		#D	V per D	% for A	% for B	Pa	Pb	Ea	Eb	E'a	E'b	E*a	E*b
(A)	S1	5	25	0.542	0.458	67.75	57.25	7		3.794	3.206	4	3
	S2	5	25	0.45	0.55	56.25	68.75		7	3.15	3.85	3	4
	S1 & S2					124	**126**	**7**	7	6.944	**7.056**	7	7
							P: B	E: tie			E': B	E*: tie	
	Consistency with the P outcome							No	No	Yes	No	Yes	
(B)	S1	6	25	0.542	0.458	81.3	68.7	8		4.336	3.664	5	3
	S2	5	25	0.45	0.55	56.25	68.75		7	3.15	3.85	3	4
	S1 & S2					**137.55**	137.45	**8**	7	7.486	**7.514**	**8**	7
						P: A		E: A			E': B	E*: A	
	Consistency with the P outcome							Yes			No	Yes	
(C)	S1	5	25	0.542	0.458	67.75	57.25	7		3.794	3.206	4	3
	S2	5	20	0.45	0.55	45	55		7	3.15	3.85	3	4
	S1 & S2					**112.75**	112.25	7	7	6.944	**7.056**	7	7
						P: A		E: tie			E': B	E*: tie	
	Consistency with the P outcome							No			No	No	

continued

Table 15 *continued*

	(1)	(2)	(3)	(4)	(5)	(6)	(7)	(8)	(9)	(10)	(11)	(12)
	#D	V per D	% for A	% for B	Pa	Pb	Ea	Eb	E'a	E'b	E*a	E*b
(D) S1	6	25	0.542	0.458	81.3	68.7	8		4.336	3.664	5	3
S2	5	25	0.42	0.58	52.5	72.5		7	2.94	4.06	2	5
S1 & S2					133.8	**141.2**	**8**	7	7.276	**7.724**	7	**8**
						P: B	E: A			E': B		E*: B
Consistency with the P outcome							No			Yes		Yes
(E) S1	6	25	0.568	0.432	85.2	64.8	8		4.544	3.456	5	3
S2	5	25	0.42	0.58	52.5	72.5		7	2.94	4.06	2	5
S1 & S2					**137.7**	137.3	**8**	7	7.484	**7.516**	7	**8**
					P: A		E: A			E': B		E*: B
Consistency with the P outcome					Yes		Yes			No		No

tions B through E illustrate small changes from that depicted in section A, with the changes appearing in bold.

This example illustrates the possibility of an inconsistent outcome under E′—the perfect proportional system. Section B shows that if the number of districts in S1 is 6 rather than 5, then the E′ outcome is inconsistent with the nationwide popular outcome while the E and the E* outcomes are consistent. Section C shows what happens when, instead of a larger number of districts in S1, the number of voters in S2 is smaller. These examples show that no Electoral College outcome is always consistent with the popular outcome.

As the first three sections of Table 15 investigate the unpleasant property of the E′ system, the outcomes under E and E* are always identical. The next two sections look into the impact on outcomes given changes in the winning margin in the popular votes. In section D, increasing the margin of victory for candidate B in S2 from section B reverses the winner between the E system and the E* system. In particular, both the E* outcome and the E′ outcome are compatible with the popular outcome while the E outcome is not. Presumably, these are the outcomes that are hoped for in this study, since alternative systems that supposedly provide better electoral presentations of the popular votes relative to the widely adopted winner-take-all system are proposed. Unfortunately, this is also not always the case.

Section E in Table 15 shows that if the winning margin for candidate A in S1 increases, the outcomes are completely different. In this case, only the E outcome is consistent with the popular vote. The table illustrates the unstable properties of all outcomes: if the numbers of districts, voter participation, or margins of victory change slightly, the popular winner can change as well as the winners under the different electoral allocation systems. Further, the lack of a fixed relationship between the outcomes of the different electoral allocation systems and the popular outcome is prominent in the example. It seems likely that any of the scenarios exhibited in Table 15 can occur in reality.

Appendix 2—Election 2000

State	T	E	Al GORE					George W. BUSH					Ralph NADER				Pat BUCHANAN			
			Pg/T	Eg	$E'g$	E^*g_1	E^*g_2	Pb/T	Eb	$E'b$	E^*b_1	E^*b_2	Pn/T	En	$E'n$	E^*n_3	Pp/T	Ep	$E'p$	E^*p
Total	103,161,312	538		267	259.89	158	105		271	261.01	166	106		0	14.61	3		0	2.49	0
Alabama	1,664,912	9	0.418	0	3.77		3	0.567	9	5.10		6	0.011	0	0.10		0.004	0	0.03	
Alaska	227,363	3	0.283	0	0.85		1	0.598	3	1.80		2	0.100	0	0.30		0.019	0	0.06	
Arizona	1,404,257	8	0.453	0	3.62		3	0.509	8	4.07		5	0.030	0	0.24		0.008	0	0.07	
Arkansas	916,779	6	0.459	0	2.75		2	0.515	6	3.09		4	0.014	0	0.09		0.012	0	0.07	
California	10,608,225	54	0.539	54	29.12	30		0.418	0	22.59	22		0.038	0	2.07	2	0.004	0	0.22	
Colorado	1,724,478	8	0.428	0	3.43		3	0.513	8	4.10		5	0.053	0	0.42		0.006	0	0.05	
Connecticut	1,406,857	8	0.566	8	4.53	5		0.388	0	3.10	3		0.043	0	0.34		0.003	0	0.03	
Delaware	326,782	3	0.553	3	1.66	2		0.419	0	1.26	1		0.025	0	0.08		0.002	0	0.01	
Dist.of Columbia ~	188,949	3	0.857	3	2.57	3		0.090	0	0.27	0		0.053	0	0.16		0.000	0	0.00	
Florida	5,939,934	25	0.490	0	12.26		12	0.490	25	12.26		13	0.016	0	0.41		0.003	0	0.07	
Georgia	2,537,761	13	0.438	0	5.69		5	0.558	13	7.25		8	0.000	0	0.00		0.004	0	0.06	
Hawaii	365,674	4	0.561	4	2.24	3		0.377	0	1.51	1		0.059	0	0.24		0.003	0	0.01	
Idaho	482,340	4	0.287	0	1.15		1	0.697	4	2.79		3	0.000	0	0.00		0.016	0	0.06	
Illinois	4,728,000	22	0.548	22	12.05	13		0.427	0	9.40	9		0.022	0	0.48		0.003	0	0.07	
Indiana	2,159,582	12	0.417	0	5.00		5	0.575	12	6.90		7	0.000	0	0.00		0.008	0	0.10	
Iowa *	1,307,663	7	0.488	7	3.42	4		0.485	0	3.40	3		0.022	0	0.16		0.004	0	0.03	
Kansas	1,052,679	6	0.373	0	2.24		2	0.586	6	3.52		4	0.034	0	0.20		0.007	0	0.04	
Kentucky	1,534,770	8	0.415	0	3.32		3	0.567	8	4.53		5	0.015	0	0.12		0.003	0	0.02	
Louisiana	1,749,802	9	0.451	0	4.06		4	0.528	9	4.76		5	0.012	0	0.11		0.008	0	0.07	
Maine *	642,999	4	0.492	4	1.97	3		0.443	0	1.77	1		0.059	0	0.24		0.007	0	0.03	
Maryland	1,919,400	10	0.570	10	5.70	6		0.402	0	4.02	4		0.027	0	0.27		0.002	0	0.02	
Massachusetts	2,671,925	12	0.603	12	7.23	8		0.328	0	3.94	4		0.065	0	0.78		0.004	0	0.05	
Michigan	4,172,659	18	0.513	18	9.24	10		0.467	0	8.40	8		0.020	0	0.36		0.000	0	0.00	
Minnesota *	2,427,334	10	0.481	10	4.81	6		0.457	0	4.57	4		0.052	0	0.52		0.009	0	0.09	
Mississippi	960,407	7	0.417	0	2.92		2	0.572	7	4.00		5	0.008	0	0.06		0.002	0	0.02	
Missouri	2,348,641	11	0.473	0	5.20		5	0.506	11	5.57		6	0.016	0	0.18		0.004	0	0.05	
Montana	407,241	3	0.337	0	1.01		1	0.589	3	1.77		2	0.060	0	0.18		0.014	0	0.04	

State	Pop																		
Nebraska	650,741	5	0.331	0	1.66		1	0.628	5	3.14	4		0.035	0	0.18		0.005	0	0.03
Nevada	601,239	4	0.466	0	1.86		1	0.502	4	2.01	3		0.025	0	0.10		0.008	0	0.03
New Hampshire *	563,747	4	0.472	0	1.89		1	0.484	4	1.94	3		0.039	0	0.16		0.005	0	0.02
New Jersey	3,100,339	15	0.564	15	8.45	9		0.404	0	6.07		6	0.030	0	0.45		0.002	0	0.03
New Mexico *	594,681	5	0.481	5	2.41	3		0.481	0	2.40		2	0.036	0	0.18		0.002	0	0.01
New York	6,260,288	33	0.602	33	19.86	20		0.357	0	11.79		12	0.036	0	1.18	1	0.005	0	0.18
North Carolina	2,852,930	14	0.433	0	6.07		6	0.563	14	7.89	8		0.000	0	0.00		0.003	0	0.04
North Dakota	288,530	3	0.333	0	1.00		1	0.609	3	1.83	2		0.033	0	0.10		0.025	0	0.08
Ohio	4,552,370	21	0.465	0	9.77		10	0.504	21	10.58	11		0.025	0	0.53		0.006	0	0.12
Oklahoma	1,227,675	8	0.386	0	3.09		3	0.606	8	4.85	5		0.000	0	0.00		0.007	0	0.06
Oregon *	1,516,099	7	0.474	7	3.32	4		0.470	0	3.29		3	0.051	0	0.36		0.005	0	0.03
Pennsylvania	4,849,053	23	0.508	23	11.69	12		0.467	0	10.74		11	0.021	0	0.49		0.003	0	0.08
Rhode Island	413,485	4	0.615	4	2.46	3		0.321	0	1.28		1	0.059	0	0.23		0.005	0	0.02
South Carolina	1,407,517	8	0.411	0	3.29		3	0.572	8	4.57	5		0.015	0	0.12		0.003	0	0.02
South Dakota	312,579	3	0.380	0	1.14		1	0.609	3	1.83	2		0.000	0	0.00		0.011	0	0.03
Tennessee	2,058,181	11	0.475	0	5.23		5	0.513	11	5.65	6		0.010	0	0.11		0.002	0	0.02
Texas	6,376,321	32	0.381	0	12.19		12	0.595	32	19.05	20		0.022	0	0.69		0.002	0	0.06
Utah	758,840	5	0.266	0	1.33		1	0.675	5	3.37	4		0.047	0	0.23		0.012	0	0.06
Vermont	289,431	3	0.512	3	1.54	2		0.412	0	1.24		1	0.068	0	0.21		0.008	0	0.02
Virginia	2,717,610	13	0.449	0	5.84		6	0.527	13	6.85	7		0.022	0	0.28		0.002	0	0.03
Washington	2,466,689	11	0.506	11	5.56	6		0.450	0	4.94		5	0.042	0	0.46		0.003	0	0.03
West Virginia	634,337	5	0.459	0	2.29		2	0.520	5	2.60	3		0.016	0	0.08		0.005	0	0.02
Wisconsin *	2,580,398	11	0.481	11	5.29	6		0.479	0	5.26		5	0.036	0	0.40		0.004	0	0.05
Wyoming ~	210,819	3	0.287	0	0.86		0	0.700	3	2.10	3		0.000	0	0.00		0.013	0	0.04

* The states that have the plurality effects.

~ The two states who allocate all the E* votes to the majority winner.

Pa/T—the fraction of popular vote going to candidate A.

Ea—the number of electoral votes allocated to candidate A under winner-take-all electoral allocation system E.

E'a—the number of electoral votes allocated to candidate A under perfect proportional electoral allocation system E'.

E*a—the number of electoral votes allocated to candidate A under integral proportional electoral allocation system E*.

(The subscript j refers to votes won because candidate A comes in jth garnering the most popular votes.)

Source: http://cbsnews.com/campaign2000results/election/index.html (Downloaded 12/16/2000)

Of Same Sex Relationships and Affirmative Action: The Covert Libertarianism of the United States Supreme Court

Richard A. Epstein*

The now discredited doctrine in Lochner v. New York, *applied a theory of constitutional review that struck down limitations on freedom of contract in economic affairs that did not protect the process of contract formation, and did not control against harmful external effects on third parties, whether by force or monopoly. Mere dislike of the practices of other parties was not a ground for regulation. Yet on matters of morals, most specifically the regulation of sexual practices, the old court applied a much laxer standard. The recent decisions in* Grutter *and* Lawrence *represent the complete reversal of the pattern, so that now on matters of sexual regulation and morals, a high standard of review is applied to state efforts to stop consensual arrangements, while a low standard of review is in practice applied when the state wishes to engage in affirmative action. The difficulties with these modern opinions lie not in their results, but in their lack of candor in the choice of standards of review. The observed pattern applies the* Lochner *standards to "intimate associations" but offers no reason why it should not be applied to all associations, regardless of their purpose.*

* James Parker Hall Distinguished Service Professor of Law, The University of Chicago; Peter and Kirsten Bedford Senior Fellow, The Hoover Institution. The second half of this lecture is based on a lecture that I gave at the George Mason Law School on Affirmative Action at the George Mason Law School. My thanks to Michael Greve for his perceptive, insistent and spirited critique of my views on affirma6tive action, and to Eric Murphy, University of Chicago Law School, class of 2005, for his instantaneous and impeccable research assistance.

I. INTRODUCTION

This past term the United States Supreme Court addressed two vital social issues that have attracted enormous attention from social theorists, but little from scholars with an economic orientation. On the first of these issues, addressed in *Grutter v. Michigan*,[1] and less importantly, in *Gratz v. Bollinger*,[2] the Supreme Court applied its revised standard of strict scrutiny to affirmative action programs for university admissions at the college and graduate level. It held, as a general matter, that these programs that stress individualized determinations and treat race as one variable among many pass constitutional muster, even though (through a different coalition) programs that give a fixed hard-edged racial preference do not. On the vexed question of same-sex relationships, in *Lawrence v. Texas*[3] the Court overruled its prior decision in *Bowers v. Hardwick*,[4] and held that state laws that prohibited sodomy between individuals of the same or different sexes had no rational basis. Thus, they could not survive the most minimal level of constitutional scrutiny.

The most casual examination of these two decisions reveals a certain level of deep irony about them. For many years it has been assumed that setting the appropriate level of review was a matter of constitutional destiny. Writing over thirty years ago, the late Gerald Gunther penned the famous phrase "strict in theory, and fatal in fact,"[5] to describe the constitutional guillotine associated with strict scrutiny. But his aphorism was explicitly disclaimed in Justice O'Connor's opinion, which held that strict scrutiny did not necessarily lead to invalidation of various state programs, including Michigan's Law School admissions program that looked to the entire record before making a decision in which race counted as only one factor.[6] The Court's approach on affirmative action, however, must be paired with its treatment of same-sex relationships. The latter once lay on the other side of the great constitutional divide in light of the once unquestioned inclusion of morals regulation within the traditional sphere of the police power. Although Gunther did not pen the correlative maxim, the conventional wisdom held, to continue the metaphor, "rational" in theory, "valid" in fact. But that maxim too was upended in *Lawrence*, for

---

[1] 123 S Ct 2325 (2003).

[2] 123 S Ct 2411 (2003).

[3] 123 S Ct 2472 (2003).

[4] 478 US 186 (1986).

[5] Gerald Gunther, *The Supreme Court, 1971 Term—Foreword: In Search of Evolving Doctrine on a Changing Court: A Model for a Newer Equal Protection*, 86 Harv L Rev 1, 8 (1972).

[6] *Grutter*, 123 S Ct at 2338.

now Texas's antisodomy statute was struck down under a rational basis standard of review because Justice Kennedy could not think of a single reason why that provision should be kept on the books. The naïve answer to this puzzle is that under the new constitutional jurisprudence, the Court upholds legislation that it likes and strikes that which it does not. It is the ultimate triumph, one might say, of a realist jurisprudence that knows no limits on judicial self-gratification.

The truth of these charges is overstated, or at least misdirected. But the combined impact of these two developments, no matter how construed, shakes the structure of modern constitutional law to its intellectual roots. For well over sixty-five years, that constitutional theory had an intelligible, albeit indefensible, intellectual structure that ran (the past tense seems appropriate) roughly as follows. Although all men were created equal, all constitutional provisions were not. Rather, before embarking on the interpretation of any particular constitutional clause, the Court had to select the level of scrutiny that it was going to bring to the inquiry. That nontextual task is not easy to discharge as an abstract matter because none of the clauses in the Constitution are written in either indelible or invisible ink. The entire document contains a set of provisions that grants powers to various branches of government or imposes specific limitations on the way in which these powers may be exercised in order to protect some individual rights. The issue is how to match the appropriate standard of review with the particular provision, often in the context of a particular case. As a matter of simple description, the Supreme Court consistently applied the lowest standard of review—rational basis—to challenges to laws on the ground that they infringed economic liberties or took private property. This standard was in marked contrast to the pre-1937 period in which these interests received greater, but not absolute, protection. That lower standard of review also attached to various forms of morals legislation that dealt with sexual relations both within and outside of marriage. Therefore, the regulation of sodomy, polygamy, and prostitution were proper subjects of state regulation along with such matters as loitering, gambling, and cockfighting. On the other side of the ledger, matters that concerned political speech and race relations were understood to be vulnerable to mischievous majorities, whose actions accordingly received far higher levels of scrutiny from the courts.

The question, therefore, is what to make of the sea change that has taken place. Here there is much truth in the realist charge that the standards of review have become a plaything in the hands of justices in search of larger game. But it is too harsh to say that these decisions are beyond theoretical reconstruction with a little bit of intellectual candor. When the dust settles, the best explanation for what the

Court has done is to revive, in the area of social rights, much of the traditional view of the somewhat misnamed laissez-faire constitutionalism that prevailed between the end of the Civil War and the New Deal revolution that culminated in 1937.

In order to make out this claim, section I traces the history of that theory of constitutional interpretation as it applies to the traditional subjects of property rights and economic liberties, and contrasts that view with the modern synthesis that displaced it in the post 1937 period. In effect there has been a full scale constitutional revolution, so that principles of freedom of association have trumped the morals head of the police power with its historical recognition of extensive discretion in the prohibition or regulation of sexual behaviors of all sort. Indeed at one time, the morals head of the police power was so broad that it was invoked to sustain explicit racial prohibitions that were avowedly designed to keep African-Americans in subordinate positions. Here is the key inversion: the older views of constitutionalism that once applied to economic liberties and property rights have now migrated to questions of affirmative action and same sex relationships, so that these are by and large judged under the loose pro-liberty standards that had once been reserved for the protection of economic liberties. *Lochner v. New York*[7] may be routinely disavowed, but it has found a new home under another name. Section II shows how the same sex sodomy cases fit within this paradigm and discusses the implications that this model has for one issue that looms large in the current political debate: that over same sex marriages. Tradition, it becomes clear, has taken a back seat to liberty. Section III applies the same analysis to the affirmative action question, which has abandoned, except in name, the strict scrutiny standard to allow a public university the freedom to manage its own enrollment, with only somewhat less freedom that was enjoyed by a private institution in the era before the antidiscrimination laws. Section IV then compares the two legal regimes with each other, and briefly with the highly intrusive system of regulation of intercollegiate athletics that has developed under Title IX.

The question is what themes unify this disparate area of law. The key here lies in how to think about voluntary decisions made by public and private groups. The Constitution should be read to give the state some greater measure of discretion when it operates its own activities than it does when it tries to limit the activities of ordinary individuals in their private affairs. In the former case, no public decision can satisfy all of the people all of the time, so we should be content largely with decisions that seem to parallel the dominant practices of

---

[7] 198 US 45 (1905).

private institutions that are not subject to direct constitutional control. But there is no reason to allow a political majority to upset the decisions made by private individuals, whether or not acting in formal groups or associations, on their own initiative. Accordingly, there is no need to show the same level of deference to political decisions because it is possible to embrace a simpler alternative that allows ordinary people, both in and out of groups, to go their separate ways. At this point, the key test for all associational liberties, whether or not intimate, is whether in fact they do cause harm to the lives and property of the majority of the population that disapproves of what they do. The nineteenth century test under the police power, which asks whether legislation or regulation is justified as a means to protect the "healthy, safety, morals, and general welfare" of the population, survives quite well under its first two heads. But it does not fare nearly so well under its elusive "morals" category, which, under the dominant transformation of our time, is banished unless it comports with the general rules that do, or at least should, limit freedom of association.[8] Both sets of the Court's recent decisions are, after a fashion, defensible, and largely correct, but we have to start from first principles in order to defend them.

II. CLASSICAL CONSTITUTIONAL THEORY

The question of what standard of scrutiny to apply to given pieces of legislation did not arise only with the welfare state, but has always been with us. In principle, the simplest approach is to argue for what might be termed a "flat Constitution," under which the same standard of review is applied to all questions: looking at the text and structure of the constitutional provision, both alone and as it relates to other provisions, does it authorize or limit the power of federal or state actors to do what they have done? This flat version of the world need not rest on any ad hoc presumptions either for or against the constitutionality of particular provisions. Nor need it cast its lots with the champions of judicial activism or judicial restraint in what has become an ever more arid debate. In its proper sense, this method of interpretation is profoundly apolitical because it regards the wisdom of the various substantive provisions of the Constitution as a philosophical given outside the scope of the interpretative sphere. Whatever theory animated the framers is the one that should be preserved to the extent possible in the interpretation of this, or indeed

---

[8] For my views on that question, see Richard A. Epstein, *Liberty, Equality, and Privacy: Choosing a Legal Foundation for Gay Rights*, 2002 U Chi Legal F 73, 90-101. For criticism, see Andrew Koppelman, *The Right to Privacy?*, 2002 U Chi Legal F 105.

any other, document. The goal of interpretation is to *preserve*, for better or worse, its basic political commitments, not to undermine them with clever exceptions that turn the original document more or less on its head. By this standard the correct interpretation of a Marxist constitution should not yield a robust protection to private property on the ground that the modest provision that says "Private Property Is Hereby Abolished" really means "except when it is more efficient than property subject to the collective ownership of the state." The Orwellian rules of construction in *Animal Farm* are the work of satire. Stated otherwise, sound interpretation proceeds in a passionless way to extract the meaning of difficult texts, much as a court would do in determining the import of a difficult or cryptic provision of a commercial contract when it is utterly indifferent, as it were, to whether the risk of the rotten cantaloupes falls on the buyer, seller, or carrier.[9]

This view of the interpretation, moreover, should not be confused with some extreme form of literalism. It is well known that the central task within nineteenth century interpretive theory was to find out whether, and if so, how various constitutional guarantees were hemmed in by the state's police power—roughly speaking the power to regulate in order to protect the health, safety, morals or general welfare—of the citizens of the United States.[10] The catch for any literal theory of interpretation is that the words "police power" nowhere appear on the face of the document in question. Therefore, the enterprise of interpretation can't be literal, but has to rest on a view that a government may regulate in order to advance the long-term advantage of all individuals who are subject to its power, or at least to prevent some individuals from engaging in activities that violate the private rights, whether to liberty or property, of their fellow citizens.

This flat view, therefore, quickly requires some sense of the purposes of government, as understood in *this* Constitution, both with an eye to explain what it is that a political body can and cannot do. In my view, this humble approach has quite startling implications. In the end, it says that the specific protections granted to property, contract, liberty and religion in the Constitution may be justifiably limited only to the extent that the limitation improves, relative to a baseline of individual liberty, the lot of all persons within that society, or protects individuals against the kind of conduct that is regarded as wrongful as between citizens under some sensible view of common

---

[9] See Henry Hart & Albert Sacks, *Legal Process: Basic Problems in the Making and Application of Law* (Foundation, 1994).

[10] For treatises on this subject, see Thomas Cooley, *A Treatise on the Constitutional Limitations Which Rest Upon the Legislative Power of the States of the American Union* (Da Capo, 5th ed 1998); Ernst Freund, *The Police Power: Public Policy and Constitutional Rights* (Callaghan & Co, 1905).

law that stresses the prohibition on force and fraud. The constitutional synthesis, as it existed from the end of the Civil War to 1937, contains clear signs that the old Court took its cue from this general theory to strike down all laws that were not designed to curb aggression, including nuisances,[11] monopoly[12] or common pool problems (e.g., hunting limitations on wild animals and oil and gas[13]). Under this view an antitrust law that breaks up monopolies, or a system of rate regulation that limits common carriers to just and reasonable rates of return, including provisions that guard against discrimination in rates charged, meets constitutional muster. But the effort to impose a general antidiscrimination law such as Title VII fails to meet constitutional standards because it violates the general norm of free association, albeit with less severe consequences, every bit as much as a law that might mandate forced marriage. The older synthesis was not inhospitable to redistribution and welfare support, at least at the state level, and made its peace with such institutions as progressive taxation and inheritance taxes. But as those issues are far from the table, I shall not trouble to analyze them here.

The question is where does this apparatus come from? Here the first point to note is life, liberty, contract, and private property receive specific protection, which (in the inverse to the Marxist example) cannot be read out of the document by a set of exceptions that swallows the rules. It is, for example, not permissible to say that the diffuse social benefits from this or that government program are always and necessarily so large as to offset the property rights taken, so that no individualized examination need be made of the benefits that the tax imposes on the taxed party. Yet just that approach, for example, is taken by Justice Stone in upholding the constitutionality of an unemployment benefits program in *Carmichael v. Southern Coal & Coke Co.*[14] when he wrote: "The only benefit to which the taxpayer is constitutionally entitled is that derived from his enjoyment of the privileges of living in an organized society, established and safeguarded by the devotion of taxes to public purposes."[15] This argument has to be wrong because it effectively concedes that all taxes are takings, but that none is unconstitutional because each is, in the eyes of the law, necessarily offset by a benefit equal to or greater than the tax imposed. The net effect is that a succession of programs all of which cost more than they are worth are constitutional because they do not send the individuals that they burden into revolution or back to the stone age.

[11] See *Northwestern Fertilizing Co v Hyde Park*, 97 US 659 (1878).
[12] See *Addyston Pipe & Steel Co v United States*, 175 US 111 (1899).
[13] See *Ohio Oil Co v Indiana* (No. 1), 177 US 190 (1899).
[14] 301 US 495 (1937).
[15] Id at 522.

On the other side, however, no matter what gloss is placed on these individual clauses, it is not credible to claim that ours is a strong libertarian Constitution if by that one means that that the government cannot use coercion or taxation to restrict liberty or take property against the will of its citizens. The Fifth Amendment—nor shall private property be taken for public use, without just compensation— makes it unmistakable that so long as just compensation is provided, the property may be taken *without* the consent of its owner so long as it is for public use. The strong libertarian takes the position that taxes are a form of theft. Yet the United States Constitution contains an explicit authorization of the power to tax, which is then subject to limitations: "The Congress shall have the Power To lay and collect Taxes, Duties, Imposts and Excises, to pay the Debts and provide for the common Defense and general Welfare of the United States; but all Duties, Imposts and Excises shall be uniform throughout the United States."[16] Note the central point is that the powers of taxation can be used to purchase what are now called public goods, which include payment of national debts, the provision of the common defense and the advancement of the general welfare. This last phrase, which is written as a limit on the objects of taxation, cannot refer to just any activity that the government wants to do, any more than the public use clause is satisfied by any "conceivable" public use.[17]

In light of this picture that allows state force to be used to advance public ends, it makes perfectly good sense to see limited government as the ideal to which the Constitution gravitates, so that the state has powers to respond to the two main areas of market failure: externalities and public goods.[18] Stated in its most general form, the use of rational basis review for state regulation of private activity is always off-limits in any system that keeps to the initial premise of limited government, which operates within the rule of law.[19] The only implied exceptions to individual rights of liberty and property cover what could be loosely called the common forms of market failure. Within this framework we can now give a precise definition to the intellectual transformation that took place during the New Deal. The three specific heads of regulation referred to above no longer defined the scope of government regulation. The New Deal frequently ratified the creation of state-supported monopolies that were wholly inconsistent with the earlier vision of limited government. Cases such as

[16] US Const Art I, § 8, cl 1.

[17] But see *Hawaii Housing Authority v Midkiff*, 467 US 986 (1984)

[18] For my defense of the clause-independent nature of this argument, see Richard A. Epstein, *The "Necessary" History of Property and Liberty*, 6 Chap L Rev 1 (2003).

[19] See generally Richard Stewart, *The Formation of American Administrative Law*, 88 Harv L Rev 1667 (1975).

Nebbia v. New York[20] marked a powerful if unfortunate transition insofar as they stood the original understanding of the aims of rate regulation on its head. The traditional preference for state support of competition was replaced by the view that the state should have the power to decide whether competition or monopoly was preferred in any given setting. How else does one explain a decision that justified the use of state power to validate *minimum* price supports for milk in what would otherwise be a competitive industry? In essence, the theory of the administrative state is that no individual or group has vested rights in any determinate set of rights. Instead, all are entitled to rights of notice and hearing before some board or agency that doles out its favor in accordance with some law-like set of principles, and is subject to judicial review as a safeguard against arbitrary and capricious behavior. That position in effect leads to the view that the residual protections to property and contract are concentrated to situations that verge on bills of attainder, namely, where an individual or small group of individuals is singled out for special treatment without justification.

Yet side by side with this transformation of property rights and economic liberties stands the reverse move with respect to morals legislation. There is little question that in the nineteenth century, all matters of moral regulation received enormous deference from the courts. In part, but only in part, morals regulation could be justified as a fumbling, but indirect, means to reach items that would be subject to regulation under the narrower views of regulation applicable to property and liberty. The regulation of a funeral home could be justified as a means to prevent waste fluids from entering local rivers, for example. And much of the regulation of promiscuous sexual behavior could be justified as a means to cut down on the incidence of sexually transmitted diseases. But lots more was done on other grounds, namely, that the practices in question, such as polygamy or premarital sexual relations, were against the dominant mores of the community. In effect, the rationale of indirect community benefit that later came to be used routinely in cases of economic regulation had its origin in the earlier cases of public morals, where it is now repudiated. Much of the tortured history of morals regulation after 1900 takes the form of adapting the standard libertarian theory on this area of law. No longer is it sufficient that certain rules appeal to the traditions and norms of our people. It has to be shown that there is a specific state justification for that peculiar form of contract known as "intimate associations." In time these took the exact same form that they assumed in the nineteenth century with liberty or property. The

[20] 291 US 502 (1934).

problems of common pools and monopoly are not serious issues in this context, and thus can be put safely to one side. The key issue, therefore, is whether sexual practices result in an increase in the incidence of sexually transmitted disease, a point that has to be pleaded and proved, which rarely was attempted outside the area of contagion and public health.

III. *LAWRENCE*, AND ECONOMICS OF SAME SODOMY AND SAME SEX MARRIAGE

At this point, the argument has progressed far enough to make clear the approach to sodomy and same sex marriage. First, these behaviors, no matter what others think of them, produce on average net gains to the parties that undertake them, so that limitations on them are justified only to protect the interests of third parties, which, in line with libertarian theory, do not include the offense that other people take toward the fact that certain actors engage in certain conduct, lest the protected zone of individual choice be overrun by an extravagant definition of harm. *Lawrence* was notable for its lack of any claim of specific harm, so that only claims of harm to community norms and values could support its judgment, and those fail categorically in a free society. Reaching this position required an inversion from the older position which gave the state unchallenged power over morals regulation. It is instructive to identify a few landmarks in this transformation.

Griswold v. Connecticut[21] struck down the Connecticut law that forbade the use of contraceptives, a clear regulation of sexual practices.[22] Under the older, categorical view of the police power, so long as the statute pertained to morals, then it hardly mattered whether it was targeted against any legitimate state object, such as teen pregnancy or the spread of sexually transmitted diseases. The statute stood regardless. To someone committed in the now-rejected *Lochner* tradition, that level of deference is not appropriate for economic liberties, so it should not be appropriate for restrictions on personal freedom either. Here there is a use of a contraceptive, like that of any other good or resource, counts as an ordinary liberty of action, so that freedom of contract need not be invoked in order to find a protected interest. But of course contractual interests are implicated because the general Connecticut law, surely valid in connection with other

[21] 381 US 479 (1965).

[22] Conn Gen Stat § 53-32 (1958) provided: "Any person who uses any drug, medicinal article or instrument for the purpose of preventing conception shall be fined not less than fifty dollars or imprisoned not less than sixty days nor more than one year or be both fined and imprisoned."

crimes, made it an offense to help other individuals (by contract of course) in the performance of any other act.[23] Indeed, the provision on accessory liability was invoked to convict Planned Parenthood officials who supplied the contraceptives to married couples. To complete the circle, there is no question that if these two statutes were valid, then any law that prohibited the *sale* of contraceptives had to be valid as well, since these sales could only be undertaken for transactions that were illegal within the state.

It is easy to see then how the full panoply of anti-contraceptive laws are a direct affront to liberty of action, freedom of association and freedom of contract. But what justification for them falls within the traditional capacity of the prevention of external harm, monopoly or common pool problems? None comes to mind so long as contraceptives are used, among other purposes, to reduce the rate of transmissible diseases. And surely none of their use is restricted within marriage, where it cannot even be argued that the availability of contraceptives increases the rate of (illicit) sexual relationships outside of marriage.

Writing in 1965, Justice Douglas and all of his colleagues treated *Lochner* like the plague. Their trick was to write an opinion that struck down the statute without invoking an opinion that seemed so well-suited to the task. Unfortunately, once the protection of ordinary liberty was out, then something else had to be in, in order to generate a constitutional claim in the first place. Here the new constitutional right of privacy rested on "the intimate relation of husband and wife," which was deemed protected under—take your pick—the penumbra and radiations of specific provisions of the Bill of Rights (Justice Douglas),[24] the Ninth Amendment (Justice Goldberg),[25] or old-fashioned substantive due process (Justice Harlan).[26] These judicial adventures were stoutly resisted by Justices Black and Stewart in dissent on the ground that *Griswold* simply brought the ghost of *Lochner* back to life, which of course is what it should have done.

What is striking about these decisions nearly 40 years later is how *illiberal* they read in the light of the subsequent sexual revolution. Justice Douglas went out of his way to limit the scope of his decision

---

[23] Id at § 54-196 provides: "Any person who assists, abets, counsels, causes, hires or commands another to commit any offense may be prosecuted and punished as if he were the principal offender."

[24] *Griswold*, 381 US at 481-84 ("The foregoing cases [dealing with religion, speech, association quartering soldiers, suggest that specific guarantees in the Bill of Rights have penumbras, formed by emanations from those guarantees that help give them life and substance.").

[25] Id at 486-99.

[26] Id at 499-502.

to the provision of information and advice to *married persons* (his italics), which recognized that the ban on the use of contraceptives, and thus their sale and any counseling function, was not touched by this decision. He noted explicitly that the protection of privacy within the institution of marriage was older than the Bill of Rights, with a clear nod to tradition, which was picked up explicitly in Justice Goldberg's concurrence. The implicit conflict between personal liberty and traditional practices, however, exerted a powerful impact on the scope of *Griswold*. The tension was best revealed by Justice Harlan, who noted that the defense of the sanctity of marriage had two components: the protection of the marriage relationship on the one side, which speaks to freedom of some intimate associations, *and* the continued illegality of "adultery, fornication and homosexual practices."[27] The entire point of his high-minded exercise was to defend liberty in the case before the court, but to do so by holding that it respectfully yield to social tradition in a wide range of other cases. The gist of the early defense of *marital* privacy carried with it the correlative barb that other relationships, equally intimate and voluntary, were outside the area of constitutional protection. In essence, the Harlan position was that the Connecticut statute could be struck down because it was an outlier to our own tradition, but that the other forms of state regulation that fell within that tradition could not be touched. The conflict between liberty, as a normative vision, and tradition, as an alternative source of authority, was postponed, not resolved.

The *Griswold* compromise, moreover, is at mortal tension with the general view that the holders of constitutional rights are not couples in relationships, but individuals. It took only a few years before the point was made explicit in *Eisenstadt v. Baird*,[28] which struck down a statute that prohibited the sale of contraceptives to unmarried persons. In an opinion that pays homage to the principle of methodological individualism, Justice Brennan wrote: "If the right of privacy means anything, it is the right of the *individual*, married or single, to be free from unwarranted governmental intrusion into matter so fundamentally affecting a person as the decision whether to bear or beget a child."[29] So *Griswold*, as it were, is reduced from bold innovation

---

[27] *Poe v Ullman*, 367 US 497, 546 (1961). Justice Harlan's full statement reads: "The laws regarding marriage which provide both when the sexual powers may be used and the legal and societal context in which children are born and brought up, as well as laws forbidding adultery, fornication and homosexual practices which express the negative of the proposition, confining sexuality to lawful marriage, form a pattern so deeply pressed into the substance of our social life that any Constitutional doctrine in this area must build upon that basis."

[28] 405 US 438 (1972).

[29] Id at 453.

to meaningless decision. But note that this particular leap from *Gris-wold* counts only as a baby-step under the forbidden *Lochner* ration-ale. Once again, the only interests that the state puts forward are the traditional offenses that other individuals take toward conduct which they regard as immoral. No tangible form of harm, sufficient to trigger an exercise of the police power, is alleged. The inversion is thus com-plete: what used to be called meretricious relationships now count as intimate associations protected by this or that constitutional clause, it hardly matters which. With the nature of the underlying interest secure, it is simply going through the motions to show that the state has no justification for its restriction.

The next stage in this development is much more controversial be-cause it applies the new rights to self-rule to abortion. As I wrote on *Roe v. Wade*[30] thirty years ago,[31] this position is in manifest conflict with the basic libertarian theory because here the third-party inter-ests, namely those of the fetus or unborn child, are harmed, and this harm has to be taken into account under any conception of the police power or liberal political theory. *Roe* thus gets matters upside down by protecting the very kinds of external harms that states are in the busi-ness to prevent. It is of course possible to contest the application of this theory at a number of levels. One is to argue that the fetus, or, at an earlier stage, the embryo, does not count as a person that is entitled to protection. Yet in response, it can be argued that the harm prin-ciple offers protection for an unborn life that will turn into a human in the ordinary course of events, even if not yet viable. It seems very hard to deny that the future child (or whatever term you wish to use) has some independent status worthy of protection. There is no ques-tion that if a third person committed acts of aggression against the mother with the intention to kill the unborn child, these acts would be two offenses and not one. And there seems equally little dispute that from a straight moral perspective no one thinks that having an abortion is equivalent to the snipping off a wart. At this point, there-fore, the argument switches to the question of whether the mother and those who assist her have a justification for the termination of unborn life. Here there is no doubt that she has a special status with respect to the child, because she bears the burdens of childbirth. Yet by the same token, this unique position carries with it special obli-gations of support, which can easily exist before as well as after birth. Children are totally dependent on their parents immediately after birth; does that give them the right to terminate them then? Within

[30] 410 US 113 (1973).

[31] Richard A. Epstein, *Substantive Due Process By Any Other Name: The Abortion Cases*, 1973 S Ct Rev 159.

this framework, it is hard to come out with a strong moral or legal case for abortion at will, although it is certainly possible to fashion more specific justifications that involve abortion to save the life of the mother, abortion in the case of rape, or abortion in the case of a severely defective child with little or no chances of a normal life. My point here is not to resolve these questions, but only to point out that *Roe v. Wade* is the worst possible case to put forward on behalf of *Lawrence* because it raises questions that are far more difficult in principle than the dispute that it is invoked to solve. *Roe* is not an extension of *Griswold* or *Eisenstadt*. Nor does it count as one more step along the road to liberty. Rather, it regulates conduct that falls squarely within the narrowest conception of the police power.

To round out this survey, it is useful to recount one more area that raises the conflict between liberty and tradition as sources of authority: state prohibitions on nude dancing, which easily fall within the nineteenth century head of morals legislation. But once the idea of sexual freedom takes over, the traditional form of deference to state power cannot survive. Here it is sufficient to consider the exchanges in *Barnes v. Glen Theatre, Inc.*,[32] which applied Indiana's public decency statute to nude dancing in private clubs. With *Lochner* still out of the picture by fiat, the state prohibition was challenged as a limitation on free speech, which led to the usual inconclusive debates over whether nude dancing was protected expression and whether the restrictions in question were but "incidental" to some legitimate state purpose. But think again of how the case must be decided if liberty and property receive a uniform level of protection. Where are the contagion, monopoly or common pool risks that would justify the restrictions in question? Who is forced to observe nude dancing against his or her will in public places? Ever alert to the challenge, Justice Scalia challenged this implicit view of the world by claiming that the offense that nude dancing gave to others who *weren't* watching it gave the state a sufficient hook on which to regulate the conduct. His answer rests on vintage, traditionalist arguments:

> Perhaps the dissenters believe that "offense to others" *ought* to be the only reason for restricting nudity in public places generally, but there is no basis for thinking that our society has ever shared that Thoreauvian "you-may-do-what-you-like-so-long-as-it-does-not-injure-someone-else" beau ideal—much less for thinking that it was written into the Constitution. The purpose of Indiana's nudity law would be violated, I think, if 60,000 fully consenting adults crowded into the Hoosier Dome to display their genitals to one another, even if there were not an offended

[32] 501 US 560 (1991).

innocent in the crowd. Our society prohibits, and all human societies have prohibited, certain activities not because they harm others but because they are considered, in the traditional phrase, "contra bonos mores," i.e., immoral. In American society, such prohibitions have included, for example, sadomasochism, cockfighting, bestiality, suicide, drug use, prostitution, and sodomy. While there may be great diversity of view on whether various of these prohibitions should exist (though I have found few ready to abandon, in principle, all of them), there is no doubt that, absent specific constitutional protection for the conduct involved, the Constitution does not prohibit them simply because they regulate "morality." See *Bowers v. Hardwick,* 478 US 186, 196.[33]

Scalia's Hoosier Dome example gets right to the crux of the dispute over what types of externalities count in the social calculus. Nudity has not been known to spread disease, and the choice of location guarantees that others do not have to watch this spectacle. The upshot is that the only form of harm that is found in this illustration is the hurt that others of supposedly good moral character sustain from the knowledge (as opposed to the observation) of the bad acts of their fellow citizens. Within the standard accounts of liberty, this type of interest falls outside the scope of the Millian harm principle,[34] which it would otherwise gut. Just imagine what would happen if freedom of speech in political matters did not protect speech that others found offensive. Or that speech which caused offense in right-minded people could be banned while other speech could not. The first case is unacceptable because it gives everyone a potential veto right over the speech of others. The second is unacceptable because it requires public officials to discriminate on the question of who can speak on the strength of viewpoint. Let them all holler, as it were, and the law of defamation and fraud can be used to defend individuals who are victimized by false statements of fact.

The defects in this argument are not cured by an appeal to principles of "contra bonos mores," which appeals to a broader, more diffuse, conception of societal harm. That kind of argument can work, perhaps, when everyone in a given culture has exactly the same views on a question, because the very fact of unanimous opinion eliminates

---

[33] Id at 584-85.

[34] John Stuart Mill, *On Liberty* 72 (Everyman's Library, 1971) (H.B. Acton, ed) (1859). The principle is, that the sole end for which mankind are warranted, individually or collectively, in interfering with the liberty of action of any of their number, is self-protection. That the only purpose for which power can be rightfully exercised over any member of a civilized community, against his will, is to prevent harm to others. His own good, either physical or moral, is not a sufficient warrant.

any question of the legitimacy of legal requirements that are only imposed by majority rule. But once the culture becomes fractured, it becomes necessary to argue that large majorities count as moral consensuses that allow for the suppression of the views of others. How large? And on what issues? These are questions that are hard to answer even when these debates take place along a single line. But they become wholly intractable in light of the numerous cross-currents that exist in any pluralistic society. In the end, the claim of contra bonos mores, without more is a way to privilege one substantive position over all others. It is a move that allows the negative utility of one group on an exquisite set of social scales to trump the sentiments of other groups, which are systematically excluded. The only way to avoid the nose counting is to claim that an objective moral view of good morals must prevail, even when it is at loggerheads with the considered views of other individuals. That form of cultural imperialism will not work. Sad but true, the only way to deal with this impasse is to keep the boundary lines between the two groups separate.

Nor does Justice Scalia make out his case with his suggestive citation to *Bowers,* which leads us smack back to the culture conflict in *Lawrence.* The most cursory examination of *Bowers* shows that Justice White's majority opinion relies on tradition to override liberty to sustain the constitutionality of Georgia's antisodomy statute. The conceptual argument for it was vintage *Griswold:* "No connection between family, marriage, or procreation on the one hand and homosexual activity on the other has been demonstrated, either by the Court of Appeals or by respondent."[35] It is homosexual practices that need justification in terms of family values. But absent any such showing, an unbroken set of anti-sodomy laws dating both from the time of the Constitution and the Fourteenth Amendment meant that democratic institutions could have their way. The dissent for its part rested on a vintage libertarian response that celebrated "the fundamental interest all individuals have in controlling the nature of their intimate associations with others," but without the once critical caveat, within the bounds of marriage.

At this point, the dissent in *Bowers* needed only a moment to dispense with the libertarian police power justifications that might have been invoked to shore up the decision. The first of these was the statute might advance "'the general public health and welfare,' such as spreading communicable diseases or fostering other criminal activity."[36] The obvious response, in line with classical theory, was that in principle these things offer legitimate types of justification, but that no evidence was advanced to support either count in the case.

[35] *Bowers,* 478 US at 191.
[36] Id at 208 (Blackmun, dissenting).

The second argument, that the statutes were in conformity with "traditional Judeo-Christian values" suffers from the converse difficulty. It was undoubtedly true, but falls outside the limited catalogue of permissible justifications. On this point, the libertarian has to agree. The leaders or members of various religious groups could, without doubt, make membership in their group conditional upon the refusal to engage in any form of sodomy. But that is their business, not that of the state, which, if anything, should distance itself from using religious rationales that could easily collide with the Establishment Clause. Finally, the *Bowers* dissent was willing to recognize that public displays of sexual activity could be limited out of the respect for the rights of others with whom they share the public commons, without deciding whether that refusal to allow nude activities in some public places creates a correlative duty to allow it in others, e.g., a special nudist beach. The *Bowers* dissent melded the classical limitations of the police power to the implicit protection of the right of intimate (as opposed to all) association. Call it *Lochner* light.

The decision in *Lawrence* simply turned that dissent into a majority view in response, no doubt, to the new groundswell of support from the strong libertarian position on matters of sexual freedom. The political lines in question were already sharply drawn, so the only question was when and where the axe would fall. The new majority could have struck down the Texas statute on equal protection grounds because it limited the offense of sodomy to individuals of the same sex. But that leaves Texas the option to pass a still *broader* statute that bans sodomy for all. Narrow rationales were not for Justice Kennedy who in his madcap dash to strike down the statute simply "concluded" that the case turned on liberty, not equality.[37] After this bold stroke, all his intellectual moves are familiar. The first task is to define the relevant liberty interests. On this, he could have taken the narrow view of liberty that meant solely the right to move about without physical restraint,[38] which kills off both *Lochner* and *Lawrence* for the same reason. Or he could have taken a more capacious definition of liberty that follows the lead of Justice Peckham who wrote:

> The liberty mentioned in that amendment means not only the right of the citizen to be free from the mere physical restraint of his person, as by incarceration, but the term is deemed

[37] See *Lawrence*, 123 S Ct at 2476 ("We conclude the case should be resolved by determining whether the petitioners were free as adults to engage in the private conduct in the exercise of their liberty under the Due Process Clause of the Fourteenth Amendment to the Constitution.").

[38] Warren, *The New "Liberty" under the Fourteenth Amendment*, 39 Harv L Rev 431, 440 (1926).

to embrace the right of the citizen to be free in the enjoyment of all his faculties; to be free to use them in all lawful ways; to live and work where he will; to earn his livelihood by any lawful calling; to pursue any livelihood or avocation, and for that purpose to enter into all contracts which may be proper, necessary and essential to his carrying out to a successful conclusion the purposes above mentioned.[39]

Justice Kennedy's definition is broad, but its emphasis carefully excluded the old-style economic liberties protected under *Lochner*, while avoiding the narrow definitions that treat liberty as the opposition to confinement.

Liberty protects the person from unwarranted government intrusions into a dwelling or other private places. In our tradition the State is not omnipresent in the home. And there are other spheres of our lives and existence, outside the home, where the State should not be a dominant presence. Freedom extends beyond spatial bounds. Liberty presumes an autonomy of self that includes freedom of thought, belief, expression, and certain intimate conduct. The instant case involves liberty of the person both in its spatial and more transcendent dimensions.[40]

Several points are worth noting about this new definition. First, Kennedy's only hesitation is contained in the reference to "certain" intimate conduct, which leaves open the continued enforcement of, for example, laws against incest. There is no attempt to explain why the subset of intimate relations exhausts the field of liberty, or why the earlier definition of Peckham, which studiously excluded sexual freedoms, was incorrect. Rather, the opinion contains a churlish criticism that the *Bowers* majority mischaracterized the issue as dealing with the criminalization of sodomy and not a general affirmation of sexual freedom:

To say that the issue in *Bowers* was simply the right to engage in certain sexual conduct demeans the claim the individual put forward, just as it would demean a married couple were it to be said marriage is simply about the right to have sexual intercourse. The laws involved in *Bowers* and here are, to be sure, statutes that purport to do no more than prohibit a particular sexual act. Their penalties and purposes, though, have more far-reaching consequences, touching upon the most private human conduct, sexual behavior, and in the most private of places, the home. The

[39] *Allgeyer v Louisiana*, 165 US 578, 589 (1897).
[40] *Lawrence*, 123 S Ct at 2475.

statutes do seek to control a personal relationship that, whether or not entitled to formal recognition in the law, is within the liberty of persons to choose without being punished as criminals.[41]

Pure word play. The *Bowers* court framed the issue narrowly because all aspects of gay freedom were not placed at risk by the statute, which only criminalized sodomy, and not lesser forms of sexual intimacy. The case does not turn on quibbles over the definition of the individual interest, but on the permissible justifications for its limitation. Here the first question on the agenda is the appropriate standard of review. But Justice Kennedy makes no explicit acknowledgement that he believes that the Texas law flunks the rational basis test. Only Justice O'Connor in her narrower concurrence—the same-sex only prohibition offends equal protection—makes copious reference to the rational basis test.[42] Thus, it was left to Justice Scalia to state that Justice Kennedy did use that standard by holding that the Texas statute "'furthers no legitimate state interest which can justify' its application to petitioners under rational-basis review.'"[43] But under the traditional view of that standard, the case had to be decided for the state so long as there was a long record of similar laws on the books. Recall that Holmes's ill-starred *Lochner* dissent defines the test in just this fashion:

> I think that the word liberty in the Fourteenth Amendment is perverted when it is held to prevent the natural outcome of a dominant opinion, unless it can be said that a rational and fair man necessarily would admit that the statute proposed would infringe fundamental principles as they have been understood by the traditions of our people and our law.[44]

Under this standard, Justice Kennedy's historical exegesis is simply beside the point. Of course, the enforcement of the anti-sodomy laws has been erratic over our history. But an ebb and flow in legislative behavior always takes place when the states make political choices through legislative processes. It would be odd to say that a once-valid statute in state A becomes unconstitutional because a like statute has subsequently been repealed in state B. It is wholly disingenuous to argue that some new constitutional tradition has arisen because segments of a deeply polarized public regard these statutes with suspicion and, in some states have supported their repeal. Indeed, my own sociological instinct is that the ambiguity of the status quo ante

[41] Id at 2478.
[42] Id at 2484 (O'Connor concurring).
[43] Id at 2488.
[44] *Lochner v New York*, 198 US 45, 76 (1904) (Holmes dissenting).

was exactly what many Americans wanted. They liked the validity of the law on the books for its symbolic disapproval of certain forms of sexual conduct, but were deeply unhappy about the criminal enforcement of those laws in individual cases. At this point, we are ever so far from showing that changed circumstances and sensibilities have eroded *Bowers*, which only stands for the proposition that antisodomy laws are permissible, not that they are required. Nothing constitutional has changed, except the votes.

Next, Justice Kennedy's evasions come at a high price for social conservatives, who disagree mightily with his results and are right to say that the decision lacks candor as to its motives and justification. No traditional account of the rational basis test allows for the invalidation of this statute. But in fact, Justice Kennedy has transformed the test from within. His first move is to limit the set of *ends* that the state may wish to achieve by legislation. The Texas statute did not address, health, monopoly, or common pool assets, including the use of public spaces. Hence, the rational basis test, if it matters, will do just fine because the statute advances none of these ends, so it hardly matters whether the means chosen are too broad, or too narrow to pass constitutional muster. The case involves only freedom of choice by consenting parties without negative external effects on outsiders. Our Justice has become a committed libertarian of sorts:

> The present case does not involve minors. It does not involve persons who might be injured or coerced or who are situated in relationships where consent might not easily be refused. It does not involve public conduct or prostitution. It does not involve whether the government must give formal recognition to any relationship that homosexual persons seek to enter. The case does involve two adults who, with full and mutual consent from each other, engaged in sexual practices common to a homosexual lifestyle. The petitioners are entitled to respect for their private lives. The State cannot demean their existence or control their destiny by making their private sexual conduct a crime.[45]

But how far can this go? One question is what weight should be attached to the words "*two* adults." If the question is whether actions are consensual between the parties without negative effects on third persons, the "two" should be treated as a simple description of the factual circumstances of *Lawrence*, and not an implicit limit on the scope of the liberty that it protects. Since marriage is not the outer limit of sexual intimacy, then what objection can Justice Kennedy have to the transcendent nature of a menage-a-trois or indeed an

[45] *Lawrence*, 123 S Ct at 2484.

adult-only orgy that is held behind closed doors? And surely polygamy falls within the scope of the new liberty as well, given the consent of all participants and the want of any additional obligations on or harms to, outsiders. Rather than fight these examples, he should throw in the towel, and treat the natural resistance to certain forms of sexual arrangements as the only state-imposed barriers to it. If some high-minded individuals find these practices repellant, they can refuse to associate for business or pleasure with those who practice them.

If the word "two" forecloses consideration of these unconventional social relationships, it invites examination of the social issue that has now worked itself into the society pages of the New York Times and into presidential politics: does the liberty found under the due process clause affords the right for two people to enter into to same-sex marriages. To be sure, *Lawrence* "does not involve whether the government must give formal recognition to any relationship that homosexual persons seek to enter."[46] But can its principles be so limited by judicial fiat. On this point Justice Scalia got right to the heart of the matter when he wrote:

> State laws against bigamy, same-sex marriage, adult incest, prostitution, masturbation, adultery, fornication, bestiality, and obscenity are likewise sustainable only in light of *Bowers'* validation of laws based on moral choices. Every single one of these laws is called into question by today's decision; the Court makes no effort to cabin the scope of its decision to exclude them from its holding.[47]

The question is whether Justice Scalia is right to forecast this chain of horribles that comes from *Lawrence* by a majority that disclaims them, at least for the moment. Here the answer in question turns in the end on how the traditional justifications of harms to others play out in the various contexts. Prostitution is a consensual but business relationship, and I have little doubt that Justice Kennedy thinks that the element of cash robs it of all expressive elements, and thus allows those laws to remain in place. The *Lochner* rationale, however, is far less confident of that judgment and would demand further evidence of how prostitution disrupts protected interests, whether by posing a health hazard or a threat to the institution of marriage by inducing men to breach their marriage vows. Laws against incest are justified to protect minors and to prevent the depression associated with in-breeding. Laws against bestiality could well be sustained on health grounds, at least if the state is prepared to meet its burden of proof.

[46] Id.
[47] Id at 2490.

The large question of course has to do with same-sex marriages, given the obvious tension between the discrete disclaimers—remember *Griswold* applies only to married couples—that it is constitutionally protected, and the broad rationales about human dignity that point in that direction, and led Massachusetts to reach just that conclusion.[48] Here, it seems to me that Scalia's prediction that same-sex marriage will become a constitutional right *should* be correct, politics apart, if *Lawrence* is rightly decided. The crux of the problem is that the state has the monopoly power over whether individuals are entitled to marry. That monopoly power is something that cannot be exercised (or not so) at the whim of the state. Rather, the doctrine of unconstitutional conditions attaches, such that it becomes imperative for the state to decide why one set of unions receives sanctification from the state when another does not. Stated otherwise, the equal protection component of the analysis makes it hard to see why the marriage license should be denied to a set of applicants when it is granted to another. If it be objected that this rationale allows for polygamy or even marriages of sorts in which three men marry four women, then so be it. The harm that others have from disliking the institution is no warrant for stopping its application to all persons who want the privileges of some particular estate so long as it is granted to others.

But this approach will doubtless offend millions who think that marriage should be reserved for their preferred arrangements. They have half a valid point. As noted earlier, any respect for a free set of institutions should make it clear that the state cannot force any private individuals, firm or church, to acknowledge these unions. A church is fully within its power to excommunicate any who engage in practices that they regard as antithetical to their religious beliefs, and no version of a state antidiscrimination law should give any person rights against the institution that holds these practices against them. Those who are excommunicated from one religious institution can establish a second of their own choosing, which is fully compatible with their beliefs, and the members of each are free to argue that the other has betrayed their highest and best religious decisions. Justice Kennedy is dead right to say that the state has no business acting as arbiter between moral positions so long as the only element of harm is the offense taken as to how others conduct their lives.

Indeed, one can go further and ask this question, which has been put forward in powerful form by my colleague Mary Ann Case: why should the state be in the business to sanction marriage of any sort at all? Why not leave that to private groups to determine, under whatever terms and conditions they see fit? If two individuals choose to marry or to cohabit, it is their own business and the state should not

---

[48] *Goodridge v Department of Public Health,* 798 NE 2d 941 (Mass 2003).

provide an edge for one type of institutional arrangements over another, any more than it should privilege partnerships over corporations in commercial life. If it be said that this position leaves children at risk, the answer is twofold: first, religious and social institutions can step forward to fill this obvious gap once the state withdraws from the field. Second, the state can show a strong and continuing interest to require both parents to support their children, just as it does today whether the parents are unmarried, married, divorced, or divorced and remarried. This state action would be legitimate because it would fit squarely with in the harm principle. Thus, private groups can peg their various benefits to whatever configuration they see fit, all without the intervention of the state. I confess that as a strong believer in the institution of marriage, I see no answer to this question when raised by individuals who wish to distance themselves from marriage on the ground that it is an institution of male dominance propped up by dubious religious values. Here is one place where competition in the world of practices and ideals can take place without the state putting a thumb on the scale.

Now this entire line of argument depends on the primacy of liberty over tradition, in a culture that finds it difficult to choose cleanly between them. So why is that choice correct? This question is especially painful to those like myself who in contracts and torts often believe in the power of customary rules and practices to interpret contracts and to supply the standard of care in routine negligence cases. If custom works well in these more limited settings, why should it be out of bounds when the question turns to larger questions of how culture and social norms mediate the actions of individuals in a larger society?

The answer runs as follows. In the usual contractual situation, custom is rightly understood as a cheap way to set default rules when parties have not written out all the terms of their agreement. Exactly how well it discharges this function is clearly subject to extensive debate. But what is clear nonetheless is that any custom that otherwise binds the parties can be displaced by explicit terms that go the contrary. The custom in question does not bind people against their own will. Nor can it bind strangers to the transaction who have had no opportunity to decide whether or not they are part of the community in which the custom has taken hold. For this reason, the proper rule about custom has two parts: as between the parties, for example, in medical malpractice cases, it is good evidence of negligence because there are no stranger issues to worry about. Thus, if negligence is the standard, then custom is the guide of choice. But in stranger cases, it should only bind those persons who are part of the community that established the custom in question. The rules for running railroads may reciprocally bind two railroads that operate on adjacent tracks, but they do not bind strangers, who have had no part in the formation of the custom and should in general be protected by a strict liability rule, absent some misconduct of their own.

These principles work well to explain this situation. The dominant cultural norms set up the rules of conduct so long as no one chose to opt out from them. But those days are past. The argument that the change in standards on gay marriage will defeat the common culture comes too late in the day to do any good. The very same day that George W. Bush railed against same sex marriage in his state of the union address, the innkeepers in Provincetown Massachusetts announced special rates for gay weddings, now made possible by the Massachusetts decision.[49] I fail to see the mysterious social externality that arises from the practice although it is easy to see why those who take deep offense at the practice are free not to attend. There is no stronger case to prohibit gay marriage than there is to ban marriages between ordinary couples. The differences in sentiment do count, but only in setting the frequency of the respective arrangements and their guest lists. In sum, if one starts with liberty as a comprehensive notion that embraces both economic and sexual activities, and subjects them to the same sorts of challenges, there is no more reason, and no less, for the state to ban gay marriage than there is for it to impose minimum wages. In both cases the cries that "I don't want to live in a society that tolerates these practices" has to fall on deaf ears lest each side find in its own indignation strong reasons to suppress the activities of others. Justice Holmes was right in *Lochner* to note that a society as large and diverse as our own must work for individuals of fundamentally different views. But he was wrong to think that the way in which this objective is best achieved is to allow the rival groups to bash each other through legislation. The state does not provide collective goods (or bads) when two people decide to marry. The best way to maintain civil peace and harmony is to make sure that the state does not put its thumb on the scale in these cultural wars, or gets out of the marriage business altogether.

IV. AFFIRMATIVE ACTION

The social issue raised by the twin decisions in *Grutter* and *Gratz* was whether to allow public universities to engage in affirmative action. At stake were two different approaches to the problem. The University of Michigan Law School adopted a loosy-goosy form of affirmative action that took race into account along with a raft of other factors relating to family background, wealth, and nonacademic achievements,

---

[49] See John Leland, *In Gay-Marriage Ruling, Boom for Provincetown*, NY Times at A1 (January 21, 2004).

with a view to obtaining a well rounded class. The undergraduate college, which is far larger, tended to rely on boards and grades, and used race to give a hefty 20 point advantage to minority candidates, which was a huge spread that could boost a marginal candidate into a sure admission. The former approach involves a preference for standards over rules; while the latter involves the reverse. But no matter what the means chosen, the objective was the same: to take race into account in order to alter the composition of the classes. In dealing with this issue, a badly fractured Supreme Court upheld the former method on the authority of *Bakke v. University of California*,[50] but struck down the undergraduate program on the grounds that its fixed rules amounted to a quota or an impermissible racial set-aside. It was clear that the splitting the baby in half did not result in a political draw. The supporters of affirmative action were ecstatic about the result and the defenders of the color-blind principle regarded the outcome as a major defeat, which for them it indeed was. But as a descriptive matter, it would also be a mistake to conclude that the rejection of the numerical admissions program in *Gratz* had no consequences apart from requiring colleges to work through to cumbersome and expensive admissions procedures to eat their affirmative action cakes. After that decision, for example, black-only scholarships are suspect, and probably illegal, so that every decision has to depend on case-by-case application of general standards.

I shall spend somewhat less time on this issue because I have set out my substantive argument on the entire matter before the Supreme Court decision,[51] and see no reason to revise that judgment in light of the unimaginative opinions that these cases have garnered from a group of tired warriors who have faced this issue too many times. Here I think that the outcome in *Grutter*, which allowed the program to proceed, was correct, but the refusal to allow numerical quantifications of the differences between races, or to use any sort of a quota system, was wrong. The argument here does not rest on whether I support or oppose affirmative action, which should be a matter of supreme indifference to the analysis. Rather, it turns in large measure on the question of whether a state university or the United States Supreme Court is best able to run an admissions program at a complex state or private institution, subject only to the usual restraints of the law of property, torts and contract. I couple private with public institutions in this analysis because Congress has under Title VI of the Civil Rights Act required private institutions to adhere to the same

[50] 438 US 265 (1978)
[51] Richard A. Epstein, *A Rational Basis for Affirmative Action: A Shaky but Classical Liberal Defense*, 100 Mich L Rev 2036 (2002).

rules that govern public institution.[52] In this particular case, the parity between these two sorts of institutions is close but not perfect, but in principle it should operate to free up public educational institutions from many of the constraints that bind the state in its nightwatchman capacity. The better approach to the problem of affirmative action is one that abolishes the Civil Rights Act of 1964 as it applies to all private institutions, and then allows state universities to follow the dominant patterns of emergent behavior as the private institutions with which they compete. My confident prediction is that affirmative action will survive, perhaps even thrive, in that environment. If the unregulated private sector mixes and matches rules and standards, public institutions should have the same degree of freedom on the familiar Hayekian ground that decentralized decisionmaking offers the best hope to balance the multiple objectives that any complex institution properly seeks. To see why this is the case, I shall first review the Court's reasoning in these decisions which involves the artificial application of the compelling state interest test, and then explain the logic that should have been used to deal with the case.

The centerpiece of modern constitutional law on race relations is the "compelling state interest" test, which is used to determine whether deviations from a color-blind norm are justified. To see why this norm was invoked, in name at least, in *Grutter* and *Gratz*, it is worth recalling that its origins go back to Justice Harlan's famous color-blind dissent in *Plessy v. Ferguson*,[53] which was the constitutional pole star during the heroic (pre-1954) era of the struggle for Civil Rights in the United States. In their post-Civil War effort to sustain racial segregation, southern states (and truth be told, some northern states as well) did not adhere to the minimal state precepts that commended themselves to Robert Nozick in *Anarchy, State and Utopia*.[54] Rather, they exercised aggressive powers that limited the choices on how ordinary individuals could lead their lives. *Plessy* sustained three different kinds of racial classifications: antimiscegenation rules, segregated common carriers, and segregated schools. The rules that banned marriage between races were a clear limitation on the ordinary freedom of contract that could not survive any serious level of scrutiny. Historically, antimiscegenation laws were, of course, sustained under a largish version of the police power, which in intermarriage did not lead to hybrid vigor, but to the compromise of the purity of the (white) race. Similarly, the limitation on the ability of railroads to organize their business as common carriers was equally indefensible under the classical liberal view. The proper use of regu-

---

[52] See Civil Rights Act of 1964 tit VI, § 606, Pub L No 88-352, 78 Stat 252, codified as amended at 42 USC § 2000d-4a (2000).

[53] 163 US 537 (1896) (Harlan dissenting).

[54] Robert Nozick, *Anarchy, State, and Utopia* (Basic Books, 1974).

lation is to prevent invidious forms of discrimination that private monopolists might engage in; how and when that power should be exercised is an enormous task, but one that is beside the point here. No matter what the proper answer to that inquiry, the *one* wrong response is to use state power to perpetuate the forms of discrimination that regulated firms do *not* wish to practice. Oddly enough, the most robust portion of *Plessy* is that which allows the state, as proprietor, to maintain segregation in public schools, and this on the deference argument that the University of Michigan advanced here: the state should have greater control over what happens in institutions under its charge than it does in the regulation of private firms. That argument works within limits in a political system in which all actors and interest groups have an equal say. But it is entitled to no respect when the levers to political power are effectively closed by denying the most vulnerable section of the population the vote, by spending tax dollars extracted from them without their consent on ends they do not share, and by backing up the entire ugly structure by an unholy mixture of the systematic public abuse of permit powers and the unofficial and private use of violence against anyone who would stand up against a system that is rotten to the core. It did not take any detailed empirical evidence to realize that white racist groups in the South, and elsewhere, did not use political power to protect private property and economic opportunity. Jim Crow is the antithesis to free markets, just as it is the antithesis to every other form of freedom. There is no question that Justice Harlan's lonely dissent set out the right constitutional solution when *all* the risks of political abuse came from one side. None of the pained rationales that carried the day in *Plessy* would have survived if the same level of scrutiny brought to a simple economic matter in *Lochner* had been applied in *Plessy*. The conundrum of the age was how it could be statist along one dimension and individualist along another—which in different permutations is the state of jurisprudence today.

The situation with race today may be explosive, but it would be foolish and perverse to argue that nothing in the calculus of domination has changed since W.E.B. du Bois announced that the color-line was the central question of the twentieth century. Today, the political constellation of forces has changed and the supporters of affirmative action do count in their number not only members of minority groups that are the direct beneficiaries of affirmative action, but large coalition of independent groups that are in sympathy with their claims. But through thick and thin, the stated version of the compelling interest test from *Adarand Constructors, Inc. v. Pena*[55] reads as follows: "all racial classifications, imposed by whatever federal, state, or

[55] 515 US 200 (1995).

local governmental actor, must be analyzed by a reviewing court under strict scrutiny. In other words, such classifications are constitutional only if they are narrowly tailored measures that further compelling governmental interests."[56] In addition, this "'standard of review . . . is not dependent on the race of those burdened or benefited by a particular classification.'"[57]

The key question is what prompts the per se use of this both ways high standard, without any attention to the particulars. In *Brown v. Board of Education*[58] the categorical attack on all racial classifications as "inherently" suspect worked well when all the errors came from one direction, namely, massive resistance to racial equality from established government institutions. The more candid way to deal with this issue is to draw an explicit connection between the level of judicial scrutiny with the perceived breakdown in the soundness of the political process:[59] As the abuse increases, the level of scrutiny also increases. These political abuses could have been easily set out chapter and verse with respect to race in the United States, but only at the cost of angering the very political institutions whose cooperation would be needed to secure the transition from segregation. Earl Warren, therefore, quite consciously chose the high-road of universalism on this matter to avoid getting caught in empirical disputes that could only undermine the single-minded nature of his conclusion. It could be describe as bad, i.e., nonfunctionalist law, but, as wise statesmanship, it is the most important decision of the twentieth century.

That lofty approach, however, comes at a price, because it makes it appear that all racial classifications are equally suspect and that the direction of the discrimination simply does not matter. That conclusion is not sustainable once the attention is placed instead on the institutional matters. There has been no history of black domination in the United States that would lead inexorably to the conclusion that any racial classifications in their favor are suspect. The concerns with the political process point to a profound asymmetry on race matters if only for the simple reason that preferences for African-American students will only make it through if there is some support from white groups, which is in fact the case. The sensible result in practice is to ratchet down the level of scrutiny to match the increased confidence in the outcomes of the political process. That approach does not generalize to all kinds of racial preferences in favor of various minority groups. There are few, if any, supporters of affirmative action

---

[56] Id at 227.

[57] Id at 224.

[58] 347 US 483 (1954).

[59] See, e.g., John Hart Ely, *Democracy and Distrust* (Harvard, 1980), for one famous attempt.

for university admissions who are likely to claim that minority burglars should receive reduced sentences in virtue of their race. Although at the empirical level, there are legions who claim that the enforcement of the law has built in biases, conscious or unconscious, against members of minority groups in general and African Americans in particular. But now the claim is not for affirmative action, but for a rededication to the color-blind principle of Justice Harlan.

That renewed quest will not do much to switch the balance in college and law school admissions, so more is needed if the balance is to be shifted. Nor will outreach, that convenient bromide, do the job because the gaps in scores are too great to be overcome by such tactics. The challenge in *Grutter* and *Gratz* was to take into account the institutional differences between discrimination in the dark days and discrimination now in the face of a formal universalism that regards those differences as irrelevant. That was indeed done, but only through the total lack of candor in the application of the *Aderand* standard— the same kind of transparently bad argument of the sort that deserves the derision it receives in *Lawrence*. Apart from her rejection of the Gunther maxim,[60] Justice O'Connor's opinion quite clearly reeks of references to deference, that unmistakable hallmark of the rational basis test, which has been applied lately to uphold the Copyright Term Extension Act,[61] and state environmental regulation against takings challenges.[62] Here it is really necessary to quote the key passages that set the mood of this opinion.

> Today, we hold that the Law School has a compelling interest in attaining a diverse student body.
>
> The Law School's educational judgment that such diversity is essential to its educational mission is one to which we defer. The Law School's assessment that diversity will, in fact, yield educational benefits is substantiated by respondents and their *amici*. Our scrutiny of the interest asserted by the Law School is no less strict for taking into account complex educational judgments in an area that lies primarily within the expertise of the university. Our holding today is in keeping with our tradition of giving a degree of deference to a university's academic decisions, within constitutionally prescribed limits.[63]

Quintessential double-talk. The words "strict scrutiny" and "deference" do not belong in the same intellectual universe. There are

---

[60] See *Grutter*, 123 S Ct at 2338.

[61] *Eldred v Ashcroft*, 537 US 186 (2003).

[62] *Tahoe-Sierra Preservation Counsel, Inc v Tahoe Regional Planning Agency*, 535 US 302 (2002).

[63] *Grutter*, 123 S Ct at 2339.

all sorts of complex judgments that can be made about how to run a university within the confines of a color-blind principle if that were thought the way to go. It is just a giant charade to say that race is only one factor among many that universities can use to make their judgments. It is just as easy to say that there are all sorts of factors that universities can take into account in making their judgments even if race is put to one side under the equal protection clause. Nor is there any reason to think that because minority students have weak board scores and grades that they somehow must have to have stronger extracurricular activities to compensate. The alternative hypothesis is that able students dominate across the board. The appeal to expertise makes sense in weighing these other factors, but it takes no more judicial expertise to rule race out of bounds here than it did in *Brown*, where deference was mercifully in short supply.

Justice O'Connor's opinion fares no better as a legal argument when it invokes the arguments for diversity that the University and its amici offered. These consisted of bare allegations that racial diversity improved educational experience in the classroom:

> The Law School's claim of a compelling interest is further bolstered by its *amici*, who point to the educational benefits that flow from student body diversity. In addition to the expert studies and reports entered into evidence at trial, numerous studies show that student body diversity promotes learning outcomes, and "better prepares students for an increasingly diverse workforce and society, and better prepares them as professionals." Brief for American Educational Research Association et al. as *Amici Curiae* 3; see, eg, W. Bowen & D. Bok, *The Shape of the River* (1998); G. Orfield & M. Kurlaender eds. *Diversity Challenged: Evidence on the Impact of Affirmative Action* (2001); M. Chang, D. Witt, J. Jones, & K. Hakuta eds.,*Compelling Interest: Examining the Evidence on Racial Dynamics in Colleges and Universities* (2003).
>
> These benefits are not theoretical but real, as major American businesses have made clear that the skills needed in today's increasingly global marketplace can only be developed through exposure to widely diverse people, cultures, ideas, and viewpoints.[64]

What is so striking about the endless recitation of academic articles and amici briefs is that the Court never once inquires whether these claims are true or inflated. It does not look at critical reviews of these contentions, nor make its own independent assessment of the sound-

[64] Id at 2340.

ness of the data on which the arguments rests.[65] In essence the entire edifice of strict scrutiny rests on little more than hearsay. Whatever illusions one might have about the case have to be dispelled by the concluding flourish, when Justice O'Connor, in pure rational basis mode, writes:

> We take the Law School at its word that it would "like nothing better than to find a race-neutral admissions formula" and will terminate its race-conscious admissions program as soon as practicable. See Brief for Respondents Bollinger et al. 34; *Bakke,* 438 US at 317-318, 98 S Ct 2733 (opinion of Powell, J.) (presuming good faith of university officials in the absence of a showing to the contrary). It has been 25 years since Justice Powell first approved the use of race to further an interest in student body diversity in the context of public higher education. Since that time, the number of minority applicants with high grades and test scores has indeed increased. See Tr. of Oral Arg. 43. We expect that 25 years from now, the use of racial preferences will no longer be necessary to further the interest approved today.[66]

The real question here is who is kidding whom. The affirmative action question was front and center on the university agenda when I entered teaching at the University of Southern California in 1968, when the gaps in performance levels between whites and blacks at the Law School, which then had less than stellar medians for its white students, were large. It would be nice to see some evidence that the gap has closed in the past 35 years to give hope to the prospect that it will be eliminated in the next 25 years. But no evidence is offered on that point, and the one sentence that points in that direction, which refers to the increase in high-quality minority applicants, studiously does not state whether it adjusts for the size of the applicant pool or the size of the increase in question. Numbers are in short supply. The blunt truth is that no one in fact "expects" that the use of racial preferences will no longer be necessary in 25 years. It is only that no member of the Supreme Court expects to be around to answer for that error when that prediction proves false.

The entire opinion in *Grutter* counts as one massive intellectual failure in argument. But the result in question can be defended, albeit with a dose of caution, once a minimal level of candor is introduced into the situation to allow for a guarded use of the rational basis test.

[65] See, e.g., Thermstrom's review of Bowen & Bok. For my views, see Richard A. Epstein, *Unexplored Tributaries, Review of William G. Bowen and Derek Bok, The Shape of the River: Long-Term Consequences of Considering Race in College and University Admissions,* 30 Reason 61 (Feb 1999).

[66] *Grutter,* 123 S Ct at 2347.

To be sure, there is an obvious concern that any relaxation of the strict scrutiny standard could trigger a return to forms of racial segregation in public (or private) institutions, which I regard as highly improbable under the circumstances. But it is not necessary to keep a uniform high two-tailed standard of scrutiny to guard against that eventuality. Rather, the baseline becomes the behavior that private institutions that compete with public universities use in deciding whether, and if so, how, to mold their own racial preferences. To this point, no one should be under any illusions that private universities perform this task with universal excellence. It is very difficult to run "nonprofit" institutions that are in the business of producing public benefits, i.e., social benefits that do not redound in revenue streams for their creators. Affirmative action policies test their limited abilities to the max.

Nonetheless, the key question in this non-Nirvana world is always compared to what? We are better off with decentralization in these decisions than with any single command from either a legislature or a court on how universities should be run. The real question is who decides, not what is decided. Autonomous universities do better than those which labor under explicit government edict. The economic and social pressures are not perfect, but they are not trivial either, and the institution that goes overboard on affirmative action will lose students and support in consequence of its decision. Stated differently, private institutions are more responsive to considerations at the margin than their public counterparts, which all too frequently lurch from extreme to extreme. Here it seems hard to believe that every private university has it wrong when it adopts some form of affirmative action. It is also hard to see why some financial level of state support, often at the 20 percent level, should transform the situation so that public institutions have to operate by a set of rules that no private university, regardless of its orientation, adopts. The colorblind solution suffers from massive overbreadth.

The one obvious point of tension with this analysis is that the willingness to adopt affirmative action programs is nothing more than a clever strategy to beat back the inevitable suits under the general antidiscrimination law, which represents a centralized decision of government. But I do not believe that to be the case: if all these laws were repealed tomorrow, the private demand for some affirmative action would remain robust, even if it might take somewhat different form, as it is driven by a sense of justice, guilt, and fear in uncertain proportions. Indeed, it is likely that the greater peril to decentralization lies in the temptation of legislatures and administrators to attach strings to the revenues they supply. It is dangerous for the legislature, or for that matter a state constitutional amendment, to either require *or* forbid an affirmative action program. My willingness to accept affirmative action programs in public universities depends critically on the ability of the state to create and respect firewalls between its own political passions and the educational choices made by its faculty. There is no doubt that this separation is hard to attain, given the need for state appropriations and the well known tendency of legislatures to overstep the limits of propriety when large political issues are on the table. But there are at least some modest steps that could be taken in the right direction. First, it should be held that the state cannot impose any specific condition in favor or against racial targets as a condition for granting money, or, less effectively, cannot link in public debate its funding for universities as a function of their performance on the affirmative action issues. The long-term hope is that state legislatures will not wish to fund institutions that they cannot manipulate. Second, the state cannot suggest classifications that respond to electoral politics instead of educational concerns. Here it would be unhappy, for example, for a state to give the preference to some blacks or some Hispanics on the ground that they have a greater electoral presence than other excluded groups. Mexican-Americans yes, Cuban-Americans no, starts to look like strong local politics independent of any sensible rationale even under a generous standard. So unless private institutions have the same patterns, and some reason for their distribution, that form of subdivision should be struck down even if more general racial preferences are allowed. I am not quite sure how these limitations would play out in practice, but I don't think that they were strongly operative here. My sense is that in this context these concerns are somewhat academic. The faculty at the University of Michigan was the author of its own program. The muddle that remains comes from the unhappy fact that state institutions of higher education do not fit well into any sensible paradigm unless and until they are privatized.

Once this rational basis test controls in the public arena, Justice O'Connor's opinion can be rewritten in a straightforward and honest sense. The deference that is afforded to public institutions because of the complex tradeoffs that have to be made is now fully defensible within the constitutional tradition. The references to what leading lights think on one side of the question, but not on the other are fine as well because the rational basis test makes it sufficient that some highly placed individuals concur on the desirability of the program even if others, more eminent, disagree. The references to the military and the titans of industry make sense as well. They are desperate for legitimate affirmative action because the litigation alternative for them is too horrible for them to contemplate. None of them could survive the constant pressures to adopt some affirmative action program in a world in which any deviation from proportionate representation could expose them to disparate impact liability under *Griggs v. Duke Power Co.*[67] The chances of any proportionate representation by race given random selection is quite low. The random flips of 1000 coins generate a normal distribution, with two tails: it is highly unlikely to see a 500/500 split. Litigation is only worse, for then astute plaintiffs, in class action mode no less, have the option to replicate the affected population in ways that accentuate the differences in some group or subgroup from the general population. No responsible military or corporate figure wants to engage in discrimination against the protected groups; timidity is their middle name. But timid or not, they rightly fear a constant stream of lawsuits from the other side. Affirmative action programs do indeed have a compelling purpose, which is that they work a partial repeal of the Civil Rights Act of 1964 in the situations where it is needed most. And if forced to choose between the inelegance of a double standard, which *Grutter* ratifies, and the relentless two-sided color-blind test, count me in favor of the former, so long as the only sensible solution—scrapping the apparatus—is out of the question in the light of current public opinion. In a word, therefore, the weak intellectual foundations of *Grutter* could be shored up by a simple recognition that the full range of relevant considerations does not lead to a subtle application of strict scrutiny in a context-sensitive way. Instead, it should be displaced by the rational basis test, which has in my view *no* place in constitutional law when the state acts as a regulator instead of a proprietor.

The question then arises, what difference does it make which approach is followed so long as the bottom line is the same. But it seems clear that the bottom line is not the same both in a social and a legal sense. To take the former first, the debates over affirmative action have been skewed by *Grutter*. It is one thing to oppose the creation or extension of an affirmative action program if the United States Supreme Court had announced that it is possible for public institutions to imitate mainstream private institutions if they so choose. At this point, it does not put its thumb on the scale one way or the other. But it is quite another to try to resist the creation or expansion of these programs now that the Supreme Court has categorically determined on the strength of testimonial evidence that diversity serves a compelling state interest, even if it doesn't. How does one deny the implementation of a program that comes with such a lofty pedigree? The debate is much more likely to be open and principled if one side does not get the boost from a decision that in no sense establishes the proposition for which it stands. Rather, the full range of voices should

[67] 401 US 424 (1971).

be heard on a level playing field. The results of that process are likely to be better than those which will emerge after the current decision, which can only polarize the local constituents between those who embrace the ruling and those who regard it as a transparent ruse.

There are also unfortunate legal consequences that attach to this decision, as *Gratz* illustrates. The gist of that decision was the determination that the UM College program that provided a 20 point advantage to members of underrepresented minorities failed the *Grutter* test because it did not meet the compelling state interest test that required "individualized consideration." At this point, the Supreme Court is caught in its own web of intellectual confusions. If strict scrutiny is indeed the norm, then I think that there is no answer to the challenge of Robert George who could not understand why if the *Grutter* program passed muster, the *Gratz* program did not. As he put it, "How can it be unconstitutional to do honesty and above board what it is constitutionally permissible to do "through winks, nods, and disguises"? Or, put the other way around: How can it be constitutionally permissible to do "through winks, nods, and disguises" what it is unconstitutional to do honestly and above board?"[68] Generally speaking, those means that are precisely tailored to reach the stated end are at least as good as those which obfuscate the issue by introducing irrelevancies before deciding the question. Here it is as though it is bad to have a quota, or more precisely, "the functional equivalent of a quota,"[69] but all right to have some more complex program that produces the same outcome. It is as though in principle the university that scrutinizes each admissions folder with an eye to get a class that is somewhere between 14 and 16 percent black has done its job while one that announces it will take 15 percent black has failed in its constitutional duty.

If George is correct about the constitutional parity of the two systems, he is wrong in my view to condemn both. Rather, both should be allowed in whatever proportions any institution wishes to match them. Here are some reasons why. The first point goes to comparative institutional competence. Once the *end* of diversity counts as a compelling state interest, who is better able to achieve that end, justices on the Supreme Court who have never done a day of admissions work in their entire lives, or full-time professionals who feel the heat each time they get the trade-offs wrong? No contest: the professionals win every time, except in front of the Court. If it is just a question of technique, then by all means go with expertise.

---

[68] Robert P. George, Gratz *and* Grutter: *Some Hard Questions*, 103 Colum L Rev 1634, 1635 (2003).
[69] *Gratz*, 123 S Ct at 2421.

The second question goes to the merits. One key point to remember is that colleges and graduate schools come in all shapes and sizes. They have different constituencies and purposes. For many programs, the question is how to fill a class, not to run an affirmative action program. For other institutions, it is quite the opposite. These issues of composition and scale matter. Viewed in this light, there are reasons why the University of Michigan Law School adopted a different path from the college. As a question of size, the college is just too large to run the individualized process of which Justice Powell spoke. It is necessary to create some formal grid that allows an institution to take some applicants without further ado, and to weed others out on summary judgment. If the academic strengths of white and black students differ, then the cut off points for the two groups would have to differ as well for this program to operate, which is exactly what the 20 point credit in *Gratz* did. It is easy to argue that the preferences given here are too large insofar as they boost black applicants from the bottom to the top tier; and it is easy to argue that they are not dramatic enough if the percentage of black students lags. But there is no constitutional principle that punishes 20 points and praises 10. The great advantage of this system is that it reduces the initial round of fine-tuning to a single process; change the number up or down until the desired population is reached.

The use of the grid has other collateral advantages in helping to reduce the influence of politics on the admissions process. Entry into the University of Michigan and other major colleges is a big deal. It gives one a leg up on both the remunerative scale and the prestige of career scale. That prize is worth seeking, and once discretion is introduced into the system, we can expect all sorts of people to seek to turn it in their direction. Since mushy criteria are the order of the day, it becomes easier to argue that the rank-order boards and grades really doesn't count at all, because they only reflect some "white-based" standard of merit. The upshot is that weak students will jump over stronger ones. The use of boards and grades offers a powerful antidote to all sorts of arguments that are best left unsaid in the context of debates over admissions and scholarship. Once the initial cut is done, then individualized determinations may be appropriate to insure that the class in question does not contain all physicists or classical guitarists. But since the initial cut has reduced the level of variance, the scope for politics is heavily constrained, and the consequences of a wrong decision are much reduced. The University of Michigan stated the right policies.

Law schools are different in both respects. Here the size of the pool is smaller so that it is easier to give individualized determinations. But even here a grid is often helpful to do the initial weeding, and if so, then it has to have different cut off points for different classes of applicants in order to work. In addition, the gain from the individualized determinations is higher. These students are older. They have life experiences and often second degrees. Their range of interests and their ages will vary, so that it pays to look more closely. Hence, the shift in relative emphasis in the program.

None of this of course makes it into Chief Justice Rehnquist's analysis, which consists of a wooden recitation of why the University of Michigan College program fails strict scrutiny because of its rigid quality. There is only one thing left for the program to do. It has to make covert the mass production decisions that were done above board before hand. There is not the personnel or time to treat thousands of applicants with the care and affection that Chief Justice Rehnquist wants, and absolutely no reason to think that his approach would lead to better classes. The most determined foe of affirmative action should prefer an affirmative action world in which both rules and case-by-case analysis applied. The advantages of the numerical setbacks are two. They reduce the level of intrigue in individual cases, and they shore up the traditional standards of merit by rejecting any argument that boards and grades are used strictly to advance the position of privileged white (and Asian) applicants.

V. THE CONNECTIONS BETWEEN *LAWRENCE* AND *GRUTTER*

We are now in a position where we can see the imperfect unity between the affirmative action and gay marriage cases. The initial impression is that these cases are oddly inconsistent because *Lawrence* strikes down state legislation under a rational basis test while *Grutter* sustains state practices in the face of a strict scrutiny challenge. But in reality these differences are more superficial than real. The correct defense of both these decisions rest on the ground that each, in its own way, seeks to promote autonomous decision making by voluntary organizations. In *Lawrence* the only way in which that could be achieved was to strike down the statutes that blocked various forms of consensual sex. In *Grutter* the only way that could be done was to allow universities and colleges massive discretion in the way in which they organize their admissions and scholarship programs. To be sure, this simple account of the two cases misses much of what is going on in both areas. There is no doubt that *Gratz* showed the inveterate desire of the Supreme Court to fine-tune the way in which ordinary voluntary processes take place. There is, of course, some concern with the levels of freedom that are rightly given to state organizations, but the test that I proposed earlier—allow the state universities and colleges to do what unregulated private institutions as a group tend to do—gives a reality check against forms of extreme behavior, and is far preferable to the uninformed fine-tuning in *Gratz*, which will only make higher education more costly and less efficient than it ought to be. For its part, it is not clear how far *Lawrence* will go either. The question of whether its logic will carry over to same-sex marriages is unclear and it is highly unlikely that this Supreme Court will go so far as to overrule *Reynolds v. United States*,[70] and find that the free exercise of religion (and freedom of association) should govern there as well. It is most unlikely that that court will allow more complex sexual alliances in which say six individuals, three male and three female, form a sexual commune, in which each has sexual relations with everyone else. It may well be that the Court will keep the state in the marriage business, and limit the new level of constitutional protection to two.

The hard question that then arises is whether this form of judicial laissez-faire on sexual and educational arrangements beats the older system of tight controls over both. I think that the answer to that question is no. One way to see the point is to look at another way in which grand social principles of equality are used to encourage state domination over athletics under Title IX of the Civil Rights Act. The parallels to the affirmative action debate are ominous. Title IX started as a modest effort to secure equal opportunity at the university level. Its most obvious targets were explicit exclusions from programs on account of sex, all of which were on their way out in any event. But that model will not work for college athletics in the face of obvious difference. So the reach of the statute was successively extended until this modest sex-blind provision became a full scale regulatory regime of inordinate complexity whose equal participation goal swamped all countervailing considerations. It has placed just about every college program for intercollegiate athletics in noncompliance with the basic norm. Just that path would have been traveled if the color-blind norm had applied to academics because the aggressive use of outcome standards would have forced in the name of color-blindness the same kinds of programs on universities. If they had resisted, then the distortions of Title IX would have taken over.[71] If they complied, then affirmative action would be relabeled "true" racial equality, and we would have affirmative action programs all under the watchful eye of the Office of Civil Rights, which we would do well to abolish. As between government programs that force equality and decentralized

---

[70] 98 US 145 (1878).

[71] For a longer discussion, see Richard A. Epstein, *Foreword: Just Do It! Title IX 01 a Threat to University Autonomy*, 101 Mich L Rev 1365 (2003).

programs that allow for differences in the institutional level, I would take the latter every time even if I believed that many of the private institutions in question would behave in scandalous ways in their implementation of the diversity ideal. The world is not a perfect place. The views that I hold on education are not shared by a majority of the population. As an outlier on many issues, who has serious reservations about the efficacy of affirmative action in many settings, I would rather take my chances on a decentralized system that permits some diversification than to work under a state monopoly in which "diversity" becomes the one true goal.

In sum, the arguments I have made do explain why we adopt strict scrutiny in fact when the government wishes to limit private associations, and rational basis when it wishes to facilitate the internal operations of public institutions that provide goods and services in competition with market institutions. That result is defensible on intellectual grounds no matter which way one comes out on any of the issues that are canvassed here. It represents a consistent application of classical liberal principles that would (if allowed) work in economic matters just as they do in the contentious social issues of our time, which are so rich in symbolism for all concerned. The Supreme Court has moved in sensible directions in both cases but for reasons that should give pause to its supporters and courage to its opponents. It would be a great national service if the Court collectively rethought its position so that its stated rationales actually supported the results that it reaches. The stakes are high, for the legitimacy of legal and social decisions depend ultimately on the strength and the candor of the arguments put forward in their defense. By that standard, much judicial work remains to be done on the most explosive controversies of our time.

The Original Meaning of the Judicial Power

Randy E. Barnett *

*In this paper, Professor Barnett refutes the claims that judi-
cial review was invented in Marbury v. Madison, or that, because it is contrary to the original meaning of the Constitution, it must be justified by some nonoriginalist interpretive
methodology. He does so, not by discerning the shadowy and
often counterfactual "intentions" of the founding generation,
but by presenting what the founders actually said during the
constitutional convention, in state ratification conventions,
and immediately after ratification. Taken cumulatively, these
statements leave no doubt that the founders contemplated judicial nullification of legislation enacted by the states and by
Congress. In short, the evidence presented here demonstrates
that, at the time of its enactment, the original public meaning
of the "judicial power" in Article III, included the power of
judicial nullification.*

*This Constitution defines the extent of the powers of the gen-
eral government. If the general legislature should at any time
overleap their limits, the judicial department is a constitutional check. If the United States go beyond their powers, if
they make a law which the Constitution does not authorize,
it is void; and the judicial power, the national judges, who, to
secure their impartiality, are to be made independent, will de-*

* Austin B. Fletcher Professor, Boston University School of Law [rbarnett@bu.edu].
This article expands upon materials presented in Randy E. Barnett, *Restoring the Lost
Constitution: The Presumption of Liberty* (Princeton, 2004). I extend my thanks to
Kate McFarland for her research assistance in the preparation of this article. Permis-
sion to photocopy this article for classroom use is hereby granted.

*clare it to be void. On the other hand, if the states go beyond
their limits, if they make a law which is a usurpation upon the
general government, the law is void; and upright, independent
judges will declare it to be so.[1]—Oliver Elsworth (1788)*

*The evidence seems to indicate that the Framers did not
mean for the Supreme Court to have authority to void acts of
Congress.[2]—Leonard Levy (1988)*

I. INTRODUCTION

In the two centuries separating Oliver Elsworth's speech to the Connecticut ratification convention from the statement by the deservedly
well-respected historian Leonard Levy, doubts developed in some
quarters concerning the historical legitimacy of judicial review at the
time of the founding—doubts I hear expressed wherever I speak on
the Constitution. The origin of these misgivings can be traced to
some distinguished legal writers and historians. In addition to Leonard
Levy, similar denials or skepticism have been expressed by such well-
known legal figures as Charles Beard, William Crosskey, Learned
Hand, Charles Hyneman, Jesse Choper, and William Nelson. Although I know that many constitutional scholars today do not share
their views, there exists no definitive originalist refutation of the
claim that judicial review was invented by Chief Justice John Marshall in *Marbury v. Madison*, a claim that has, over the years, crept
into the legal consciousness and law school classrooms.[3]

In this article, I intend to refute any claim that judicial review was
invented in *Marbury v. Madison*, or that, because it is contrary to the
original meaning of the Constitution, it must be justified by some
nonoriginalist interpretive methodology. I will do so, not by discerning the shadowy and often counterfactual "intentions" of the founding generation, but by presenting as comprehensively as I can what the
founders actually said during the constitutional convention, in state
ratification conventions, and immediately after ratification. These
statements, taken cumulatively, leave no doubt that the founders
contemplated judicial nullification of legislation enacted by the

---

[1] 2 Jonathan Elliot, *The Debates In The Several State Conventions On The Adoption Of The Federal Constitution* 196 (J.B. Lippincott, 1859) (Oliver Elsworth in the
Connecticut ratification convention January 7, 1788).

[2] Leonard Levy, *Original Intent and the Framers' Constitution* 100 (MacMillan,
1988).

[3] See, e.g., Shawn Gunnarson, *Using History to Reshape the Discussion of Judicial
Review*, 1994 BYU L Rev 151, 152 (1994) ("A conventional interpretation of *Marbury*
is that the Supreme Court, under the leadership of Chief Justice Marshall, invented judicial review without supporting precedent or significant historical antecedent.").

states and by Congress. In short, I will demonstrate that the original meaning of the "judicial power" in Article III, included the power of judicial nullification.

This evidence should not be of interest solely to originalists. Many constitutional scholars who do not consider themselves to be originalists nevertheless acknowledge that originalism provides the starting point of constitutional interpretation or at least is a factor to be considered among others.[4] It is equally important that these nonoriginalists are made aware of the substantial evidence that the original meaning of the "judicial power" included the power to nullify unconstitutional laws.

II. THE SOURCE OF THE CONTROVERSY

Most people today assume that judges are authorized by the Constitution to declare statutes unconstitutional. Yet the Constitution does not seem to grant this power expressly. Article III says: "The judicial Power of the United States, shall be vested in one Supreme Court, and in such Courts as Congress may from time to time ordain and establish." In sharp contrast with the presidential veto power,[5] nowhere in the Constitution does it say explicitly that the "Supreme Court, and such inferior courts as may be established by Congress, shall have power to nullify a Law enacted by Congress and signed by the President if the Law is unconstitutional."

The absence of a clearly expressed grant of power has moved some critics of judicial review to question its legitimacy. One of these, Charles Hyneman, argued that the Constitution "expressly endows the president with powers to restrain Congress and the judiciary," and it "expressly endows Congress with powers enabling it to check the president and the judiciary."[6] Nevertheless, "it contains no provision which asserts that the Supreme Court or any other court may exercise a specific power which would restrain the president or Congress in the exercise of their powers."[7] Hyneman contended that the most reasonable inference to draw from the "silence about a restraining

---

[4] See, e.g., Philip Bobbit, *Constitutional Interpretation* 13-14 (Oxford, 1991) (counting both "historical" and "textual" as useful and legitimate "modalities" of constitutional argument); Lawrence Lessig, *Fidelity and Constraint*, 65 Fordham L Rev 1365 (1997) (advocating the method of translating original meaning into contemporary terms).

[5] See US Const Art I, § 7 ("Every Bill . . . shall, before it becomes a Law, be presented to the President of the United States; If he approve he shall sign it, but if not he shall return it, with his Objections to the House in which it shall have originated. . .").

[6] Charles S. Hyneman, *The Supreme Court on Trial* 125 (Atherton, 1963).

[7] Id.

power" for the judiciary is that the courts "should not exercise significant restraint on the other two"[8] departments.

Hyneman was not alone. Apart from Leonard Levy, he was joined in his skepticism (in chronological order) by such writers as Louis Boudin (1911): "There is absolutely no evidence whatever of an intention on the part of [the constitutional convention] to invest the judiciary with any sort of control over federal legislation, or over state legislation in matters admittedly within the legislative competence of the states."[9] Charles Beard (1912): "The direct intention of the framers and enactors not being clearly expressed on this point, we may have recourse to the reason and spirit of the Constitution."[10] William Crosskey (1953): "The rationally indicated conclusion is that judicial review of congressional acts was not intended, or provided, in the Constitution."[11] Learned Hand (1958): "In spite of authority which I am certainly not qualified to challenge, I cannot, however, help doubting whether the evidence justifies a certain conclusion that the Convention would have so voted, if the issue had been put to it that courts should have power to invalidate acts of Congress."[12]

More recently doubts have been expressed by Alexander M. Bickel (1962): "At worst it may be said that the intentions of the Framers cannot be ascertained with finality; that there were some who thought this and some that, and that it will never be entirely clear just exactly where the collective judgment—which alone is decisive—came to rest. In any debate over the force of tradition, such is the most that can be said against the claims of judicial review."[13] Jesse Choper (1980): "Whether the framers originally intended to vest the Supreme Court with such an extensive authority has been the subject of powerful and painstaking scholarship. . . . The reported evidence appears—at least to a nonhistorian who has not carefully culled it for himself—to be inconclusive."[14] William Nelson (2000): "What makes [*Marbury*]

[8] Id.

[9] Louis B. Boudin, Government by Judiciary, 26 Pol Sc Q 238, 248 (1911); see also Hyneman, *The Supreme Court on Trial* (cited in note 6) ("There is ample historical proof that, whatever the hope of some, from the complete silence of the document, as to possible future development—the great majority of the framers never suspected that a general power of the judiciary to control legislation could be interpreted into the new Constitution. They evidently assumed that such an extraordinary power could not be exercised unless expressly granted.").

[10] Charles Beard, *The Supreme Court and the Constitution* 76 (The Lawbook Exchange, Ltd, 1912).

[11] William Crosskey, 2 *Politics and the Constitution* 1000 (Chicago, 1953).

[12] Learned Hand, *The Bill of Rights* 7 (Atheneum, 1958).

[13] Alexander M. Bickel, *The Least Dangerous Branch* 16 (Yale, 1986).

[14] Jesse Choper, *Judicial Review and the National Political Process* 62-63 (Chicago, 1980).

even more important is the absence of any clear plan on the part of the Constitution's framers to provide the Court with this power."[15]

All these prominent writers have certainly influenced the legal culture, but were they right? While virtually all constitutional scholars accept the legitimacy of judicial review, there has developed a veritable cottage industry in producing defenses of the practice. My purpose is not to rehearse all (or any) of these defenses here. Few of these elaborate analyses would have been necessary, however, if the Constitution contained words whose plain meaning made it irresistibly clear that courts may declare acts of Congress unconstitutional. The absence of this plain language provides an opening for Hyneman et al. to dismiss such "inferences" as depending "too much on imagination, too little on the plain meaning of plain words."[16] And it leads some to rest the justification for judicial review on highly contestable nonoriginalist interpretive techniques.

Also contributing to the controversy is confusion and disagreement about originalism itself. Some of these skeptics may have been led to their conclusions by their efforts to discern the original *intentions* of the founders. Given that they involve inquiries into the often hidden and conflicting subjective intentions of myriad people who lived a long time ago, a single prevailing "original intention" is often notoriously difficult to establish beyond dispute. In contrast, I have defended elsewhere the need to look at the original public meaning given the text of the Constitution at the time of the founding, rather than the intentions of those who wrote or ratified it.[17]

Because a unique or dominant original public meaning is much easier to discern from the historical record many of the well-known practical difficulties of originalism abate if not disappear with this version. As important, so too do the normative objections to originalism. Original meaning originalism need not rest on any appeal to the authority of long-dead framers. Rather originalism is based on the fact the Constitution is an effort to place rules and restrictions on lawmakers and enforcers; that the Constitution was put in writing to better preserve these restrictions; that this purpose for putting these restrictions in writing would be severely undermined if lawmakers (or judges) could change the rules by which laws are made. Hence, originalism is justified because we, right here and right now, are or

[15] William Nelson, Marbury v Madison: *The Origins and Legacy of Judicial Review* 1 (Kansas, 2000).

[16] Hyneman, *The Supreme Court on Trial* at 124 (cited in note 7).

[17] See Randy E. Barnett, *An Originalism for Nonoriginalists,* 45 Loyola L Rev 611 (1999). I expand the normative justification for this approach, and better explain how it works in Randy E. Barnett, *Restoring the Lost Constitution: The Presumption of Liberty,* chapters 4 & 5 (Princeton, 2004).

profess to be committed to a written constitution to help ensure that those who make, enforce, and interpret the law are subject to rules that they cannot change on their own. And for this to be accomplished, *the meaning of a written constitution should remain the same until it is properly changed.* This last proposition is the essence of original meaning originalism.

Original meaning interpretation is not, however, always sufficient to yield a rule of law to apply to a case or controversy. When the Constitution's provisions are relatively abstract, there is room to, indeed an imperative to, construe the Constitution in a manner that does not conflict with the original meaning of what the Constitution does say. In other words, where the original meaning of the Constitution is underdeterminate, constitutional construction is needed to provide sufficient determinacy to decide a case, provided that any such construction is consistent with the original meaning of the text.

While some originalists would use the original intentions of the framers or ratifiers to provide specificity, others would look to tradition and history as it has developed since the founding. Unlike original meaning interpretation, neither of these techniques of construction is mandated by a commitment to a written constitution. Elsewhere I explain at greater length the distinction between interpretation and construction and argue that underdeterminate text should be construed in a manner that enhances the qualities that render the Constitution legitimate.[18] All that is important for present purposes, however, is to note that original meaning provides a frame within which choices must be made in the form of supplementation of abstract textual provisions by constitutional construction.

With this approach to originalist interpretation (and its limits) in mind, the overwhelming majority of courts and scholars are correct, I submit, to accept the historical legitimacy of judicial review. Judicial nullification of unconstitutional laws is not only consistent with the frame provided by original meaning, it is expressly authorized by the text and is entirely justified on originalist grounds. Hyneman and other dissenters are wrong, therefore, to reject its historical pedigree. Hyneman does not consider evidence that the original meaning of the "judicial power" found in Article III was more specific than what today is its plain meaning and that, at the founding, it included a power of judicial nullification. If this is established by the weight of the evidence of usage, then some power of judicial review would be

---

[18] See Barnett, *Restoring the Lost Constitution,* chapters 4 & 5 (cited in note 17). For a discussion of the distinction between interpretation and construction see Keith E. Whittington, *Constitutional Interpretation: Textual Meaning, Original Intent, and Judicial Review* 7 (Kansas, 1999). For an examination of what I mean by "legitimacy," see Randy E. Barnett, *Constitutional Legitimacy,* 103 Colum L Rev 111 (2003).

justified by an originalist interpretation even if it is not within today's "plain meaning" of the text. In this regard, the "dead" constitution provides a better foundation for judicial review than the ordinary meaning given its words today.

III. THE "JUDICIAL POWER" INCLUDED THE POWER OF NULLIFICATION

Far more evidence exists to suggest that the original public meaning of the term "judicial power" included the power to nullify unconstitutional legislation than even many constitutional scholars who acknowledge its historical pedigree realize. In this section I present the evidence to be found in the records of the Constitutional Convention, in the ratification conventions, and in some of the controversies and writings that immediately followed ratification. The evidence in these sources is remarkably uniform.

A. Evidence from the Constitutional Convention

Several members of the Constitutional Convention in Philadelphia explicitly assumed that the power to nullify unconstitutional legislation resided in the judiciary even before they settled on the particular wording of the various clauses. Several statements were made in the context of a proposed power of Congress to nullify state laws. Roger Sherman of Connecticut argued that such a power was "unnecessary, as the Courts of the States would not consider as valid any law contravening the Authority of the Union."[19] James Madison of Virginia favored such a negative because states "will accomplish their injurious objects before they can be . . . set aside by the National Tribunals."[20] He then cited the example of Rhode Island, where "the Judges who refused to execute an unconstitutional law were displaced, and others substituted, by the Legislature."[21] Gouverneur Morris of Pennsylvania argued that the legislative negative was unnecessary because "A law that ought to be negatived will be set aside in the Judiciary department."[22] No one in this discussion disputed the power of the judiciary to set aside unconstitutional laws passed by states.

Nor did anyone question that federal judges would have the same power to set aside unconstitutional legislation from Congress. Much is made by critics of judicial review of the Convention's rejection of

---

[19] James Madison, *Notes of Debates in the Federal Convention of 1787* 304 (Norton, 1987) (statement of R. Sherman).

[20] Id (statement of J. Madison).

[21] Id at 305.

[22] Id (statement of G. Morris).

the proposed council of revision. They infer from the refusal to adopt such a council an intention of the framers that the judiciary defer to legislative will. They rarely mention, however, that the most discussed and influential reason for rejecting the council of revision proposal was the acknowledged existence of a judicial negative on unconstitutional legislation. So powerful is this and other evidence that it strongly supports the conclusion that judicial nullification was included within the original public meaning of the "judicial power."

During a debate concerning whether judges should be included with the executive in a council empowered to revise laws, the comments of several delegates revealed their assumption that federal judges had the inherent power to hold federal laws unconstitutional. Luther Martin of Maryland stated that "as to the Constitutionality of laws, that point will come before the Judges in their proper official character. In this character they have a negative on the laws."[23] George Mason of Virginia observed that "in their expository capacity of Judges they would have one negative. . . . They could declare an unconstitutional law void."[24] While he favored the idea of the council, James Wilson of Pennsylvania conceded that there "was weight in this observation" that "the Judges, as expositors of the Laws would have an opportunity of defending their constitutional rights."[25]

The assumption that judges possess the inherent power to nullify unconstitutional laws crops up in a variety of other contexts during the Convention. For example, Gouverneur Morris favored ratification of the Constitution by the people in convention because legislative ratification of the new Constitution was prohibited by the terms of the Articles of Confederation. "Legislative alterations not conformable to the federal compact, would clearly not be valid. The Judges would consider them as null & void."[26] James Madison argued that a difference between a league or confederation among states and a constitution was precisely its status as binding law on judges. "A law violating a treaty ratified by a pre-existing law, might be respected by the Judges as a law, though an unwise or perfidious one. A law violating a constitution established by the people themselves, would be considered by the Judges as null & void."[27] Hugh Williamson of North Carolina argued that an express prohibition on ex post facto laws by states "may do good here, because the Judges can take hold of it."[28]

What is striking in light of these statements is that, throughout the duration of the Convention, I could find no one who disputed the ex-

---

[23] Id at 340 (statement of L. Martin).
[24] Id (statement of G. Mason).
[25] Id at 336-37 (statement of J. Wilson).
[26] Id at 351 (statement of G. Morris).
[27] Id at 352-53 (statement of J. Madison).
[28] Id at 511 (statement of H. Williamson).

istence of a judicial power to nullify unconstitutional laws. No one. Still, the fact that judicial nullification was taken as given by all members of the Constitutional Convention does not mean everyone liked this power. John Mercer of Maryland said he "disapproved of the Doctrine that the Judges as expositors of the Constitution should have authority to declare a law void."[29] Instead he "thought laws ought to be well and cautiously made, and then to be uncontroulable."[30] But Mercer's was a lone voice. Even John Dickenson of Delaware who "was strongly impressed with the remark of Mr. Mercer as to the power of the Judges to set aside the law,"[31] said he "was at the same time at a loss to know what expedient to substitute."[32] Gouverneur Morris took issue with Mercer more sharply, stating that he could not agree that the judiciary "should be bound to say that a direct violation of the Constitution was law. A control over the legislature might have its inconveniences. But view the danger on the other side."[33]

The principal criticism of judicial nullification was not its existence but its *weakness*. Some framers were not sanguine about the ability of courts to stand up for constitutional principle when necessary (and our history has borne out their skepticism). James Wilson thought that Congress should have the power to nullify state laws because "[t]he firmness of Judges is not itself sufficient."[34] Moreover, he argued (in words that assume a judicial power to declare "improper" laws unconstitutional[35]) that it "would be better to prevent the passage of an improper law, than to declare it void when passed."[36] Despite this concern, a congressional negative on state laws along with the council of revision was rejected by the Convention, leaving the other structural constraints, including the doctrine of judicial nullification, to keep state and national governments from exceeding their proper powers.

Although I contend that we are not bound by the original *intentions* of the framers, their expressions of intention are evidence of the original public meaning of the "judicial power." Drafters typically strive to choose words whose public meaning reflects their intentions. Moreover, this evidence of framers' intentions should also quiet the concerns of those originalists who do care about original intent because the evidence of such intent is overwhelming. Originalist crit-

---

[29] Id at 462 (statement of J. Mercer).

[30] Id.

[31] Id at 463 (statement of J. Dickenson).

[32] Id.

[33] Id (statement of G. Morris).

[34] Id at 518 (statement of J. Wilson).

[35] A point I stress in Randy E. Barnett, *The Original Meaning of the Necessary and Proper Clause*, 6 U Pa J Const Law 183, 215-20 (2003).

[36] Madison, *Notes of Debates in the Federal Convention of 1787* at 518 (cited in note 19) (statement of J. Wilson).

ics of judicial review would also have to disregard the evidence that suggests that the original public meaning of "judicial power" at the time of ratification included the power of judicial review. For the fact that judges were to be empowered to nullify unconstitutional legislation was no secret intention held only by delegates to the Constitutional Convention in Philadelphia.

B. Evidence from the State Ratification Conventions

The state ratification debates are replete with assertions of the power of judicial nullification. Supporters of the Constitution offered this power as a means of limiting the powers of the general government. Speaking to the Pennsylvania convention, James Wilson stated: "If a law should be made inconsistent with those powers vested by this instrument in Congress, the judges, as a consequence of their independence, and the particular powers of government being defined, will declare such law to be null and void; for the power of the Constitution predominates. Any thing, therefore, that shall be enacted by Congress contrary thereto, will not have the force of law."[37] To the objection that judges would "be impeached, because they decide an act null and void, that was made in defiance of the Constitution," Wilson replied: "What House of Representatives would dare to impeach, or Senate to commit, judges for the performance of their duty?"

In the Virginia convention, future chief justice John Marshall openly stated the principle of nullification he would later enunciate (and then expand upon) in *Marbury v. Madison.* If the government of the United States "were to make a law not warranted by any of the powers enumerated," said Marshall, "it would be considered by the judges as an infringement of the Constitution which they are to guard. They would not consider such a law as coming under their jurisdiction. They would declare it void."[38]

This article began by quoting Oliver Elsworth's ringing endorsement in the Connecticut convention of the judicial power to nullify unconstitutional acts of both Congress and state legislatures which is worth repeating here:

[37] Elliot, *The Debates In The Several State Conventions On The Adoption Of The Federal Constitution* at 2:489 (cited in note 1) (James Wilson in the Pennsylvania ratification convention December 4, 1788).

[38] Id at 3:553 (John Marshall in the Virginia ratification convention, June 20, 1788). Notice too Marshall's invocation of the enumerated powers scheme to quiet the fears of opponents—the scheme he did so much to undermine in his opinions in *McCulloch v. Maryland,* 17 US (4 Wheat.) 316 (1819) and *Gibbons v. Ogden,* 22 US (9 Wheat.) 1 (1824). See Barnett, *Restoring the Lost Constitution,* 166-84, 291-94, 301-02 (cited in note 17).

This Constitution defines the extent of the powers of the general government. If the general legislature should at any time overleap their limits, the judicial department is a constitutional check. If the United States go beyond their powers, if they make a law which the Constitution does not authorize, it is void; and the *judicial power*, the national judges, who, to secure their impartiality, are to be made independent, will declare it to be void. On the other hand, if the states go beyond their limits, if they make a law which is a usurpation upon the general government, the law is void; and upright, independent judges will declare it to be so.[39]

The power of the federal judiciary to strike down unconstitutional state laws was also asserted in the North Carolina convention by William Davie, who stated that "Every member will agree that the positive regulations ought to be carried into execution, and that the negative restrictions ought not to [be] disregarded or violated. Without a judiciary, the injunctions of the Constitution may be disobeyed, and the positive regulations neglected or contravened."[40] He then argued that, should states impose duties on imported goods, "the Constitution might be violated with impunity, if there were no power in the general government to correct and counteract such laws. This great object can only be safely and completely obtained by the instrumentality of the federal judiciary."[41]

Even opponents of the Constitution conceded the existence of judicial nullification, though as at the Philadephia convention some again questioned its efficacy. In his statement to the legislature of Maryland, Luther Martin said: "Whether, therefore, any laws or *regulations* of the Congress, any acts of *its President or other officers*, are contrary to, or not warranted by, the Constitution, rests only with the judges, who are appointed by Congress, to determine; by whose determinations every state must *be bound.*"[42] In the Virginia ratification convention, Patrick Henry made a similar charge in a manner that suggests he included judicial nullification within the meaning of the word "judiciary":

The honorable gentleman did our judiciary honor in saying that they had firmness to counteract the legislature in some cases. Yes, sir, our judges opposed the acts of the legislature. We have this landmark to guide us. They had fortitude to declare that

[39] Id at 2:196 (Oliver Elsworth in the Connecticut ratification convention, January 7, 1788) (emphasis added).

[40] Id at 4:156 (July 29, 1788).

[41] Id at 157.

[42] Id at 1:380 (Martin Luther in the Maryland ratification convention, January 27, 1788).

they were *the judiciary*, and would oppose unconstitutional acts. Are you sure that your federal judiciary will act thus? Is that judiciary as well constructed, and as independent of the other branches, as our state judiciary? Where are your landmarks in this government? I will be bold to say you cannot find any in it. I take it as the highest encomium on this country, that the acts of the legislature, if unconstitutional, are liable to be opposed by the judiciary.[43]

Also in Virginia, William Grayson, another opponent of the Constitution, observed that "If the Congress cannot make a law against the Constitution, I apprehend they cannot make a law to abridge it. The judges are to defend it."[44] This evidence is another example of how original meaning originalism transcends disputes between contending political parties in ways original intent originalism often cannot. Both sides typically used the same words to describe the same thing. I could find no dissent from this interpretation of the "judicial power" in any of the ratification debates.

C. Evidence from Immediately After Ratification

Nor was this conception of judicial power short-lived. Two years after ratification of the Constitution, Representative James Madison delivered his speech to the first session of the House explaining his proposed amendments to the Constitution. In it he asserted the importance of judicial nullification:

If they are incorporated into the constitution, independent tribunals of justice will consider themselves in a peculiar manner the guardians of those rights; they will be an impenetrable bulwark against every assumption of power in the legislative or executive; they will be naturally led to resist every encroachment upon rights expressly stipulated for in the constitution by the declaration of rights.[45]

No one in Congress rose to object to this assertion of "judicial power."

Similarly instructive is the understanding of Thomas Jefferson. Because Jefferson was in France during the drafting and ratification of the Constitution, some originalists disparage any reliance upon his views. Yet the very fact that Jefferson did not participate in writing or debating the meaning of the Constitution makes his reading of the

---

[43] Id at 3:324-25 (Patrick Henry in the Virginia ratification convention, June 12, 1788) (emphasis added).

[44] Id at 567 (William Grayson in the Virginia ratification convention, June 21, 1788).

[45] Joseph Gales ed, 1 *Annals of Congress* 457 (Buffalo, 1790).

text relevant to an assessment of its original public meaning. Added to this is the fact that Jefferson was less of a partisan at this time. While he generally supported the Constitution, Jefferson had serious reservations about several of its features particularly the absence of a bill of rights and rotation in office (what we call today "term limits"). As he put it, "I am neither federalist nor antifederalist; . . . . I am of neither party, nor yet a trimmer between parties."[46]

Of special interest are statements in two letters written closely in time to James Madison. In the first, a well-known exchange, Jefferson attempts to persuade Madison of the value of a bill of rights, which Madison had previously disparaged in a letter to Jefferson as mere "parchment barriers."[47] Madison contended that "experience proves the inefficacy of a bill of rights on those occasions when its controul is most needed."[48] In Jefferson's reply he invoked the importance of judicial nullification:

> In the arguments in favor of a declaration of rights, you omit one which has great weight with me, the legal check which it puts into the hands of the judiciary. This is a body, which if rendered independent, and kept strictly to their own department merits great confidence for their learning and integrity.[49]

Jefferson's affirmation of a judicial power to nullify unconstitutional laws is of special significance in light of an earlier objection to the Constitution he had made in a letter to Madison: "I like the negative given to the Executive with a third of either house, though I should have liked it better had the Judiciary been associated for that purpose, or invested with a similar and separate power."[50] A judicial "negative," which the Constitution omitted, like the presidential veto to which Jefferson referred, could be exercised for any reason, not just on the ground that a law was unconstitutional. From Jefferson's later exchange with Madison asserting the existence of judicial review, we can discern that the omission of a judicial negative or veto on legislation in the Constitution did not undermine Jefferson's view that the judicial power included a power to nullify unconstitutional laws.

Finally, Madison's early skepticism of the *merits* of judicial re-

---

[46] Julian P. Boyd et al, eds, 14 *The Papers of Thomas Jefferson* 651 (Princeton, 1950) (Letter to Francis Hopkinson, March 13, 1789).

[47] Charles F. Hobson and Robert A. Rutlands eds, 11 *Papers of James Madison* 297 (Virginia, 1977) (Letter to Thomas Jefferson, October 17, 1788) ("Repeated violations of these parchment barriers have been committed by overbearing majorities in every State.").

[48] Id.

[49] Boyd et al, eds, 14 *The Papers of Thomas Jefferson* at 14:659 (cited in note 46) (Letter to James Madison, March 15, 1789).

[50] Id at 12:440 (Letter to James Madison, December 20, 1787).

view confirms, rather than undermines, the conclusion that the original meaning of the "judicial power" included the power of nullification. In his *Observations on the "Draught of a Constitution for Virginia,"* written within days of his "parchment barriers" letter to Jefferson, Madison proposed that vetoed or nullified bills reenacted by specified supermajorities in either or both houses should become law over the objection of either the executive or the judiciary stating: "It sd. not be allowed the Judges or the Ex to pronounce a law thus enacted, unconstitul. & invalid."[51] Nevertheless, he acknowledges that in the Constitution then pending ratification, only the executive veto may be overridden by a supermajority of both houses. As a result,

> In the State Constitutions & indeed in the Fedl. one also, no provision is made for case of a disagreement in expounding them; and as the Courts are generally the last in making their decision, it results to them, by refusing or not refusing to execute a law to stamp it with its final character. This makes the Judiciary Dept paramount in fact to the Legislature, which was never intended, and can never be proper.[52]

I disagree with Madison here. Being last does not make the judiciary in any sense "paramount" but merely equal to the other branches. After all, Congress may refuse to enact a law because it deems it to be unconstitutional and, because it is first, the bill never reaches the courts who may disagree. This does not render Congress paramount to the courts. By the same token, if the president vetoes a bill and his veto is sustained, the courts do not get to reverse that decision and uphold the bill as constitutional. Instead, in our system, absent a legislative supermajoritarian override of a presidential veto, all three branches must concur before it is found constitutional. Any one branch may scuttle a law because it alone deems it unconstitutional. If the judiciary deferred to Congress, this would double count the opinion of legislative branch. Of course, as we have seen, by the time he introduced his proposed amendments in the first Congress, Madison came to be persuaded by Jefferson (and presumably others) to change his mind on the propriety of judicial nullification and he strongly asserted the need for such a power.

More importantly, by bemoaning this feature of the pending Constitution as written, Madison nevertheless assumes, rather than denies, that the text includes the power of nullification. That Madison admits the existence of the power of nullification in the text at the

[51] Charles F. Hobson and Robert A. Rutlands eds, 11 *Papers of James Madison* at 11:293 (cited in note 47) ("Observations on the 'Draught of a Constitution for Virginia,'" ca. October 15, 1788).
[52] Id.

very moment he is objecting to its propriety is particularly potent evidence that the original meaning of the "judicial power" included the power of nullification.

Madison's objection confirming the original meaning of the "judicial power" is also another vindication of the practicality of original meaning originalism and shows its advantages over original intent. While Madison's intent may have changed or conflicted with that of other framers, the meaning of the term "judicial power" in the Constitution remained constant and readily discernable by historical evidence. Like the statements of antifederalists discussed above, this example illustrates how original meaning can be discerned from the contemporaneous statements of those who opposed no less than those who supported a particular provision.

I have presented so many different statements asserting the existence of the power of judicial nullification because there are those today who question whether the doctrine was widely held by the founding generation. Like Charles Hyneman, they suggest that it was invented in 1803 by John Marshall in *Marbury v. Madison*. Given the weight of the historical evidence (which Hyneman, for example, does not discuss), their argument ultimately rests on the fact that the power of nullification is not explicit in the Constitution. Rarely do they examine the original meaning of "judicial power," however, choosing to rely instead on the "plain meaning" that term has today.

D. Construing the Power From Other Provisions of the Text

A power of judicial nullification is warranted not only by interpretation of the term "judicial power" but also by construing other provisions. According to Article III, Section 2: "The judicial Power shall extend to all Cases, in Law and Equity, arising under this Constitution and Laws of the United States. . . . [and] to Controversies to which the United States shall be a party." Second, the Supremacy Clause of Article VI provides that "This Constitution, and the Laws of the United States which shall be made in Pursuance thereof; and all Treaties made, or which shall be made, under the Authority of the United States, shall be the supreme Law of the Land; and the Judges in every State shall be bound thereby, any Thing in the Constitution or Laws of any State to the Contrary notwithstanding."

These provisions support the following construction: Courts are empowered under Article III to decide "all cases . . . arising under this Constitution and Laws of the United States." When deciding such a case, a court is required to apply the laws that are applicable to the case at hand. In cases where both the Constitution and a statute apply and the latter is in conflict with the former, the court must decide which is the superior authority. The Supremacy Clause suggests that the Constitution should take precedence over a statute. (I say "suggests," because the Supremacy Clause speaks of the superiority of the Constitution only to state laws and constitutions, not to acts of Congress.) Therefore, when the court finds that a statute is in conflict with the Constitution, it is bound to obey the Constitution and disregard the statute.

This was the construction provided by Alexander Hamilton in *Federalist* 78:

> The interpretation of the laws is the proper and peculiar province of the courts. A constitution is, in fact, and must be regarded by the judges as, a fundamental law. It therefore belongs to them to ascertain its meaning as well as the meaning of any particular act proceeding from the legislative body. If there should happen to be an irreconcilable variance between the two, that which has the superior obligation and validity ought, of course, to be preferred; or, in other words, the Constitution ought to be preferred to the statute, the intention of the people to the intention of their agents.[53]

Why is the Constitution "superior" to an act of Congress? "There is no position which depends on clearer principles than that every act of a delegated authority, contrary to the tenor of the commission under which it is exercised, is void. No legislative act, therefore, contrary to the Constitution, can be valid."[54] Moreover, Hamilton argued: "To deny this would be to affirm that the deputy is greater than his principal; that the servant is above his master; that the representatives of the people are superior to the people themselves; that men acting by virtue of powers may do not only what their powers do not authorize, but what they forbid."[55] Hamilton also rejected the idea that this construction makes the judicial branch "superior" to Congress.

> Nor does this conclusion by any means suppose a superiority of the judicial to the legislative power. It only supposes that the power of the people is superior to both, and that where the will of the legislature, declared in its statutes, stands in opposition to that of the people, declared in the Constitution, the judges ought to be governed by the latter rather than the former. They ought to regulate their decisions by the fundamental laws rather than by those which are not fundamental.[56]

[53] Clinton Rossiter ed, *The Federalist No. 78* at 467 (Alexander Hamilton) (Penguin Books, 1961).

[54] Id.

[55] Id.

[56] Id at 467-68.

Hamilton's argument is undoubtedly a constitutional construction rather than a straightforward interpretation of the "judicial power." This becomes even clearer when he bases his analysis on the premise that "[t]he complete independence of the courts of justice is peculiarly essential in a limited Constitution. By a limited Constitution, I understand one which contains certain specified exceptions to the legislative authority; such, for instance, as that it shall pass no bills of attainder, no ex post facto laws, and the like."[57] If the legislature is to be limited in this manner, who besides the courts can police this limitation?

> Limitations of this kind can be preserved in practice no other way than through the medium of courts of justice, whose duty it must be to declare all acts contrary to the manifest tenor of the Constitution void. Without this, all the reservations of particular rights or privileges would amount to nothing.[58]

Notice that nothing in this rationale for judicial review would empower the judiciary to permit Congress to exceed the limits on its powers by changing via "interpretation" the written Constitution. To the contrary, *this whole justification for judicial review assumes that the Constitution provides written limitations that Congress is to follow and judges to enforce.* In short, this construction permitting judicial nullification provides still more support for originalist interpretation.

Is Hamilton's argument for judicial review undermined because it is a "mere" construction rather than a straightforward interpretation of the text? Hardly. First, it is entirely consistent with evidence of the original meaning of the "judicial power." Second, the contrary position that the Constitution's silence is to be taken as support for congressional supremacy is also a construction. Indeed, Hamilton himself appreciated this:

> If it be said that the legislative body are themselves the constitutional judges of their own powers and that the construction they put upon them is conclusive upon the other departments it may be answered that this cannot be the natural presumption where it is not to be collected from any particular provisions in the Constitution. It is not otherwise to be supposed that the Constitution could intend to enable the representatives of the people to substitute their *will* to that of their constituents. It is far more rational to suppose that the courts were designed to be an intermediate body between the people and the legislature in

---

[57] Id at 466.
[58] Id.

order, among other things, to keep the latter within the limits assigned to their authority.[59]

In this passage, Hamilton shows that the opposing view is itself one of construction, but a construction inferior to the one he advocates. Where the text of the Constitution is silent ("where it is not to be collected from any particular provisions in the Constitution") and therefore not subject to straightforward interpretation, we ought not adopt a construction ("this cannot be the natural presumption") that Congress is to be "the constitutional judges of their own powers and that the construction they put upon them is conclusive upon the other departments." Rather, in light of the purposes for which the Constitution was adopted and the limitation of power it imposes upon Congress, "It is far more rational to suppose that the courts were designed to be an intermediate body between the people and the legislature in order, among other things, to keep the latter within the limits assigned to their authority."[60]

However, this last formulation that courts were designed "to keep [the legislature] within the limits assigned to their authority" is vague. Because Hamilton does not add "by nullifying the enforcement of unconstitutional statutes that come before them," his formulation could also be taken to justify a broader power to order or compel other branches of the government to keep them "within the limits assigned to their authority." To claim this power for the judiciary would be to move beyond judicial nullification to something that could be called judicial supremacy. Hamilton, of course, said no such thing and, in context, it is not clear that such meaning could fairly be attached to his words. Yet in 1803, this power was claimed for the courts in the landmark case of *Marbury v. Madison.*

IV. JUDICIAL SUPREMACY IS A CONSTRUCTION

We speak today of the power of "judicial review," not judicial nullification. The modern power of judicial review is not limited to refusing to enforce an unconstitutional law being applied to an individual, a power that is warranted by the original meaning of the "judicial power." Modern judicial review also includes a power to command or order other branches of the government to follow the judiciary's interpretation of the Constitution, a power that is sometimes called "judicial supremacy." Although I am not entirely satisfied with this term,[61] I

[59] Id at 467.
[60] Id.
[61] "Supremacy" strikes me as needlessly pejorative. I would prefer a term to describe this power that does not prejudge the outcome of an inquiry into its propriety.

will use it to distinguish between a conception of judicial review limited to judicial nullification and one that extends as well to the power to command or direct other branches and levels of government to conform to the judiciary's view of what the Constitution requires.

The distinction between judicial nullification and judicial supremacy can be hard to grasp because nullification seems like a subset of supremacy. A power of nullification gives the judiciary the last word on whether a statute is "law" that is binding on the individual and this seems like "supremacy," but the appearance is misleading. As was discussed above, the explicit division of the government into three departments, commonly said to be "coequal" (though this term also does not appear in the text), suggests that the judicial branch must reach its own decision on what the Constitution requires in cases of conflict between the Constitution and an act of Congress when deciding which to enforce. A power of nullification is not one of supremacy, but one of judicial equality. Were it absent, the legislative and executive branches alone would decide on the constitutionality of their laws. Judges would have to merely take their orders. This would render the judiciary inferior to the other branches rather than their equal.

The confusion of judicial nullification with judicial supremacy arises if one ignores the proposition that *judicial negation is not legislation*.[62] If Congress refuses to enact a statute, perhaps because in its opinion it would be unconstitutional, it does not matter if a court would uphold it as constitutional. Courts cannot mandate the passage of a statute. On the issue of which statutes to enact the legislative power the legislature is "supreme." Only if the Congress enacts a measure because enough of its members believe it to be constitutional (or do not care) and the president signs the bill believing it is constitutional (or does not care) may the Court have the opportunity to express its opinion on its constitutionality. A court's power to negate unconstitutional legislation renders it equal, not superior, to the other branches.

Just as a power to negate legislation does not imply a power to enact it, neither does it imply a judicial power to mandate that the executive branch exercise its powers in a particular mode. True, judicial nullification would extend to refusing to hold a person liable for disobeying an unconstitutional command of the executive branch. Nullification, however, does not include the further power to order or "mandate" that someone act in a particular manner or to desist from acting in a manner a court finds to be unconstitutional. Whether or not this additional power can be justified on the basis of interpretation or construction is a separate question. While historical evidence strongly supports the conclusion that the original meaning of "judi-

[62] I thank Leonard Liggio for providing this helpful formulation.

cial power" included the power to nullify, there is little if any evidence to support a claim that the original meaning of "judicial power" also included a power to command other branches.

Nor was such a power actually exercised by the Supreme Court in *Marbury v. Madison*.[63] This famous case grew out of legislation enacted by a lame-duck Congress dominated by Federalists to create numerous judicial positions that could be filled with Federalists by outgoing President Adams before the newly elected Republican Thomas Jefferson could assume the presidency. In a bizarre twist by today's lights, all these "midnight commissions" had been sealed by John Marshall himself, who was not only chief justice but also the outgoing secretary of state, and delivered by his brother James. In the haste to seal and deliver the commissions, Marbury's was left behind. At the instruction of incoming President Jefferson, James Madison, the incoming secretary of state, refused to deliver it.

Marbury then brought suit in the Supreme Court to issue a writ of mandamus to compel the secretary of state "either to deliver the commission, or a copy of it from the record."[64] The Court rejected this request because the Judiciary Act that authorized the Court to grant writs of mandamus on government officials exceeded the powers of Congress and was unconstitutional.[65] By avoiding the issue of whether a judicial command of this kind to the executive branch would exceed the judicial power, Marshall needed only to justify in his opinion the judicial power to nullify the Judiciary Act as beyond the powers of Congress to enact. Although this conclusion could have been well-supported by evidence of the original meaning of the "judicial power," Marshall's opinion in *Marbury* is entirely an exercise in constitutional construction—and perhaps this absence of originalist justification is the source of the cloud over the judicial power of nullification ever since.

Marshall begins by recourse to "certain principles, supposed to have been long and well established."[66] Among these is the principle that the Constitution is "superior law . . . unchangeable by ordinary means."[67] Although the text says the Constitution is superior to state constitutions and statute, it does not say it is superior to acts of Congress. Nor

[63] *Marbury v Madison*, 5 US 137 (1803).

[64] Id at 173.

[65] The ruling was based on the distinction between "original" and "appellate" jurisdiction explicit in Article III rather than on any inherent constitutional limitation on the judiciary. The Court found that the act improperly allowed for such relief in cases initiated in the Supreme Court instead of only those cases that the Court heard on appeal from the suit commenced in lower court.

[66] *Marbury*, 5 US at 176.

[67] Id at 177.

does it say that it cannot be changed by ordinary means, though this can be implied by the extraordinary mechanisms of amendment it provides in Article V. Marshall notes that "all those who have framed written constitutions contemplate them as forming the fundamental and paramount law of the nation."[68] He concludes from all this that "legislative act contrary to the constitution is not law."[69]

Marshall then claims that it is "emphatically the province and duty of the judicial department to say what the law is. Those who apply the rule to particular cases, must of necessity expound and interpret that rule."[70] Like Hamilton, Marshall notes that "[i]f two laws conflict with each other, the courts must decide on the operation of each."[71] In such a case, "the court must determine which of these conflicting rules governs the case. That is of the very essence of judicial duty."[72] Like Hamilton, he finds the answer in the superior authority of the Constitution. "If, then, the courts are to regard the constitution, and the constitution is superior to any ordinary act of the legislature, the constitution, and not such ordinary act, must govern the case to which they both apply."[73]

Marshall emphasizes that to hold otherwise would be to thwart the idea of a written constitution and would violate the first principles of this particular system of government:

> This doctrine would subvert the very foundation of all written constitutions. It would declare that an act which, according to the principles and theory of our government, is entirely void, is yet in practice, completely obligatory. It would declare, that if the legislature shall do what is expressly forbidden, such act, notwithstanding the express prohibition, is in reality effectual. It would be giving to the legislature a practical and real omnipotence, with the same breath which professes to restrict their powers within narrow limits. It is prescribing limits, and declaring that those limits may be passed at pleasure.[74]

Most modern admirers of Marshall and of *Marbury* fail to realize how the "principles and theory of our government" he advances for the power of judicial nullification also argue strongly for originalist interpretation. For only if the Constitution has a meaning independent of the judiciary, and that must remain the same until properly changed,

[68] Id.
[69] Id.
[70] Id.
[71] Id.
[72] Id at 178.
[73] Id.
[74] Id.

does the existence of the "superior" law that is the written Constitution justify judges nullifying the "ordinary" authority of a statute.

Not until the end of his opinion does Marshall reinforce his analysis with "additional arguments" furnished by inferences drawn from "the peculiar expressions of the constitution of the United States."[75] With respect the "judicial power," Marshall argues that it "is extended to all cases arising under the constitution."[76] He asks: "Could it be the intention of those who gave this power, to say that, in using it, the constitution should not be looked into? That a case arising under the constitution should be decided without examining the instrument under which it arises?"[77]

Marshall then lists various explicit prohibitions and restrictions in the Constitution and concludes, "From these, and many other selections which might be made, it is apparent, that the framers of the constitution contemplated that instrument, as a rule for the government of *courts*, as well as of the legislature."[78] In this way, "the particular phraseology of the constitution of the United States confirms and strengthens the principle, supposed to be essential to all written constitutions, that a law repugnant to the constitution is void; and that *courts*, as well as other departments, are bound by that instrument."[79]

Notice that none of Marshall's arguments presented to this point support a judicial power to command another coequal branch of government. Indeed, he explicitly denies that the court may issue a writ of mandamus to the president himself, confining his attention only to whether the secretary of state can be compelled to perform a merely "ministerial act." He concludes that

> where the heads of departments are the political or confidential agents of the executive, merely to execute the will of the President, or rather they act in cases in which the executive possesses a constitutional or legal discretion, nothing can be more perfectly clear than that their acts are only politically examinable. But where a specific duty is assigned by law, and individual rights depend upon the performance of that duty, it seems equally clear that the individual who considers himself injured, has a right to resort to the laws of his country for a remedy.[80]

Later in the opinion Marshall denies that a court may "enquire how the executive, or executive officers, perform duties in which they

[75] Id.
[76] Id at 178.
[77] Id at 179.
[78] Id at 179-80.
[79] Id at 180 (emphasis added).
[80] Id at 166.

have discretion. Questions, in their nature political, or which are, by the constitution and laws, submitted to the executive, can never be made in this court."[81]

Because I do not wish to question whether courts may properly compel executive branch officials to perform acts required by law, I shall not rehearse here all the arguments made by Chief Justice Marshall on behalf of such a judicial power. My point is simply that, unlike the case of judicial nullification, there is little or no evidence that such a power can be justified by the original meaning of the "judicial power," and Marshall offered none. Further, because it held that the power was improperly granted to the Court by Congress, any suggestion in *Marbury* that a court has power to mandate behavior is dicta.

Marshall's dicta that courts may sometimes have such a power is a construction, rather than an interpretation, of the Constitution, though this is not to say that it is necessarily improper. Also a construction is the contrary position favored, for example, by President Jefferson who was of the opinion that federal courts "cannot issue a mandamus to the President or legislature, or to any of their officers."[82] Although the writ existed at common law, "the constitution [controls] the common law in this particular."[83] Because he was speaking of judicial supremacy, not judicial nullification, Jefferson was not contradicting his earlier endorsement of judicial review as some have charged.[84] To resolve this dispute would require an inquiry into whether a constructive judicial power of mandamus sometimes or always conflicts with the original meaning of the text and, if not, whether such a power enhances or detracts from constitutional legitimacy.[85] I express no opinion on this issue here.

[81] Id at 170.

[82] Paul Leicester Ford, ed, 10 *The Writings of Thomas Jefferson* 140 (Putnam's 1892-99) (Letter to Spencer Roane, September 6, 1819).

[83] Id.

[84] Jefferson has been accused of changing his position on judicial review when Federalist judges obstructed his political agenda. A more nuanced account is provided by David Mayer, who shows that while Jefferson never wavered in his support for judicial nullification, his objection was to affirmative judicial interference with the "Revolution of 1800." See David N. Mayer, *The Constitutional Thought of Thomas Jefferson* 257-94 (Virginia, 1994).

[85] It might, for example, be improper to issue a mandamus to the President or Congress perhaps because it violates the original textual allocation of executive or legislative powers, but not improper for a court to command some lesser employee of another branch. I offer this possibility only to illustrate the potential relationship between interpretation and construction in answering this question. Of course it is also possible to advance additional evidence that judicial supremacy was within or in conflict with the original meaning of the judicial power and therefore is either mandated or prohibited by the text.

V. CONCLUSION

We are now in a position to understand why the Constitution did not contain a passage reading something like: "The Supreme Court, and such inferior courts as may be established by Congress, shall have power to nullify a Law enacted by Congress and signed by the President if the Law is unconstitutional." The evidence from the Constitutional Convention and from the state ratification conventions is overwhelming that the original public meaning of the term "judicial power" included the power to nullify unconstitutional laws. In contrast, because the "executive power" did not include the inherent power to veto legislation, it had to be added expressly. So too did the legislative override.

The evidence found in these crucial records of public meaning is so consistent that the discovery of a few counterexamples would not greatly undermine this conclusion. Nevertheless, I found no such counterexamples in my search through these records (though one never can be completely sure about what one has missed). Will the evidence marshaled here end all further controversy over whether judicial review is authorized by the original meaning of the text? Long-standing academic debates are rarely settled so cleanly. Still, one of the virtues of original meaning originalism is that those seeking to dissent from this conclusion must go out and find direct evidence of original meaning in the form of statements from the conventions (or, less relevantly, from elsewhere) to the contrary. Speculation under the guise of historical "context" or counterfactual channeling the framers will not do. I look forward to examining the fruits of their labor.

Irrationality and the Criminal Sanction

*Michael Edmund O'Neill**

In this article, Professor O'Neill examines the interaction between cognitive limits and criminal sanctions by reasoning that perfectly rational decisions are inhibited because of inherent biological limitations. O'Neill explains that rationality must be understood both in subjective and objective ways. Whether a result of genetic anamoly, mental illness, or catastrophic neurological trauma, internal, biological causes may prevent an indivudual from engaging in objectively rational behavior. Accordingly, O'Neill argues that policy makers must take cognitive limits and irrationality into consideration, because typical methods of punishment will not always deter misbehavior.

"Man is obviously made for thinking. Therein lies all his dignity and his merit; and his whole duty is to think as he ought."[1]

* Associate Professor of Law, George Mason University; Commissioner, United States Sentencing Commission. I would like to thank Terrence Chorvat, Margaret O'Neill, Jeff Parker and Todd Zywicki for their helpful comments in thinking through these rather difficult issues. I would also like to thank Frank Buckley and the Law & Economics Center for such generous financial support, and Meghan Fatouros and Suzette Hurley for their invaluable research assistance. Finally, by way of disclaimer, I would note that the opinions expressed within this article do not reflect the policy or positions of the United States Sentencing Commission.

[1] See Blaise Pascal, *Pensees* (A.J. Krailsheimer trans, Penguin Books, 2d ed 1995).

I. INTRODUCTION

In Fritz Lang's fascinating portrait of abnormal sexuality, M,[2] Peter Lorre plays a murderous pedophile who prowls the dark environs of 1920's Berlin. A masterpiece of German expressionism, the film follows Lorre's character (Hans Beckert) as he systematically preys upon young children, first gaining their confidence by plying them with treats, and then abducting and ultimately murdering them. As Beckert's murderous rampages go unchecked, the unsavory elements of Berlin's underworld, whose economic interests are jeopardized by the increased police scrutiny, ferret out the killer and bring him before a jury of his true peers: fellow criminal offenders. Apparently, even the most hardened criminals have their limits and by preying upon children, Beckert has transgressed the informal rules that guide even members of the underworld.

Beckert's capture and mock-trial are the subjects of the film's final act. A group of rough-looking men hustle him down into a cavernous warehouse to face his accusers. Beckert's trial is a justly famous scene, animated by Lorre brilliantly laying out the template for all future cinematic psychopaths. An ideal casting choice with his pudgy frame, bulging, mournful eyes, and panicked grimaces, he is sinister without outwardly appearing so. As the assembled criminal mob finds him guilty and demands his execution, Beckert loses his cool facade, once so helpful in luring children to their doom. Breaking down before the mob's judgment, he does not deny that he is the killer, but instead cries out for the mercy. The mercy he seeks is that reserved for those compelled by forces seemingly beyond their control: "But can I . . . can I help it?" he asks rhetorically. "Haven't I got this curse inside me?" he screams, "The fire? The voice? The pain? . . . Who knows what it feels like to be me?"[3] Beckert fully acknowledges the wrongfulness of his actions, but confesses his utter inability to control himself.

Beckert represents the classic criminal psychopath—the individual who is unable to conform his behavior to legal dictates. Although a common feature of the criminal law (and popular cinema), such an archetype is at odds with the standard neoclassical model of human behavior. That model posits that human behavior is innately self-directed and rational. The question to be addressed is whether Beckert is acting *rationally* or whether he's exhibiting what some might deem *irrational* behavior.

[2] Theau Harbou and Fritz Land, M (1931) (movie directed by Fritz Lang) . M is based on the real-life case of child-killer Peter Kurten, the aptly dubbed "monster of Dusseldorf," whose crimes of the 1920s were quite notorious and particularly grisly.
[3] Id.

Irrationality is not a particularly well-mined topic in the law, save perhaps among those interested in criminal law.[4] In part, this is a result of the difficulty legal scholars have in viewing human behavior as being anything but the product of self-conscious choice. This understanding, that adult human behavior is the product of willful choice, undergirds the criminal law. Although the literature contains scattered references to the unconscious and to internal compulsion, the law has remained remarkably resistant to the methods and insights of psychiatry or biological causation generally, and the study of irrationality in particular.[5] Although iconic Supreme Court Justice Oliver Wendell Holmes, Jr. emphasized the influence of unconscious ideas on the development of law,[6] his lasting contribution has been the reasonableness standard of legal liability. Other than musings on the legal insanity defense, law and biology remains a somewhat underdeveloped field.[7]

The neoclassical economic model necessarily demands the use of certain simplifying assumptions. The most important of these may be that people behave rationally.[8] The behavioral model posited by neoclassical economics assumes that the individual is a rational actor self consciously choosing utility maximizing behaviors. Rationality dominates, both as a descriptive model of human behavior and as a pre-

---

[4] Stephen J. Morse, *Excusing and the New Excuse Defenses: A Legal and Conceptual Review,* 23 Crime & Just 329 (1998); Owen D. Jones, *The Evolution of Irrationality,* 41 Jurimetrics 289 (2001); Ahmed A. White, *Victims Rights, Rule of Law, and the Threat to Liberal Jurisprudence,* 87 Ky L J 357 (1999).

[5] The seminal application of psychoanalytic ideas in the law was carried out by Jerome Frank in *Law and the Modern Mind.* Jerome Frank, *Law and the Modern Mind* (Smith Peter, 1930). A few prominent scholars attempted to integrate psychoanalysis into law earlier in this century. See Jay Katz et al, *Psychoanalysis, Psychiatry and Law* (Free Press, 1967); C.G. Schoenfeld, *Psychoanalysis and the Law* (Charles C. Thomas, 1973); Joseph Goldstein, *Psychoanalysis and Jurisprudence,* 77 Yale LJ 1053 (1968); Robert S. Redmount, *Law as a Psychological Phenomenon,* 18 Am J Juris 80 (1973); Alan A. Stone, *Psychoanalysis and Jurisprudence: Revisited,* in S.C. Post, *Moral Values and the Superego Concept in Psychoanalysis* (Intl Univ Pr, 1972). Perhaps the earliest discussion of psychoanalytic ideas in the legal literature appears to be Theodore Schroeder, *The Psychologic Study of Judicial Opinions,* 6 Calif L Rev 89 (1918). Karl Llewellyn, for one, described the influence of psychoanalytic ideas on legal realism: "In 1920, as a result of James Harvey Robinson's Mind in the Making, a Freudian interpretation of judicial opinions broke upon the little world of legal scholarship." Karl N. Llewellyn, *The Common Law Tradition: Deciding Appeals* 12 (Hein & Co,1960).

[6] See Anne C. Dailey, *Holmes and the Romantic Mind,* 48 Duke L J 429 (1998).

[7] See Michael Edmund O'Neill, *Stalking the Mark of Cain,* 25 Harv J L & Pub Pol 31 (2001); David C. Rowe, *Biology and Crime* (Roxbury, 2002).

[8] Owen D. Jones, *Time-Shifted Rationality and the Law of Law's Leverage: Behavioral Economics Meets Behavioral Biology,* 95 Nw U L Rev 1141 (2001); Jon D. Hanson and Douglas A. Kysar, *Taking Behavioralism Seriously: Some Evidence of Market Manipulation,* 112 Harv L Rev 1420 (1999).

scriptive norm for the development of legal rules. Today, the rational actor is a canonical figure in the law; indeed, policy makers craft legislation to further the aims of this mythical person and legal scholars develop intricate theories to predict how this individual will behave in response to changes in legal norms. The success of the neoclassical model of human behavior is, at least in part, attributable to this model's elegant simplicity and its oft-touted ability to predict human behavior.[9]

"Rationality," however, is a notoriously difficult concept to understand.[10] Because it is devoid of an operational definition, it remains hard to critique as a concept. Like the sands upon a beach, the definition of rationality is an ever-shifting concept, changing to meet whatever demands the user may place upon it. Nevertheless, most often the term rationality is assumed to mean that individuals are *rational maximizers of personal utility.*[11] The concept of "personal utility" is necessarily subjective and thus may be individually defined. Rational actors will "pursue consistent ends using efficient means [as a function of] preferences which are complete, reflexive, transitive, and continuous."[12] Employing this assumption, scholars have modeled behavior under a variety conditions, and legislators have attempted to craft public policy with an eye towards the assumption that individuals will behave in accordance with this understanding of rationally.[13]

But do people truly behave rationally? Some deny the existence of irrationality, claiming that all behavior is necessarily rational from the individual's perspective. The argument is that if we understood the individual's subjective motivations, we would realize that his outwardly bizarre behavior was, in fact, rational. As a purely epistemological matter, however, it is difficult to label behavior as "rational" unless its converse can be acknowledged. In our everyday experience it is not uncommon to witness acts of seeming irrationality. Those who have dealt with children, substance abusers, or the chronically depressed doubtless have observed behavior that seemingly defies ra-

---

[9] See generally, Robert Cooter and Thomas Ulen, *Law and Economics* (Pearson Education, 3d ed. 2000); Richard A. Posner, *Economic Analysis of Law* (Aspen Law & Business, 5th ed. 1998).

[10] The various rationality constructs are detailed in Robert H. Frank, *Microeconomics and Behavior* (McGraw-Hill Co, 3d ed. 1997); Russell B. Korobkin and Thomas S. Ulen, *Law and Behavioral Science: Removing the Rationality Assumption from Law Economics*, 88 Cal L Rev 1051, 1060 (2000).

[11] Jones, 41 Jurimetrics at 318 (cited in note 4).

[12] Nicholas Mercuro and Steven G. Medema, *Economics and the Law: From Posner to Post-Modernism*, 57 (Princeton, 1997).

[13] See Erin Ann O'Hara and Douglas Yarn, *On Apology and Consilience*, 77 Wash L Rev 1121 (2002); Korobkin and Ulen, 88 Cal L Rev 1051 at 1053 (cited in note 10); Jones, 95 Nw L Rev at 1141 (cited in note 8).

tionality. Human behavior is complex and is oftentimes difficult to predict with any reliability. As a consequence, scholars have increasingly scrutinized this central tenant of law and economics.[14] Critics complain that theoretical models of human behavior employed by the neoclassical school are overly simplistic and do not withstand the gale force of empirical analysis.[15] They observe that real people often behave irrationally in that they are prone to become emotional, they accede to costly social norms, and they both make logical errs and base decisions on false (or incomplete) premises.[16] These criticisms may be particularly apt in the context of criminal law, where many offenders act on the basis of raw emotion, tend to be exceptional risk takers, or are incapable of engaging in basic cost-benefit analysis. Despite occasional attempts to demonstrate otherwise,[17] for example, addictive behavior (typified by the use of illegal drugs) often seems to defy rational explanation. Once-respectable people will sacrifice personal health, family, employment, and friends to satisfy a drug habit. Similarly, the widely acknowledged age and gender components to criminality—ie, young men are consistently more likely to engage in violent criminal acts than women or the elderly[18]—suggests that a pure rationality calculus fails to account adequately for certain types of commonly observed behavior.

A central question, however, is whether these criticisms are of sufficient weight to dislodge the rational actor theory from its privileged place in the world of legal and economic analysis.[19] After all, it is highly unlikely that *any* model of human behavior will account for

[14] See Christine Jolls, Cass R. Sunstein and Richard Thaler, *A Behavioral Approach to Law and Economics*, 50 Stan L Rev 1471 (1998); Jon D. Hanson and Douglas A. Kysar, 112 Harv L Rev at 1420 (cited in note 8); Korobkin and Ulen, 88 Cal L Rev 1051 at 1053 (cited in note 10).

[15] See Korobkin and Ulen, 88 Cal L Rev 1051 (cited in note 10); Thomas F. Cotter, *Legal Pragmatism and the Law and Economics Movement*, 84 Georgetown L J 2071 (1996); Donald C. Langevoort, *Behavioral Theories of Judgement and Decision Making in Legal Scholarship: A Literature Review*, 51 Vand L Rev 1499 (1998).

[16] See Gregory Mitchell, *Why Law and Economics Perfect Rationality Should not be Traded for Behaviroal Law and Economics' Equal Incompetence*, 91 Georgetown L J 67 (2002); Owen D. Jones, *Law, Biology and Emotions*, 39 Jurimetrics J 283 (1999); John Elster, *When Rationality Fails*, in Karen S. Cook and Margret Levi, *The Limits of Rationality* 19 (Chicago, 1990).

[17] Gary S. Becker and Kevin M. Murphy, *A Theory of Rational Addiction*, Working paper No. 41, (Univ of Chicago, Center Study Econ and State, Sept 1986).

[18] See, e.g., Michael P. Ghiglieri, *The Dark Side of Man: Tracing the Origins of Male Violence* (Perseus,1999); James Q. Wilson and Richard J. Herrnstein, *Crime and Human Nature* (Free Press,1985); Richard Wrangham and Dale Peterson, *Demonic Males: Apes and the Origins of Human Violence* (Houghton Mifflin Co,1996).

[19] Thomas Ulen examines why economists are so enamored of their assumptions regarding human rationality. Thomas S. Ulen, *Rational Choice and the Economic Analysis of Law*, 19 Law & Soc Inquiry 487, 487-491 (1994).

the myriad behavior human beings exhibit. The question is simply whether the rational actor model is sufficiently serviceable that to further complicate it in the name of "accuracy" is worth the costs of creating something that is more difficult to learn or to implement.[20] Part of the trouble of course, is that without developing working alternatives, it will be hard to know whether they are either more accurate, or more (or less) costly than present constructs.

Despite the confounding definitional debates concerning what constitutes rationality or irrationality, a cadre of scholars have started both to identify and to catalogue seemingly irrational behavior and have examined whether such behavior may have implications for broader legal analysis.[21] This scholarship, operating under various guises,[22] seeks to mesh empirical studies of human behavior with neoclassical economic modeling. As with much modern legal analysis, these efforts draw from both the social sciences (such as economics, psychology, and sociology) and the hard sciences (neurobiology and biological psychiatry) in an effort better to understand human behavior as it exists, not how we might wish it to exist. Unfortunately, social science based initiatives are presently more suitable for describing irrationality and documenting individual cases of behavioral anomaly than they are at explaining *why* people exhibit such behavior and *under what conditions* such anomalous behaviors

[20] See Douglas G. Baird, *The Future of Law and Economics: Looking Forward*, 64 U Chi L Rev 1129, 1146-48 (1997); Gregory S. Crespi, *Does the Chicago School Need to Expand its Curriculum*, 22 Law & Soc Inq 149, 154 (1997).

[21] See, e.g., Cass R. Sunstein, ed, *Behavioral Law and Economics* (Cambridge, 2000); Jennifer Arlen, *Comment: The Future of Behavioral Economic Analysis of Law*, 51 Vand L Rev 1765 (1998); Melvin Aron Eisenberg, *The Limits of Cognition and the Limits of Contract*, 47 Stan L Rev 211 (1995); Jolls et al, 50 Stan L Rev at 1471 (cited in note 14); Russell B. Korobkin, *The Status Quo Bias and Contract Default Rules*, 83 Cornell L Rev 608 (1998); Korobkin and Ulen, 88 Cal L Rev 1051 at 1053 (cited in note 10); Timur Kuran and Cass R. Sunstein, *Availability Cascades and Risk Regulation*, 51 Stan L Rev 683 (1999); Langevoort, 51 Vand L Rev at 1499 (cited in note 15) (compiling bibliography of behavioral law and economics scholarship); Richard A. Posner, *Rational Choice, Behavioral Economics, and the Law*, 50 Stan L Rev 1551 (1998); Matthew Rabin, *Psychology and Economics*, 36 J Econ Literature 11 (1998); Jeffrey J. Rachlinski, *The "New" Law and Psychology: A Reply to Critics, Skeptics, and Cautious Supporters*, 85 Cornell L Rev 739 (2000); Cass R. Sunstein, *Behavioral Analysis of Law*, 64 U Chi R 1175 (1997); Thomas S. Ulen, *Cognitive Imperfections in the Economic Analysis of Law*, 12 Hamline L Rev 385 (1989); Thomas S. Ulen, *The Growing Pains of Behavioral Law and Economics*, 51 Vand L Rev 1747 (1998); Owen D. Jones, *Time-Shifted Rationality and the Law of Law's Leverage: Behavioral Economics Meets Behavioral Biology*, 95 Nw U L Rev 1141 (2001).

[22] This scholarship seems to operate under such titles as "behavioral economics," "behavioral law and economics," "behavioral economic analysis of law," "behavioral analysis of law," "law and behavioral science," "law and the 'new' psychology." See, e.g., David Laibson and Richard Zeckhauser, *Amos Tversky and the Ascent of Behavioral Economics*, 16 J Risk & Uncertainty 7 (1998).

surface.[23] Economics, however, doesn't fare much better in that it posits a model of human behavior that *ought* to exist, and then builds legal rules around it.

To this end, it has been argued that those advancing the idea that human irrationality must be incorporated into behavioral analysis will not have a claim to modify the rational actor model unless and until critics are both able to prove the existence of such irrationality and then demonstrate that it arises in discernable patterns and under particular conditions.[24] Already, some are dismissing the empirical observations of psychologists and others working in the behavioral sciences as simple "noise" constituting merely random behavioral anomalies for which sound public policies could never be developed.[25] Traditionalists assert that without an overarching and coherent explanatory framework for irrationality, such random insights can never be successfully incorporated into existing rational actor models.[26] These incidental observations must be marshaled in such a way both to explain why people behave irrationally and under what circumstances they so behave. The thrust of these criticisms is that mere empirical observation can have no predictive power and thus no realistic effect upon shaping legal policy. After all, it must be acknowledged that sound public policy can never be designed solely for outliers.

This difficulty may be on the verge of being addressed, if not yet solved. It must always be remembered that economics is essentially a theory of human behavior. Behavior is the product of the brain, and its complicated interactions with the environment: the so-called (and oft-debated) "nature versus nurture" question, which most now concede to be "nature plus nurture."[27] Any theory seeking to explain human behavior is at bottom a theory about the brain.[28] Science

---

[23] See, e.g., Ariel Rubinstein, *Modeling Bounded Rationality* 3-4 (MIT, 1998) ("We have clear, causal, and experimental observations that indicate systematic deviations from the rational man paradigm. We look for models that will capture this evidence.").

[24] Owen D. Jones, *The Evolution of Irrationality*, 41 Jurimetrics 289, 291 (2001).

[25] See Gregory Mitchell, *Taking Behavioralism Too Seriously? The Unwarranted Pessimism of the New Behavioral Analysis of Law*, 42 Wm & Mary L Rev 1907 (2002).

[26] As Kahneman, Knetsch, and Thaler have explained:

"Parsimony requires that a new behavioral assumption should be introduced only of it specifies conditions under which observations deviate significantly from the basic model and only if it predicts the direction of these deviations."

Daniel Kahneman, Jack Knetsch, and Richard Thaler, *Fairness and the Assumptions of Economics*, 59 Journal of Business S285-300, 233 (1986).

[27] Grant R. Steen, *DNA and Destiny: Nature and Nurture in Human Behavior* (Plenum Press, 1996); Francis Fukuyama, *Is it all in the Genes? Nature versus Nurture Controversy*, 104 Commentary 30, 30-36 (1997).

[28] Dr. Eric Kandel has explained that "the central tenant of modern neural science is that all behavior is a reflection of brain function." Eric R. Kandel, *Brain and Behavior*, in Eric R. Kandel, ed, *Principles of Neural Science* 5-17 (Appleton & Lange, 1991). See also Owen D. Jones, *The Evolution of Irrationality*, 41 Jurimetrics 289, 291 (2001).

presently stands at the edge of a precipice looking down into a valley with a great many important discoveries to be unearthed: science is only at the most rudimentary stages of understanding basic brain biology, how evolutionary forces may have shaped the brain, and how behavior flows from that well-spring. But the future holds substantial promise, particularly in criminal law, where mental state is such a well ingrained part of the juridical landscape.

In constructing a theory of how behavior may be influenced by biology, however, certain ground rules must be established. For example, scholars need to construct operative definitions of "rationality" and "irrationality." The devil resides in the definitional details. One person's *rationality* may be another's *irrationality*, rightly understood. For purposes of this discussion, I offer two distinctive definitions of rationality: objective, or *social* rationality, and subjective, or *private* rationality. *Social* rationality consists of those behaviors that can be empirically verified as occurring in a wide spectrum of human behavior. In other words, *ceteris paribus*, human beings prefer eating chocolate to being punished. As a consequence, we can say that those individuals who avoid punishment and maximize their eating of chocolate are acting objectively rational. Other individuals, however, may exhibit the seemingly anomalous behavior of preferring corporeal punishment to eating chocolate. Those individuals may be described as acting subjectively, or privately rational if they eschew chocolate in favor of punishment, but objectively irrational because their behavior does not lie within the mean of observed human activity.

This distinction is particularly important in the criminal law, for (at least from a utilitarian standpoint) we craft punishments designed with social rationality in mind. At a fundamental level, we assume that most people prefer freedom to prison or keeping their money as opposed to paying it to the government in the form of fines. This assumption is not merely theoretical myth-making; rather, it is the product of observing human behavior over time. Parents punish their young children as a means of deterring future bad conduct because they know that children prefer sweets to punishment. If most people failed to respond to incentives and to disincentives, then it would be difficult to use law as a tool to shape behavior. The entire enterprise of deterrence would be futile if lawmakers did not believe that punishments could be fashioned to deter certain behaviors. Society thus labels certain behaviors as socially deviant and then seeks to create punishments in order to deter people from engaging in those behaviors. For example, Congress believes that stealing property is inappropriate. It assumes that people prefer living in freedom to being jailed. As a consequence, Congress creates a regime in which the costs of stealing property (being convicted and going to prison) outweigh the benefits of obtaining additional property. This relatively simple example demands, however, that policy makers make certain fundamental assumptions about how people are likely to respond to these legislative efforts. Unfortunately, experience with criminal law demonstrates that such deterrence efforts, while in the main successful, are not *uniformly* successful.

The prescriptive analysis offered here is based upon the slowly unfolding understanding of basic neuro-biology, and the ability of scientists to uncover the foundations of human behavior from a biological standpoint. At its core, it must be understood that life sciences *are* social sciences. The venerable Cartesian mind/brain duality postulate that has so long persisted is becoming increasingly difficult to support scientifically.[29] Evidence suggests that the mind and brain appear in actuality to be an archetype of the religious trinity, except that here, the two are one.

Lest one think this integration of neuroscience with social science will yield little in terms of predicting behavior, one need only consider three obvious examples that have stood the test of time: the way in which we treat children, the aged, and the insane. Policy makers have long accepted the fact that children are sufficiently different from adults such that it is necessary to place limits on their ability to enter into contracts and to hold them to a different standard when apportioning responsibility for criminal activity.[30] Moreover, the behavior of the young is often predictable: we know they assess risk poorly and often fail to consider the consequences of their actions.[31] Only recently, however, has science been able to demonstrate, as a result of sophisticated brain scanning techniques, *why* the young are poor at assessing risk. Neuroscience has revealed that a child's brain is anatomically different from that of an adult, and those differences yield fairly predictable behavioral results.[32]

Similarly, the criminal law has long understood that some individuals—even if chronologically adults—are unable properly to care for themselves or have little ability to act in what we would consider a

[29] Patricia Smith Churchland, *Brain-wise: Studies in Neurophilosophy* 6-10 (MIT, 2002); Antonio R. Damasio, *Descartes' Error: Emotion, Reason, and the Brain* 247-52 (HarperCollins,1994).

[30] See Elizabeth S. Scott and Thomas Grisso, *The Evolution of Adolescence: A Developmental Perspective on Juvenile Justice Reform*, 88 J Crim L & Criminology 137, 172-176 (1997) (discussing developmental differences between adolescents, adults, and very young children, and arguing for a reduced criminal responsibility standard for adolescent offenders); Peter Arenella, *Convicting the Morally Blameless: Reassessing the Relationship Between Legal and Moral Accountability*, 39 UCLA L Rev 1511, 1521 (1992).

[31] Clifford R. Maynatt and Michael E. Doherty, *Understanding Human Behavior* (APA, 1999).

[32] Alexander J. Field, *Altruistically Inclined? The Behavioral Sciences, Evolutionary Theory, and the Origins of Reciprocity* 238 (2001).

responsible fashion.[33] Those persons, which the law has labeled "insane" (a term foreign to medical literature)[34] often act in ways that are both predictable and seemingly irrational. Schizophrenia, for example, which at one time was merely a clinical diagnosis based upon certain agreed-upon (and universally recognized) patterns of behavior, may be now diagnosable on the basis of a brain scan.

While clinical diagnoses do not a theory make, they do provide a foundation for better understanding the complexities of human behavior and likely will enable us not only to identify patterns of irrationality, but to predict them as well. As of yet, the science is still too new to provide useful tools to legal scholars, but it will have an effect upon current models of human behavior. I hope to demonstrate that a useful reservoir of biological knowledge exists about the manner in which the brain dictates behavior that may prove useful in reshaping the current legal and economic model's assumptions about behavior.

II. CRIMINAL LAW POSTULATES AND THE ASSUMPTIONS OF ECONOMICS

A. Of Mens Rea and the Criminal Law

The defining feature of criminal law is the concept of *mens rea:* the guilty mind.[35] Under the American criminal justice system, for a crime to have been committed the defendant must have performed an *actus reus* (a socially undesirable act) and must have done so with the appropriate *mens rea* (guilty mind). Absent either requirement, even if a socially undesirable act may have been committed, no legal crime exists.[36]

This simple definition belies the complexity hiding behind the term *mens rea*, for it is shorthand for a broad range of concepts relating to the interaction between individuals, acts, and legal rules. The lynchpin of *mens rea*, however, is the notion of rationality. To exhibit a guilty mind, one must be capable of reasoned and free choice. In other words, in order for an individual to be criminally responsible he must have the capacity rationally to choose to engage in criminal conduct. The law's reach thus may extend only to creatures who are able to understand its requirements and to abide by its prescrip-

[33] *Dusky v United States*, 362 US 402, 402 (1960) (concluding that a defendant have sufficient present ability to consult with his lawyer with a reasonable degree of rational understanding and whether he has a rational a well as factual understanding of the proceedings against him).

[34] *Kansas v Hendricks*, 521 US 346 (1997) (holding that potentially indefinite detention is permissible when a special justification, such as dangerous mental illness, outweighs the individuals constitutionally protected interest in avoiding physical restraint).

[35] Joshua Dressler, *Criminal Law* 131-55 (Aspen,2d ed 1999)

[36] Id.

tions.[37] A rampaging bull who gores a farmhand is no more guilty of a criminal act than a tree branch that inadvertently falls and kills a weary traveler seeking shelter from a storm.

The ancients understood and appreciated this concept. In Plato's Laws, for example, the Stranger illustrates how Athenian law deals with rational motivation and the ability to understand the consequences of one's actions.[38] He explains that the laws have been enacted in order to bring justice to those who would steal from the gods, commit treason against the state, or abuse the state's protection to satisfy their own selfish ends. Those who choose to engage in such actions, he observes, merit severe punishment.[39] He notes, however, that not all who commit such heinous crimes are deserving of equal punishment.[40] The Stranger acknowledges that such crimes may be committed: "in a state of madness or when affected by disease, or under the influence of extreme old age, or in a fit of childish wantonness, himself no better than a child."[41] Presumably, it is the common observation that such individuals are unable to act rationally, that permits the state to excuse (but not to condone) their behavior.[42] If suffering from such debilities in reasoning, the just state spares the uncomprehending offender from punishment.

This notion of the reasoning malefactor was carried over into the early English legal tradition, where the concept arose that criminal liability entails that the offender freely choose to undertake the proscribed conduct. By the time of Coke, the maxim "actus non facit reum nisi mens sit rea" (an act does not make one guilty unless his mind is guilty)[43] had become well ingrained in the common law.[44] It remains a central precept of Anglo-American criminal law today.[45]

---

[37] See Stephen J. Morse, *Rationality and Responsibility*, 74 Cal L Rev 251 (2000).

[38] Plato, *Laws, Book IX*, 864 (Jowett Trans).

[39] Id.

[40] Id.

[41] Id.

[42] Under these special circumstances, the offender merits deferential treatment. For, "if this be made evident to the judges elected to try the cause, on the appeal of the criminal or his advocate, and he be judged to have been in this state when he committed the offense, he shall simply pay for the hurt which he may have done to another; but he shall be exempt from other penalties. . . ." Plato, *Laws* at 864 (cited in note 38).

[43] Wayne R. LaFave & Austin W. Scott, Jr., *Criminal Law* 212 (West Group, 2d ed 1986).

[44] Edward Cooke, *Third Institute* 107 (1641).

[45] Richard G. Singer and Martin R. Gardner, *Crimes and Punishment: Cases, Materials and Readings in Criminal Law* 213 (Matthew Bender & Co, 1989)("For well over five hundred years, [this] maxim has guided criminal law. . . ."). Commenting on the persistence of the mens rea requirement in modern law, the United States Supreme Court stated:

The contention that an injury can amount to a crime only when inflicted by intention [or some other culpable state of mind] is no provincial or transient no-

Recognizing that neither jurors nor judges are mind readers, society permits them to infer the defendant's intent from the commission of the act. Society allows this inference to be drawn largely because it has adopted the assumption that individuals are rational actors and that any acts they commit are the product of their intentional desire to bring about the proscribed conduct. If this assumption were not made, it might be difficult for a jury ever to hold anyone responsible for their conduct because proof of rationality is not something easily obtained. The exemptions, namely the young, the very old, and the outwardly demented, gain a special status presumably because the proof of their inability to act rationally is widely acknowledged within society. The weight of anecdotal experience demonstrates that children lack the same capacity for reason that adults do. These broad inter-generational observations founded in personal experiences that are repeated over time are the virtual equivalent of modern empirical observation.

B. The Law, Economics, and Rational Behavior

Criminal law thus assumes objective rationality, but makes broad allowances for behavioral states that appear irrational. As a concept, however, "rationality," tends to be an ephemeral and fast-moving target. Rationality is somewhat akin to Potter Stewart's famous statement regarding obscenity: "that he knew it when he saw it."[46] Yet, despite the difficulty scholars have in agreeing as to rationality's definition, it remains perhaps the most significant insight into human behavior that economics employs; namely, that people respond to incentives and seek to maximize their own utility. The behavioral premises of the economic model on which rational choice theory is based are the subject of an enormous body of scholarly literature.[47]

---

tion. It is as universal and persistent in mature systems of law as belief in freedom of the human will and a consequent ability and duty of the normal individual to choose between good and evil. A relation between some mental element and punishment for a harmful act is almost as instinctive as the child's familiar exculpatory "But I didn't mean to.". . . Unqualified acceptance of this doctrine by English common law . . . was indicated by Blackstone's sweeping statement that to constitute any crime there must first be a "vicious will."

Morissette v United States, 342 US 246, 250-51 (1952) (footnotes omitted).

[46] *Jacobellis v Ohio,* 378 US 184, 197 (1964) (Stewart, J., concurring) ("shall not today attempt further to define the kinds of material I understand to be embraced within that shorthand description; and perhaps I could never succeed in intelligibly doing so. But I know it when I see it, and the motion picture involved in this case is not that.").

[47] See, e.g., Jeffrey Freidman, ed, *The Rational Choice Controversy: Economic Models of Politics Reconsidered* (Yale, 1996) (defending the validity of public choice despite criticisms); Donald P. Green & Ian Shapiro, *Pathologies of Rational Choice Theory: A Critique of Applications in Political Science* (Yale, 1994) (arguing that public choice is not empirically well-founded).

Max Weber was among the first to treat rationality as a mode of social interaction.[48] This is important, because the rationality assumption is itself an axiom of human behavior. It arises from the common observation of the human condition. Differentiating between the personal and the political, Weber identified two distinct types of contextual rationality. The first, which forms the cornerstone of microeconomic rational choice theory, is the concept of *instrumental* rationality, which is "determined by the expectations as to the behavior objects in the environment of and other human beings."[49] The second, *values* rationality, is "determined by a conscious belief in the value for its own sake of some ethical, aesthetic, religious, or other form of behavior, independent of its prospects for success."[50] In other words, instrumental rationality suggests that people seek to achieve their goals in an optimally efficient fashion. Such rationality is value-neutral in that it only describes the means by which an end is reached, it does not pass judgement upon the ends sought to be obtained. Values rationality, on the other hand, is a mode of social action that determines the end itself.

Instrumental rationality undergirds micro-economics. Economists modeling choice under conditions of scarcity assume that individuals will act rationally to maximize their own personal utility.[51] The concept of values rationality, however, is given somewhat short shrift. Economists tend to believe that the end result of the rational deliberative process is best left up to the individual. They have a point. Ex ante, it is difficult to know what individual preferences may be.

Although the precise definition of rationality is often the subject of heated debate,[52] Gary Becker has identified the basic principles of standard economics as involving individuals who "(1) maximize their utility (2) from a stable set of preferences and (3) accumulate an optimal amount of information and other inputs in a variety of markets."[53] Of course, neither Becker nor any one else for that matter, asserts that human beings *never* err; the softer claim is merely that individuals adopt behavioral strategies that are optimal within the particular in-

[48] Max Weber, *Economy and Society* 24 (California, 1978).

[49] Id.

[50] Id at 24-25.

[51] See generally, David W. Barnes and Lynn A. Stout, *Cases and Materials on Law and Economics* (West Group,1992); Henry N. Butler, *Economic Analysis for Lawyers* (Carolina Academic,1998); Cooter and Ulen, *Law and Economics* (cited in note 9); Posner, *Economic Analysis of Law* (cited in note 9).

[52] "Rationality" has meant many things to different scholars. For useful distinctions between different kinds of rationality, see Robert H. Frank, *Microeconomics and Behavior* (cited in note 10); Korobkin and Ulen, 88 Cal L Rev 1051 at 1053 (cited in note 10).

[53] Gary Becker, *The Economic Approach to Human Behavior* 14 (Chicago, 1976).

ternal and external constraints that exist.[54] The real world dictates that human beings have differing cognitive abilities and must function with limited knowledge and within limited time frames. Nevertheless, scholars argue that the sub-optimal choices these limitations produce do not violate the premise of human rationality. Individuals still act rationally within their limited spheres of understanding. For example, we would describe a bank robber planning an elaborate heist as adopting an instrumentally rational strategy to steal from a bank even if he were unaware of every possible means of surreptitiously entering the bank or if he lacked either the time or the technical expertise to determine how to open any possible safe he might encounter. Provided he makes the best use of the information at his disposal, and executes the plan most likely to result in his successful theft of money from the bank, his behavior could be described as rational.

Rational choice theory thus presumes that individuals will act so as to maximize their expected utility, which generally involves comparing various outcomes that might result from alternative behaviors discounted by their likelihood of transpiring. From this powerful insight spring two important observations. First, the law may serve as a tool to encourage certain types of socially desirable behaviors and to discourage undesirable behaviors. This has important consequences for criminal law. For example, penalty structures can be designed to deter what society has chosen to label criminal conduct or used to shape preferences by encouraging people to trade one form of conduct for another.[55] A state might adopt the death penalty to deter premeditated murderers or increase penalties for heroin in order to press addicts to substitute less harmful drugs. Second, economic theory forces policy makers to acknowledge that law has important efficiency, as well as distributive consequences. The selection of legal rules will therefore have real-world effects on human behavior.

As a result, the economic analysis of law is essentially a human behavioral theory. The entire discipline seeks to examine how individuals in a given legal system respond to incentives disguised as policy directives. However, in understanding how people respond to various policy directives, it is necessary to have an underlying theory of human behavior. One has to accept, for example, that human beings will respond to incentives. If human beings did not respond to incentives, then the entire project of classical economics would be hopelessly flawed. Similarly, in order to predict how individuals will respond to incentives, one has to assume certain characteristics of human behavior are commonly shared—the desire to avoid pain, for example.

---

[54] Id.
[55] Neal Katyal, *Deterrence's Difficulty*, 95 Mich L Rev 2385 (1997).

Without reliance upon such basic assumptions, it is impossible accurately to predict how individuals will respond to specific policy directives and incentives.

The rational actor, as defined in economic terms, has as the reason for his actions the maximization of utility. A clarification of sorts is in order, however. First, what does it mean to have a "reason" for one's action? And second, how does outwardly manifested behavior follow from those reasons? An economist might say that the reason for an action is some self-determined calculation of utility. A psychologist might identify that calculation as being an internal drive. Regardless of how one defines it, it is some collection of knowledge and beliefs that lead to behavior. If I am uncomfortably hot, and believe that by turning up my air conditioner, I will be cooled down, it follows that I will do so. Based upon my desire to be cool, and my knowledge that the air conditioner would work to bring me relief from the heat, I would engage in the behavior of adjusting the air conditioning unit.

Rational choice thus may be understood as action an agent chooses out of a belief that it will bring about a desired end.[56] Behaviors or decisions may be defined as rational when they are consistent with the individual's broader system of beliefs and desires. In this respect, the concept of rationality turns on the individual's ability to give a full or coherent account of her actions by situating those actions within a larger system of beliefs, desires, and intentions. Animals might act purposefully, and in that sense act for reasons, but only humans "are able to think about what they want, to subject their desires and beliefs to self-conscious scrutiny, and to modify them in the light of criticism."[57] This conveys the Socratic view that some presumption of rationality is built into the very ideas of mind and action. Nevertheless, moments of irrationality, when one's actions fail to fit within the larger context of the actor's beliefs and desires, are not only common, but are an inescapable factor of human experience. And, far from being random occurrences, these seemingly irrational moments may be identified and catalogued.

The criminal law has long treated two classes of persons quite outside of the working assumption of rationality: children and the (legally) insane.[58] The law treats children differently because common human experience demonstrates that they do not possess the same faculties of reason found in adults. One need not perform a battery of tests to

---

[56] See Jules L. Coleman, *Rational Choice and Rational Cognition*, 3 Legal Theory 183, 183 (1997); John C. Harsanyi, *Advances in Understanding Rational Behavior*, in *Rational Choice* 82, 83 (Springer-Verlag New York, 1986).

[57] Jonathan Lear, *Open Minded: Working Out the Logic of the Soul* 81 (Harvard, 1998)

[58] Calvin Woodard, *Listening to the Mockingbird*, 45 Ala L Rev 563, 584 (1994).

determine what conventional wisdom has demonstrated over time; namely, that children have internal limitations that cabin their ability to reason. Children doubtless respond to incentives and have the capacity to seek the satisfaction of their immediate needs, but they are poor at assessing risk or of comprehending fully the consequences of their actions. No rational adult, for example would routinely place a five year old child in sole charge of her baby brother for the weekend.

Similarly, the criminal law has long refused to assign criminal responsibility to those persons who may suffer from a "mental disease or defect," which renders them "unable to appreciate the nature or quality" of their actions.[59] Such individuals are deemed "legally" insane, a shorthanded way of saying that their actions are not the product of rational thought. While some might quibble with the operational definitions of legal insanity, the common law has consistently recognized *some* sort of insanity that removes culpability from the sufferer.

These are not the only examples of situations in which people behave in ways that seem to belie their own properly considered interests. A growing body of scholarship empirically demonstrates that people frequently act in ways seemingly at odds with their own interests; and do so in consistent and predictable ways.[60] Before turning to those considerations, however, let us first consider how rationality affects the imposition of criminal sanction.

C. Rationality and the Criminal Sanction

If behavior is a social modality, as Weber claimed, and rational, as economists assume, then certain behaviors may be labeled "anti-social" and the costs of indulging in that behavior may be increased so as to discourage it. This utilitarian approach to the criminal sanction was championed by Cesare Beccaria, who first applied the Enlightenment's social contract tradition to issues of punishment,[61] and Jeremy Bentham, who laid the theoretical groundwork for the movement away from retribution to more rational punishment schemes.[62] Implicit in both scholar's understanding of human behavior was their belief that

[59] *M'Naughten's Case*, 8 Eng Rep 718 (1843) (concluding that a defendant must establish that he either was not conscious of the nature of the act he was committing, or that he was not aware that is was considered wrongful).

[60] See, e.g., Sunstein ed., *Behavioral Law and Economics* (cited in note 21); Langevoort, 51 Vand L Rev at 1499 (cited in note 15).

[61] See Cesare Beccaria, *On Crimes and Punishments* 23 (Hacknet, David Young ed 1986).

[62] Jeremy Bentham, *An Introduction to the Principles of Morals and Legislation* 166 (Continuum International, J.H. Burns & H.L.A. Hart eds 1970) ("The value of the punishment must not be less in any case than what is sufficient to outweigh that of the profit of the offence.").

crime resulted from the informed and rational choices of individuals.[63] For these proponents of utilitarianism, an appropriately crafted legal sanction demanded an understanding of the nature of human rationality. In other words, if a legislator could know why an individual would choose to commit a crime, a law could be adopted to alter her decision.

The utilitarians have largely triumphed in the public policy arena. The utility premise of rational choice theory has an obvious affinity for deterrence doctrine in the criminal law. Deterrence theory applies utilitarian philosophy to crime.[64] Pursuant to standard deterrence theory, the rational calculus of the pain of legal punishment offsets the motivation for the crime (presumed to be roughly constant across offenders but not across offenses), thereby deterring criminal activity. Classic rational choice theory, of course, takes no account of ends and thus assumes that one takes those actions, criminal or lawful, which maximize payoff and minimize costs.[65]

This important link between deterrence and rational choice has become well-established in the legal literature[66] and is the foundation of so-called optimal penalty theory.[67] This theory posits that an appropriately constructed sanction will be no harsher than necessary to prevent the rational individual from engaging in criminal conduct.[68] Individuals will thus be deterred from acting unlawfully when the sanction as-

---

[63] In contrast, the positivist school rejected the idea that (most) crime resulted from a rational choice that could be made by anyone. These scholars argued instead that crime was "atavistic," the failure of an individual to evolve to a truly human state. Thus, criminal behavior resulted not from what the offender had in common with other individuals, but rather from his distinct physical or mental defects-defects that were often the product of environmental influences.

[64] See Richard G. Singer and John Q. La Fond, *Criminal Law* 18-28 (Aspen Law & Business, 1997); J. Gibbs, *Crime and Punishment and Deterrence* (Elsevier, 1975); Scott Decker & Carol Kohfield, *Crimes, Crime Rates, Arrests, and Arrest Ratios: Implications for Deterrence Theory*, 23 Criminology 437 (1985).

[65] Owen D. Jones, *The Evolution of Irrationality*, 41 Jurimetrics J 289-318 (2001).

[66] See Derek Cornish & R. V. Clarke eds., *The Reasoning Criminal: Rational Choice Perspectives on Offending* (Springer-Verlag New York, 1986); Williams & Hawkins, *The Meaning of Arrest for Wife Assault*, 27 Criminology 721 (1989); Steven Klepper & Daniel Nagin, *The Deterrent Effect of Perceived Certainty and Severity of Punishment Revisited*, 27 Criminology 721 (1989);Raymond Paternoster, *Decisions to Participate In and Desist From Four Types of Common Delinquency: Deterrence and the Rational Choice Perspective*, 23 Law & Soc Rev 7 (1989); Raymond Paternoster, *Absolute and Restrictive Deterrence in a Panel of Youth: Explaining the Onset, Persistence/Desistance, and Frequency of Delinquent Offending*, 36 Soc Probs 289 (1989); Irving Piliavin, Craig Thorton, Rosemary Gartner & Ross Matsueda, *Crime, Deterrence and Rational Choice*, 51 Am Soc Rev 101 (1986).

[67] Richard A. Posner, *Optimal Sentences for White-Collar Criminals*, 17 Am Crim L Rev 409, 410 (1980); Gary S. Becker, *Crime and Punishment: An Economic Approach*, 76 J Pol Econ 169 (1968).

[68] Id.

sociated with the illegal behavior fully compensates society for the harm inflicted by the criminal behavior, while at the same time depriving the individual wrong-doer of the benefit of his illegal conduct.[69]

We generally accept the fact that, at some level, deterrence works. Parents routinely employ deterrence strategies in preventing their children from engaging in inappropriate behavior. Legislators similarly tout "tough on crime" proposals, claiming that harsh penalties will deter would-be criminals.[70] Unfortunately, validating the effect deterrence-based punishment schemes have on behavior has been difficult to demonstrate. Research on *specific* deterrence—the effect of a sanction on the person who receives it—suggests that even sophisticated offenders who receive harsher penalties are not appreciably deterred. David Weisburd compared recidivism rates between federal white collar offenders who were similar in many respects, except that some received only probation and others received imprisonment.[71] He detected no difference in the recidivism rates between the two groups of offenders, however. Weisburd concluded that if a deterrent effect could not be found with this group of offenders—who are generally considered the most rational and calculating—finding such an effect for other types of crime is unlikely.[72] But why is it that such effects have

---

[69] Daniel S. Nagin, *Criminal Deterrence Research at the Outset of the Twenty-First Century,* 23 Crime & Just 1 (1998). Perhaps the most interesting example of an attempt to form public policy pursuant to optimal penalty theory is the United States Sentencing Guidelines. Deterrence figures prominently as a goal of the federal Sentencing Reform Act. Besides its inclusion on the list of purposes of sentencing, deterrence is singled out in 28 USC § 994(c)(6), which directs the Commission to consider "the deterrent effect a particular sentence may have on the commission of the offense by others." The Commission includes deterrence along with the other statutory purposes in its explanation of the guidelines in Chapter One, and also cites it as the primary reason for several particular guideline provisions. E.g., USSG § 2R1.1. concerning antitrust offenses: "The Commission believes that the most effective method to deter individuals from committing this crime is through imposing short prison sentences coupled with large fines. The controlling consideration underlying this guideline is general deterrence." There is good reason to think that the guidelines support deterrence. Some research suggests that the criminal justice system as a whole provides a substantial deterrent effect and criminal sentencing is doubtless an important element in that system. Nagin, 23 Crime & Just 1 (cited above).

[70] Bush vows tough penalties for corporate fraud, DAWN, internet edition, (July 9, 2002), http://www.dawn.com/2002/07/10/ebr12.htm; CBS News.com, House Gets Tough on Business Fraud, (July 20, 2002) http://www.cbsnews.com/stories/2002/07/20/politics/main515751.shtml; Consumers' Union, CU Urges Legislature To Get Tough On Telemarketers, http://www.consumersunion.org/other/telemarketsw300.htm.

[71] David Weisburd et al, *Specific Deterrence in a Sample of Offenders Convicted of White-Collar Crimes,* 33 Criminology 587 (1995). This research was conducted using offenders sentenced prior to implementation of the guidelines. The guidelines make this kind of matched-group design more difficult, because offenders who are similar now receive similar sentences.

[72] Id.

been hard to demonstrate? If criminal act rationally, it is safe to assume that their behavior ought to be predictable and thus deterrable.

III. RATIONALITY, THE BRAIN, AND BEHAVIOR

The rational choice model is an elegantly simple paradigm for human behavior, which is an attractive characteristic in a theoretical model. Simple models are easy to explain, and elegant models, particularly those that rely upon mathematical formulae, engender a feeling that they are somehow superior to other behavioral constructs. Despite the allure of simplicity, however, scholars have begun to acknowledge the neoclassical assumption of rationality often fails as either a descriptive or a predictive model of individual behavior.[73] Turning to experimental work in cognitive psychology, researchers have borrowed the concept of bounded rationality (a term coined by Herbert Simon[74]) to help explain seemingly non-rational behavior. The theory of bounded rationality does this by identifying systematic, and therefore purportedly predictable, deviations from rational behavior.[75] The theory focuses on cognitive biases, heuristics, and limitations that lead individuals to depart from outcomes otherwise predicted by the neoclassical rational choice model.[76] Bounded rationality is not a refuta-

---

[73] See generally Jolls et al, 50 Stan L Rev at 1471 (cited in note 14) (examining "how law and economics analysis may be improved by increased attention to insights about actual human behavior"); *Symposium: The Legal Implications of Psychology: Human Behavior, Behavioral Economics, and the Law*, 51 Vand L Rev 1495, 1497 (1998) (examining behavioral research and the impact of behavioral economic analysis of law on scholarship and policy).

[74] Herbert A. Simon, *A Behavioral Model of Rational Choice*, 69 Q J Econ 99 (1955).

[75] See John Conlisk, *Why Bounded Rationality?*, 34 J Econ Literature 669 (1996) (surveying empirical studies of cognitive biases suggesting that people are capable of substantial and systematic reasoning errors relevant to economic decisions). For an example of the genre, see Daniel Kahneman et al, *Experimental Tests of the Endowment Effect and the Coase Theorem*, 98 J Pol Econ 1325 (1990); see also Langevoort, 51 Vand L Rev at 1502 (cited in note 15) ("Transaction cost economics accepts that the rationality of economic actors is "bounded," to use Herbert Simon's phraseology, and bounded rationality can include cognitive imperfection as well as informational limits.").

[76] For a useful listing of the cognitive biases, heuristics, and limitations discussed in the economic literature, see Langevoort, 51 Vand L Rev at 1499 (cited in note 15) (containing useful bibliography of other behavioral law and economics scholarship); Donald C. Langevoort, *Selling Hope, Selling Risk: Some Lessons for Law from Behavioral Economics About Stockbrokers and Sophisticated Customers*, 84 Cal L Rev 627 (1996). See also Jon D. Hanson and Douglas A. Kysar, *Taking Behavioralism Seriously: The Problem of Market Manipulation*, 74 NYU L Rev 630 (1999) ("In place of the rational actor model, [cognitive psychologists, behavioral researchers, probability theorists, and others] were developing a human decision maker model replete with heuristics and biases, unwarranted self-confidence, a notable ineptitude for probability, and a host of other nonrational cognitive features."); Jon D. Hanson and Douglas A. Kysar, *Tak-*

tion of the rational actor model; to the contrary, it seeks to recalibrate the neoclassical model to take account of predictable cognitive limitations and biases.[77] Despite occasional references to irrationality in the literature,[78] there is nothing especially irrational about bounded rationality.[79] Indeed, bounded rationality is often an attempt to reconcile the rational actor model with empirical research.

The model of bounded rationality represents a useful modification of abstract conceptions of human nature to a more empirically grounded behaviorism. Nevertheless, it may not go far enough in examining inherent biological limitations to rational thought processes. Unlike neoclassical economists, who often defy claims to subjective accuracy in their models, behavioral law and economics scholars seek to lay claim to better descriptive accuracy in their behavioral models. The goal of work in this field, as described by several leading authors, "is to advance an approach to the economic analysis of law that is informed by a more accurate conception of choice, one that reflects a better understanding of human behavior and its well springs."[80]

The principles of cognitive psychology informing behavioral law and economics scholarship recognize the important role of unconscious processes in human decision making.[81] The difficulty is that it fails fully to capitalize on this important insight. The behavioral economist Herbert Simon once observed that "we cannot, of course, rule

---

ing Behavioralism Seriously: A Response to Market Manipulation, 6 Roger Williams U L Rev 259 (2000); Hanson and Kysar, 112 Harv Rev at 1420 (cited in note 8).

[77] See Hanson and Kynsar, 74 NYU L Rev at 633 (cited in note 76) ("These researchers claim not merely that we sometimes fail to abide by rules of logic, but that we fail to do so in predictable ways."). In the economics literature, the debate over rationality goes beyond cognitive biases to include alternative models of behavior such as learning theory and evolutionary psychology.

[78] See, e.g., Gary S. Becker, *Irrational Behavior and Economic Theory*, 70 J Pol Econ 1 (1962).

[79] Langevoort, 51 Vand L Rev at 1506 (cited in note 15) (noting that "identifying a departure from rationality is not the same as discovering irrationality").

[80] Jolls, 50 Stan L Rev at 1473-74 (cited in note 14) ("The unifying idea in our analysis is that behavioral economics allows us to model and predict behavior relevant to law with the tools of traditional economic analysis, but with more accurate assumptions about human behavior, and more accurate predictions and prescriptions about law."); Herbert A. Simon, 69 Q J Econ 99 (cited in note 74) ("The task is to replace the global rationality of economic man with a kind of rational behavior that is compatible with the access to information and the computational capacities that are actually possessed by organisms, including man, in the kinds of environments in which such organisms exist.").

[81] See Morris N. Eagle, *The Psychoanalytic and the Cognitive Unconscious*, in R. Stern, *Theories of the Unconscious and Theories of the Self* 155, 155 (Analytic Pr, 1987) (noting that "the concept of unconscious mental processes has gained a new respectability on the basis of recent experimental work in cognitive psychology and perception—work that demonstrates the existence of ubiquitous and remarkably complex and intelligent operations even in the absence of awareness.") (footnote omitted).

out the possibility that the unconscious is a better decision-maker than the conscious,"[82] The "unconsciousness" is best understand as being a collection of the neurological activity that exists within the brain. And, researchers are only now uncovering the way in which that activity leads to behavior.

A. Rationality, Rightly Understood

A major difficulty with the rationality assumption, however, is that people are often observed to behave seemingly at odds with their own articulated preferences and, even when they seek to attain those preferences, often employ inefficient means to pursue them.[83] This is not a particularly novel insight, but rather one that sociologists and psychologists have long recognized. This differential between actual observed behavior and the theoretical behavior constructed by economic models may have contributed to the reluctance of social scientists to pay greater attention to economic behavioral constructs. Writing in the 1950s, Herbert Simon sought to bridge this gap. He borrowed from the empirical efforts of psychologists to conclude that people do not behave as true utility maximizers, but instead act as "satisficers."[84] A satisficer does not acquire complete information about a decision nor does he use a dispassionate, cooly rational decision-making process to arrive upon an optimal decision. Instead, Simon coined the term bounded rationality to explain that certain *internal* physiological limits (such as one's innate intelligence, defined as human computational and memory abilities) as well as the *external* costs of rational decision-making (such as the cost of obtaining the proper information to make an optimal decision) cabin rational decision making. Simon's bounded rationality suggested that in certain instances, given both internal and external limitations, it would be irrational to make the otherwise rational choice. People are thus satisficers because the constraints of bounded rationality demand that they employ habits, rules, and educated guesses to make "satisfactory" instead of "optimal" decisions.[85]

Cognitive psychologists employing the traditional tools of social science have sought to determine whether the rationality assump-

---

[82] Simon, 69 Q J Econ 99 at 104 (cited in note 74).

[83] See generally, Stephen J. Morse, *Rationality and Responsibility*, 74 S Cal L Rev 251 (2000); Stephen J. Morse, *Crazy Reasons*, 10 J Contemp Legal Issues 189 (1999); Robert Nozick, *The Nature of Rationality* 139-40 (Princeton, 1993).

[84] Simon, 69 Q J Econ 99 at 104 (cited in note 74).

[85] See also Mark D. Seidenfeld, *Cognitive Loafing, Social Conformity, and Judicial Review of Agency Rulemaking*, 87 Cornell L Rev 486, 492 (2002); Jeffrey J. Rachlinski and Cynthia R. Farina, *Cognitive Psychology and Optimal Government Design*, 87 Cornell L Rev 549, 555 (2002); Herbert A. Simon, *Theories of Bounded Rationality*, in James G. March, *Decisions and Organizations* 161, 165-71 (Blackwell, 1988).

tion holds up under empirical examination. Professors Kahneman and Tversky, in a series of well-known laboratory experiments, ascertained that people tend to rely heavily on mental short cuts, allow their decisions to be influenced by extraneous factors, and often fail to exhibit stable preferences.[86] A hypothetical bank robber might not think through all of the plausible schemes to obtain his goal, but rather impatiently undertake certain risks or adopt some unproven heuristic. In many respects, Kahneman and Tversky's research vindicated Simon's theory of bounded rationality.

These criticisms need not be assumed to be a refutation of instrumental rationality, but instead a refinement of it. They serve as a useful caution against naive assumptions about instrumental rationality and provide researchers with a more realistic view of human behavior. Few scholars would be willing to abandon the idea that people act instrumentally rational on a variety of occasions. However, *striving* for rationality may be the most we can expect from human beings. Since Milton Friedman made a similar observation,[87] some economists have taken the position that people possess bounded rationality, but that "they act as if unboundedly rational."[88] From a neurobiological perspective, however, this "as if" defense of rationality fails to acknowledge the ways in which acting "as if rational" can be used, defensively, to hinder expected utility maximization.

Although there may be numerous examples of irrational behavior, there are certainly numerous other counter-examples where people's behavior perfectly comports with the model of instrumental rationality. Newtonian physics did not become fodder for the scrapheap when Einstein came along. Of course, the advantage of asserting that all human behavior results from the desire to maximize material self-interest is that such behavior is easy to understand, subject to fairly unambiguous observation, and is easily modeled. The disadvantage is that this model of human behavior is woefully incomplete. Presumably, a more complete understanding of human behavior will result in more complete—and accurate—models.

1) Objective and Subjective Rationality

Some constraints upon rational decision-making identified by scholars advancing the idea of bounded rationality—such as the costs asso-

---

[86] See Daniel Kahneman and Amos Tversky, eds, *Choices, Values, and Frames, in Choices, Values, and Frames* 1 (Cambridge, 2000); Daniel Kahneman and Amos Tversky, *Prospect Theory: An Analysis of Decision Under Risk,* 47 Econometrica 263 (1979); Amos Tversky and Daniel Kahneman, *Judgment Under Uncertainty: Heuristics Biases* 1, 3-20 (Cambridge, 1982).

[87] Milton Friedman, *Essays in Positive Economics* (Chicago, 1953).

[88] See John Conlisk, *Why Bounded Rationality?,* 34 J Econ Literature 669 (1996).

ciated with gathering all the necessary information to make a choice—
are external.[89] Other constraints—such as how an individual's brain
is able to process information—are internal. Taken together, these in-
ternals and external constraints create obstacles for yielding completely rational decisions. Although Simon acknowledged internal
limitations that inhere in human beings,[90] he perhaps did not push
his analysis far enough to understand that internal limitations may
not only be of the kind that all people suffer from, but may also include biological anomalies.

Rationality is based upon a conceptual (and significant) distinction between a decision's rationality, and its objective merits. It may
occasionally be rational to engage in criminal conduct, if all the
available information happens to point to that decision. However, not
every seemingly rational decision is "right" (a loaded term over
which philosophers may disagree[91]), nor is every mistaken decision
necessarily irrational. Oftentimes, when we talk about "rationality"
we are referring to social, or objective rationality. By *social* rationality, I mean rationality that is exhibited by most human beings upon a
spectrum of behavior. Those who adhere to traditional notions of deterrence within the criminal law assume that most people prefer freedom to prison. For a more concrete example, it is safe to say that *most*
human beings do not enjoy cutting or biting their own flesh. As a
consequence, if we examine any given group of individuals, we will
observe that the majority of them do not engage in self-destructive,
physically harmful behavior of this type. Thus, we might say that it
is *objectively* rational behavior not maliciously to injure one's self.

However, in any randomly selected group, there might be people
who do enjoy self mutilation. In fact, a clinically observable symp-
tom of a disease known as Lesch-Nyhan Syndrome is that the individual tears and bites uncontrollably at her own flesh.[92] If the person's
hands are not bound, she will injure herself repeatedly. It can be assumed that the rational individual would not choose to harm herself
in this way. Thus, from the perspective of social rationality, this person is acting deviantly—or irrationally—because this person is acting contrary to the way in which most individuals would behave.

One could, however, say that this person is acting in accordance

[89] Herbert A. Simon, *Models of Bounded Rationality* 295-98 (MIT, 1997); Herbert A.
Simon, *Rationality in Psychology and Economics* in *Rational Choice: The Contrast
Between Psychology and Economics* 25 (Chicago, 1987); John Conlisk, *Why Bounded
Rationality?*, 34 J Econ Lit 669 (1996).

[90] Herbert A. Simon, *Models of Man* 1999 (Taylor & Francis, 1957).

[91] Gregory Mitchell, *Taking Behavioralism Too Seriously? The Unwarranted Pessimism of the New Behavioral Analysis of Law*, 43 Wm & Mary L Rev 1907 (2002);
Korobkin and Ulen, 88 Cal L Rev 1051 at 1114 (cited in note 10).

[92] See generally *The New England Journal of Medicine*, Massachusetts Medical Society (2002) *at* http://content.nemj.org .

with her own *private* or subjective rationality. For some reason, perhaps this particular individual places a high value on cutting or biting her own flesh. She therefore chooses to mutilate herself. To the extent this is willed behavior, then it is privately rational behavior. In my view, however, to accept this vision of subjective rationality is to render the concept of rational behavior devoid of any operational meaning. Were a child intent upon mutilating herself, for example, I doubt many parents would say: "Well, her insistence on slashing her arms and wrists is acceptable behavior because she is merely acting in accordance with her own personal utility, and therefore, we should not intervene." No rational parent would allow her child to indulge in such destructive behavior.

If an actor makes a decision that does not maximize net expected benefits to him, then he violates the behavioral predictions of the expected utility version of rational choice theory. One of the troubles of the microeconomic model is that ends are seldom taken into account. It is difficult to know, ex ante, what choices are optimal for a particular decision maker without knowing the profile of his utility function. Because utility functions are difficult to elicit, absent individualized examination, the behavioral predictions of expected utility theory often are not directly verifiable or falsifiable.

More salient versions of rational choice theory start from expected utility theory's predictions about the manner in which individuals will attempt to achieve their personal utility, and then add predictions about the actors' goals and preferences.[93] If we can figure out what course of action will most profit the decision maker, we will be able to predict his course of action. This intuition suggests falsifiable predictions about substantive behaviors, not just predictions about decision-making procedures. Most of these predictions will be based upon objective behavioral observations. Consider, for example, the simple prediction that if there is no punishment for overstaying one's time at a parking meter, people will monopolize parking spaces (the cost to an individual of parking in a lawful manner exceeds the cost to him of inappropriately dominating scarce parking spaces). This prediction implicitly relies on the assumption that individuals are

---

[93] Perhaps the most common assumption about ends, that actors will seek to maximize what is in their self-interest, can be traced to Adam Smith's famous justly statement:

> It is not from the benevolence of the butcher, the brewer, or the baker that we expect our dinner, but from their regard to their own interest. We address ourselves, not to their humanity but to their self-love, and never talk to them of our necessities but of their advantages.

Adam Smith, *An Inquiry into the Nature and Causes of the Wealth of Nations* 15 (Clarendon Press, 1869).

concerned with punishments they might receive, not with the disutility others will suffer from not being able to find a parking space. Thus, the self-interested version of rational choice theory may lead to the creation of directly falsifiable behavioral predictions.

But, from where do these assumptions spring? They must come from an understanding of human behavior, which is, in turn, an understanding of how the brain functions. Individual rationality may be predictive of social rationality to the extent that sufficient numbers of people have similar utility functions. But this runs deeper than the mere selection of preferences. I know many people who enjoy chocolate. Indeed, I am willing to say—without having made an empirical study of this question—that *most* people enjoy eating chocolate. Even so, I would not label someone as irrational who steadfastly refused to eat chocolate. In contrast, consider again the example of the individual who enjoyed repeatedly mutilating herself. We may be unable to ascertain her odd preference, ex ante; thus our ability to predict her behavior is impaired. As a consequence, social rationality may not be predictive of each individual's own particular utility curve. But, by observing human behavior in general, we can then posit certain assumptions.

If we simply define any expressed behavior as "freely chosen" behavior and the best evidence of personal utility, then "rational" action becomes little more than a tautology. Nevertheless, although the expected utility version of rational choice theory rises above mere tautology, it is scarcely more satisfactory for generating behavioral predictions.[94] Without accounting for social rationality as a baseline, however, there is no way to determine the content of any individual's utility function. This has important consequences for legal policy. If, for example, society wishes to reduce crime, assuming all other policy decisions are held constant, should it increase or decrease the length of prison sentences? Although the former appears to be the obvious answer, it is only correct if we assume that most people prefer to live outside of prison than to be incarcerated. In order to make appropriate public policy determinations, it is thus necessary for the theory to include some predictions about the content of preferences. In fact, without reference to preference content, it is difficult to label any behavior as "criminal."

B. The Neurobiological Roots of Rationality

In order to act rationally one must be able to exercise choice and reason. Reason, in particular, is a function of neurological activity. Be-

---

[94] See, e.g., Russell B. Korobkin, *Behavioral Analysis and Legal Form: Rules vs. Standards Revisited*, 79 Or L Rev 23, 44 (2000).

cause the brain controls behavior, any theory of human behavior is at its core a theory about the human brain. Because the brain is the product of evolution, many seemingly anomalous behaviors, as Owen Jones has observed, may be traced to evolutionary forces.[95] Aggression, which may occasionally present as a social problem, is an adaptive behavior that doubtless may have performed an important function for our ancestors. Nevertheless, just as the eye—also a product of evolutionary change—can fail, so may the brain. While healthy individuals can be expected to follow behavioral patterns that reflect reasoned choice, individuals who suffer from impairments to the brain may defy such expectations.

Moreover, neurological dysfunction of this sort often yields predictable behavioral results. Neurologists have long understood that when a patient presents in the emergency room with partial paralysis and slurred speech, they can make a clinical diagnosis that this person has likely suffered a stroke.[96] In fact, the entire Diagnostic and Statistical Manual IV,[97] which is routinely employed by psychiatrists and psychologists as a means of guiding clinical diagnosis, is premised upon the examination of groupings of individuals who suffer from the same observable behaviors.[98] Once the behavior is clinically observed, the brain can then be examined to determine whether consistent damage is present to thereby link, when possible, the damaged area with the clinical observation.

Seemingly aberrant behavior may not be the result of trauma per se. Instead it may be the result of environmental (such as lead paint exposure)[99] or developmental factors (as in the case of malnutrition).[100] Sometimes those developmental factors are quite natural and widely recognized. For example, as previously discussed, the law routinely treats children differently from adults because people have long understood that children act differently from adults. A child's ability to understand the consequences of his actions, or to control his anger dif-

[95] See, e.g., Owen D. Jones, *Time-Shifted Rationality and the Law of Law's Leverage: Behavioral Economics Meets Behavioral Biology*, 95 Nw UL Rev 1141 (2001); Owen D. Jones, *Evolutionary Analysis in Law: An Introduction and Application to Child Abuse*, 75 NC L Rev 1117 (1997); Owen D. Jones, *Law and Biology: Toward an Integrated Model of Human Behavior*, 8 J Contemp L Issues 167 (1997); Owen D. Jones, *Sex, Culture, and the Biology of Rape: Toward Explanation and Prevention*, 87 Cal L Rev 827 (1999).

[96] Robert Berkow, M.D., ed., *The Merck Manual of Medical Information* 351 (Merck Research Lab, 1997).

[97] American Psychiatric Association, Diagnostic and Statistical Manual of Mental Disorders (APA, 4th ed 1994) [hereinafter DSM IV].

[98] See, e.g., S.S. Sharfstein, *Values, Mental Disorders and the DSMS*, 347 N Engl J Med 1289, 1289-1290 (2002).

[99] David C. Rowe, *Biology and Crime* 118 (Roxbury Pub Cal, 2002).

[100] Id.

fers markedly from an adult's. If one sees a screaming three-year old in a restaurant throwing a tantrum because he wanted a hot dog but none was on the menu, one reacts quite differently than if one saw a screaming 35 year-old man throwing a tantrum given the same circumstances. We would understand, based upon our personal experience, that it might be quite normal for a three year old to throw a tantrum in public when he could not obtain the dinner he wanted, but quite unusual for an adult to throw a screaming fit when his selection of dinner was not available. Human beings have long acknowledged behavioral differences between adults and children, but not until fairly recently has science been able to locate, within the brain, the cause of those differences.[101]

1. Biology and Causation: A Cautionary Tale

Although researchers may seek to link behavior and biology, determining biological causation is quite a difficult undertaking. When we talk about rational action, we are really talking about a complicated and dynamic process originating in the brain. Proximate causation relates to the internal mechanisms, physical processes, and organic development that comprise the immediate predicates to behavior.[102] The underdeveloped child's brain leading to "childish" behavior or the stoke victim's damaged brain yielding an inability to form words properly may be deemed proximate causes. Ultimate causation is more properly deemed the "why" cause, which describes the evolutionary processes by which a behavior came to be commonly observable in a given species.

Proximate causation may relate to a particular individual exhibiting a specific behavior, while ultimate causation seeks to explain why a certain species engages in behavior that is common to that species. Essentially, ultimate causation may give rise to understanding why certain preferences are selected, thus defining socially rational ends. Proximate causation, however, may be a useful tool for determining why and under what conditions, a given individual will deviate from socially rational norms.

Human behavior necessarily requires perception, information processing, and action. Each of these facets of behavior is dependent upon brain function. Therefore, behavior—the principal output of the brain—is a product of that brain's ability to function properly. The implications for criminal law are significant. Criminal law defines socially rational ends and labels and punishes behavior that deviates

[101] Id at 53.
[102] Id at 118.

from those ends in a harmful—either to the individual or to society—manner. Although, as Owen Jones has explained, "some behaviors currently ascribed to cognitive limitations reflect not defect, but rather finely tuned features of brain design,"[103] plainly some instances of observed behavior *do* reflect defects. This may be the province of much of the criminal law that proscribes seemingly irrational behavior.

Indeed, as an epistemological matter, there can be no "rationality" *without* irrationality. We define rationality, in part, by reference to observable human behavior. Human beings lie upon a spectrum of mammals. When we examine animals, we observe certain instinctual behaviors that appear hardwired. I have a cat. Whenever he takes a drink from his water dish, his paws knead the ground, a reflexive action that is a result of what he needed to do to obtain milk while he was a mere nursing kitten. Similarly, my childhood dog, a beautiful collie, instinctively herded things—animals or people—without having received training to herd. These inbred, instinctual characteristics exhibited by these two animals were not the result of specific learning—they are hard-wired in the animals' brains. Humans have hard-wiring that guides behavior as well. We act altruistically in circumstances that would seemingly belie predictions of self-interest, have evolved mechanisms for detecting dishonesty, and tend to be maximizers of individual utility.

However, deviations from such "normal" behaviors occasional transpire. My cat once suffered severe head trauma, and as a result, developed odd neurological problems. He could not smell food for a brief period of time, and, as a result, would have starved had he not been force fed. In addition when a certain area along his spinal column was touched, his hind legs would give way, and he would begin uncontrollably to lick himself. Much in the same way this cat suffered from neurological damage that "caused" him to act in a particular way, human actions can also be governed by neurological deficiencies.

Such deficiencies, while yielding predictable behavioral patterns, may nevertheless "cause" individuals to behave abnormally. If abnormal behavior may be defined as behavior that deviates from the norm, then we may be able to define "irrational" behavior as behavior that fails to conform to social norms. Although social irrationality could be nothing more than private rationality, if that private rationality is something more that mere atypical preference selection, and violates deeply ingrained notions of social rationality, we could choose to label it "irrational."

Irrationality might thus be defined as behavior that falls outside the range of generally accepted social rationality, or behavior that

[103] Owen Jones, *Time-Shifted Rationality and the Law of Law's Leverage: Behavioral Economics Meets Behavioral Biology*, 95 Nw UL Rev 1141, 1168 (2001).

fails to enable the individual to obtain the self-selected ends. For example, someone who suffers from obsessive compulsive disorder (OCD) may strongly desire *not* to wash her hands until they are raw and bleeding. Absent her disorder, she may freely choose not to wash. However, part of the diagnosis of OCD is that the individual is unable internally to control her ability to wash incessantly.[104] Thus, if she continues to wash her hands in the face of her desire to put an end to that behavior, we can say that she is acting irrationally.[105]

Returning to our example of the nefarious (or unfortunate) Mr. Beckert, we can gain something of an insight into rationality. If Beckert enjoys raping and murdering children, and is willing to take substantial personal risks in order to feed his appetite, we can say that he is acting subjectively rationally. However, because society condemns such actions, we might say that Beckert is acting objectively irrationally, because his behavior is socially irrational.

We might also say that Beckert is acting subjectively irrational if he truly believes that raping and murdering little children is evil and he does not wish to do it, but like the woman suffering from OCD, he is nevertheless so internally compelled to perform those acts that he can't stop himself. If we can assume that this truly represents his deeply held belief—that he does not wish to kill children—then we might say that he is acting subjectively irrationally as well. From the outsider's viewpoint, however, who has no access to Beckert's deepest thoughts and beliefs, he may externally perceive that Beckert is acting subjectively rationally. All the outsider can witness is Beckert's actions. He may then assume that actions speak louder than words and that Beckert is acting subjectively rational.

Social or objective rationality is useful as a means of predicting group behavior. This is precisely why economic analysis works so well much of the time. Most of us do act as utility maximizers much of the time. Unfortunately, however, the assumptions underlying economic analysis do not consistently predict individual behavior. As a consequence, social systems that rely upon an understanding of objective rationality may not always work as predicted. The United States sentencing guidelines, which are premised upon certain theories of human behavior, may thus act as a deterrent against most people, most of the time, but they may not deter all of the people all of the time. While we cannot expect perfection in any human engineered system, we can nevertheless make improvements upon such systems. To this end, we must integrate an understanding of human psychology and basic brain biology with our public policy predilections.

[104] DSM IVat 417-424 (cited in note 97).
[105] See generally *The New England Journal of Medicine,* Massachusetts Medical Society (2002) *at* http://content.nemj.org .

2. Deviations from Social Norms: Neurological Damage and Behavior

Violence is certainly a human characteristic. Indeed, the ability to *be* violent may have helped to assure our survival as a species. Nevertheless, using violence to resolve conflict is not applicable to all situations. What motivates one from *thinking* about taking violent action and *actually engaging* in violent behavior is significant. Psychologists Douglas Kenrick and David Buss independently surveyed men and women in several different countries about attitudes towards violence.[106] They discovered that 80 percent of women and more than 90 percent of men fantasize about killing disliked acquaintances, including romantic rivals, step-parents, and people who had publically humiliated them. Similarly, if entertainment tastes are any sort of indication of popular preferences, it is interesting to note the popularity of murder mysteries, crime dramas, horror movies, and violent sports. While a draw towards violence appears to be part of human nature, and the use of violence may occasionally be a quite rational strategy for maximizing one's utility, what is it that differentiates the individuals who keep their violent acts confined to their imaginations, and those who consistently express violence in their behavior? Is it only the calculation of reasoned choice? What circumstances may exist in which behavior may be the product of irrationality, here defined as the inability to constrain violent impulses when social norms would dictate that restraint is rational?

The basic model for how violence arises in the brain is that the initial impulses originate in deep regions of the limbic system, or emotional brain. After that, it's the job of the prefrontal cortex to decide whether to act on these impulses or not.[107] In other words, the function of prefrontal lobes is "executive function," that is, planning, integrating information and generally serving as a mechanism to control emotional impulses that originate in deeper brain regions.[108] If

---

[106] Steven Pinker, *The Blank Slate: the Modern Denial of Human Nature* (Viking, 2002).

[107] See, e.g., Steven J. Gould, *Mismeasure of Man* 151-75 (Norton W W & Co, 1996) (debunking "projects" purporting to find biological causes of violence); Steven P. R. Rose, *Lifelines: Biology Beyond Determinism* (Oxford, 1998) (critiquing studies purporting to find biological or medical causes of violent behavior); Carolyn Abraham, *Doctor Pinpoints Key to the Criminal Mind, Research Cites Damage to Brain's Frontal Lobes, Globe and Mail* at A1 (Toronto, 2000) (citing twenty years of research by Dr. Daniel Tranel, neuropsychologist at the University of Iowa, suggesting that injury to the ventromedial prefrontal cortex results in anti-social and violent behavior); Adrian Rain, *New Scientist*, May 13, 2000, available at http://www.newscientist.com/opinion223819.html (arguing that biology turns certain individuals into rapists and serial killers); Robert Berkow, M.D., ed., *Merck Manual of Medical Information* 279-278 (Merck Research Lab, 1997).

[108] See generally Berkow, *Merck Manual of Medical Information* at 279-278.

that region is damaged, or otherwise developmentally challenged, predictable irrational behaviors will emerge.

Violent behavior thus may be the result of neurological misfunction. Consider the example of ill-fated railway worker Phineas Gage, easily the most celebrated brain damage case of the modern era. In 1848, Gage accidently sparked an explosion while using a piece of an iron rod to tamp blasting powder into place in order to remove rock for railroad bed construction.[109] The resulting explosion propelled the 1.25 inch-thick, yard-long tamping iron directly through Gage's head. Although the iron caused catastrophic frontal lobe damage, it neither killed him, nor even knocked him unconscious. Gage not only survived the severe head trauma, but remained functional; indeed, he retained both memory and intelligence, as well as basic motor functions. Interestingly, however, his personality changed dramatically after the accident. Gage became uncharacteristically vulgar and obstinate He was unable to carry through planned activities and was subject to frequent temper outbursts.[110] In light of his prior history, Gage's sudden predilection to obdurate behavior appears less a rational decision and more a result of his head injury.

If Gage were the only individual to have so behaved, we might be able to dismiss his conduct as mere happenstance and therefore treat him as an outlier. After all, brain damage of the sort Gage suffered is doubtless uncommon. His survival was nothing short of miraculous. Evidence, however, continues to mount illustrating the importance of the prefrontal cortex to controlling behavior and influencing rational decision making. This area of the brain is associated with the ability to assess risk, understand the consequences of action, and to anticipate and comprehend the future.

At the National Institute of Neurological Disorders and Stroke, Dr. Jordan Grafman, chief of the cognitive neuroscience section, studied wounded Vietnam veterans and found that those with penetrating head injuries that caused damage to parts of the prefrontal cortex, as shown on computed tomography (CT) scans, were at increased risk for violent behavior.[111] Not unlike the personality changes that plagued Phineas Gage, these individuals suffered from similar neurological deficits.

In a similar vein, Antonio Damasio has illustrated a possible neu-

[109] Hanna Damasio et al, *The Return of Phineas Gage: Clues about the Brain from the Skull of a Famous Patient*, 264 Science 1102 (1994); Alexander Field, *Altruistically Inclined? The Behavioral Sciences, Evolutionary Theory, and the Origins of Reciprocity* 250-51 (Michigan, 2001).

[110] J.M. Harlow, *Recovery from the Passage of an Iron Bar through the Head*, 2 Publications of the Massachusetts Medical Society, 327-47 (1868); H. Damsio, et al, *The Return of Phineas Gage: Clues about the Brain from the Skull of a Famous Patient*, 264 Science 1102-05 (1994).

[111] R. Greenwood, *Head Injury for Neurologists*, 73(8) J Neurol Neurosurg Psychiatry 16 (2002).

rological underpinning for abnormal preference selection and behavior.[112] In well-publicized research, Damasio studied two research subjects, one male and one female, who had suffered injuries to the prefrontal cortex during infancy.[113] Although each of these individuals had grown up in stable, middle class families with college educated parents and otherwise normal biological siblings, neither had made a satisfactory transition into adulthood. They lacked friends, were dependant upon parental support to survive, and both had engaged in criminal behavior during adolescence. Interestingly, researchers tested both subjects on their ability to respond to the uncertainty of punishment and reward—vital to determining whether they could respond to classic deterrence efforts. Using a simple deck of cards, the subjects were instructed that rewards to the "bad" card deck were high and immediate, whereas payoffs to the "good" card deck were immediately low, but substantially better long-term. A control group of participants was able easily to determine that it was better to draw from the "good" deck for later and better payoffs. Neither research subject, however, was able to master the use of the long term deck, suggesting that classic deterrence strategies might have little effect upon them.[114] This provocative study demonstrates that while deterrence strategies may generally be effective, there may be people upon whom they simply will not work.

Along these same lines, Dr. Robert Hare and his colleagues have done research on subjects believed to be psychopathic.[115] His research demonstrates that the criminal psychopath lack of emotional empathy stems from a neural defect in the brain's frontal lobes. An irregularity in the mechanisms of the amygdala and related frontal circuits causes abnormal emotions or a lack of certain emotions altogether.[116] Such deficits may even defeat the evolved mechanisms such as reciprocal altruism that help guide human behavior.[117]

Such defects not only have distinctive patterns, but when recog-

[112] A.R. Damasio, D. Tranel, and H. Damasio, *Somatic Markers and the Guidance of Behavior*, reprinted in *Frontal Lobe Function and Dysfunction* (Oxford, 1991); A.R. Damasio and G. Van Hoesen, *Emotional Disturbances Associated with Focal Lesions of the Limbic Frontal Lobe*, reprinted in *Neuropsychology of Human Emotion*, 268-299 (Guilford, 1983).

[113] Antonio R. Damasio, *Descartes' Error: Emotion, Reason and the Human Brain* 212 (Penguin Group, 1994).

[114] Id at 212-220.

[115] R.D. Hare, *Comparison of the Procedures for the Assessment of Psychopathy*, 53 J of Consulting & Clinical Psychology 7-16 (1985).

[116] R.D. Hare, *Without Conscience: The Disturbing World of the Psychopaths Around Us* (Guilford Press, 1993).

[117] Alexander J. Field, *Altruistically Inclined? The Behavioral Sciences, Evolutionary Theory, and the Origins of Reciprocity* (Michigan, 2001).

nized, predict specific behaviors. It was recently reported that the existence of a brain tumor in an 40-year-old man caused him to become obsessed with sex and to molest young children[118] The married schoolteacher first began secretly visiting child pornography websites and soliciting prostitutes at massage parlors. His wife evicted him from the family home after discovering he had made subtle sexual advances to young children. The unfortunate man, who had no previous history of sexual misconduct, had an egg-sized tumor in the right lobe of the orbifrontal cortex.[119] Doctors opined that the tumor's location impaired his ability to reason and to control his sexual appetites.

Perhaps the most intriguing visual evidence for the link between brain damage and violence has occurred in the work of Adrian Raine, a clinical neuroscientist at the University of Southern California in Los Angeles.[120] Among other things, Raine has performed positive emission tomography (PET) scans[121] on 41 murderers and 41 normal people of similar age. In each group, 39 of the 41 people were male. The murderers consistently registered lower glucose metabolism in the prefrontal cortex, a sign that this region was not functioning as it should to inhibit aggressive impulses.[122]

But murderers are clearly not all the same. Significantly, when Raine divided his subjects into those who had committed cold-blooded, premeditated murder, and those who killed impulsively, it was the impulsive killers who showed the poorest functioning in the prefrontal cortex.[123] This suggests that premeditated killers, unlike their more impulsive cousins, might be amenable to deterrence strategies. Furthermore, the deep brain regions where neuro-scientists believe primitive emotions like fear and aggression originate,[124] were more active in

[118] Right Orbitofrontal tumor with Pedophilia symptoms and constructional Apaxia, Sign; Jeffrey Burns and Russell H. Swerdlow, 60 Archives of Neurology (March 2003). See Brain Tumor Caused Paedophilla, BBC News Online, Oct. 21, 2002, at http://news.bbc.co.uk/2/hi/health/2345971.stm (Last visited April 27, 2003).

[119] Id.

[120] A. Raine et al, *Reduced Prefrontal Gray Matter Volume and Reduced Automatic Activity in Antisocial Personality Disorder,* 57 Archives of General Psychiatry, 119, 119-127 (2000).

[121] PET scans, which measure glucose uptake by brain cells, show which brain regions are most active.

[122] A. Raine et al, *Reduced Prefrontal Gray Matter Volume and Reduced Automatic Activity in Antisocial Personality Disorder,* 57 Archives of General Psychiatry, 119, 119-127 (2000); Adrian Rain, *New Scientist,* May 13, 2000, available at http://www.newscientist.com/opinion223819.html (arguing that biology turns certain individuals into rapists and serial killers).

[123] Id.

[124] For an interesting discussion of the neurobiology of emotion, see Gene V. Wallenstein, *Mind, Stress, and Emotions: The New Science of Mood* (Commonwealth Press, 2002).

the brains of murderers than control subjects. For instance, Raine has used a magnetic resonance imaging, (MRI) which looks at the structure, as opposed to the functioning, of different brain regions, to look at people with antisocial personality disorders.[125] He found that brain cells within the prefrontal cortex regions of these people with antisocial personality disorder—who show a psychopathic lack of remorse and a penchant for breaking rules and violent crime—were on average 11 percent smaller than normal, yet another clue that damage or dysfunction in this area may predispose people to hostility and aggression.

3. Genetic Anomalies and Behavior

Genes also doubtless play a role in behavior. Just as genes may have evolved to promote rational self-interest, they may sometimes go awry. A recent study reported that children who suffer abuse and who have a common variation in a gene linked to behavior are much more likely to become aggressive, anti-social adults than those who have similar environmental circumstances, but lacked the genetic anomaly. This report was particularly important because it represented the first clear link between anti-social behavior and a specific interaction of genes and environment.[126] This could explain why childhood mistreatment increases the risk of criminality by 50 per cent, even while most abused children do not themselves become delinquents.[127]

Similarly, science can point to the (in)famous Inmate X from Holland , who suffers from the only known gene linked directly to violent behavior in humans.[128] After a troubled history of violent, impulsive conduct, 23 year old Inmate X was ultimately convicted of raping his sister. Although he was generally deemed a model inmate, he was prone to violent outbursts, and on one occasion inexplicably stabbed a guard in the chest with a pitchfork.

[125] A. Raine et al, *Reduced Prefrontal Gray Matter Volume and Reduced Automatic Activity in Antisocial Personality Disorder*, 57 Archives of General Psychiatry, 119, 119-127 (2000).

[126] Erik Strokstad, *Violent Effects of Abuse Tied to Gene*, 297 Science 752 (2002). The study of 1037 males in New Zealand, now aged about 30, revealed that the low-activity form of the gene alone is not linked to antisocial behavior. But those who had the gene variation and who had experienced moderate or severe mistreatment as children were much more likely to commit crimes. That group made up only 12 per cent of the study group but were responsible for 44 per cent of offences.

[127] Id.

[128] See H.G. Brunner et al, *Abnormal Behavior Associated with a Point Mutation in the Structural Gene for Monoamine Oxidase A*, 262 Science 578, 578-80 (1993); H.G. Brunner et al, *X-Linked Borderline Mental Retardation with Prominent Behavioral Disturbance: Phenotype, Genetic Localization, and Evidence for Disturbed Monoamine Metabolism*, 52 Am J Hum Genetics 1032, 1032-39 (1993); see also William Wright, *Born that Way: Genes, Behavior, Personality* 149-50 (1998) (discussing Brunner's case study of Inmate X).

A female relative of Inmate X visited a physician and explained that she wanted her children genetically tested because she believed her violent relative's behavior was not an aberration, but in fact a long-standing deviant behavioral trait within her family. Researchers undertook a study of the family and discovered Inmate X was not the only member of his family who was prone to violence. In fact, the researchers learned that eight male family members had engaged in repeated sexual misconduct and had been involved in other incidents of violence. It was uncovered that problems of this sort extended back some five generations in the family tree.

Dr. Hans Brunner, who supervised this research, conducted a genetic analysis of the male members of the family to determine whether any identifiable abnormalities could be uncovered.[129] He discovered that each of the afflicted family members, all blood-related males, had an odd mutation in the monoamine oxidase A gene. The gene affects the production of an enzyme that normally regulates serotonin. Due to the mutation, this enzyme was rendered effectively non-functional. Brunner showed that Inmate X and his troubled male family members each had the same odd genetic mutation, but that the twelve healthy male family members did not. In light of the understanding that serotonin is a key to regulating impulse control, it was assumed that this genetic defect prevented Inmate X and his similarly afflicted male relatives from controlling their impulsive behavior.

4. Serotonin and Aggression

Impulsive aggressive behavior in patient populations exhibiting personality disorders is a common clinical phenomenon.[130] Researchers have long been aware that patients diagnosed with borderline and antisocial personality disorders report a high rate of self-mutilation and episodic control problems, resulting in aggressive attacks on others. For example, in an important study of repeat violent offenders and impulsive fire setters, some 47 percent of the subjects were found to have a personality disorder diagnosis. In a sample of spouse abusers, significantly higher scores on a measure of borderline personality organization were found compared with control groups.[131] To quiet concerns suggesting this is merely freely chosen behavior that is the product of rational deliberation, it is worth noting that abnormalities in serotonin levels have consistently been associated with personality disorders in which impulsive and violent behavior plays a role.

[129] *See* Brunner et al, *Abnormal* at 578-80 (cited in note 128); Brunner et al, *X-Linked* at 1032-39 (cited in note 128).
[130] DSM IV at 629-673 (cited in note 97).
[131] Jonathan Benjamin et al, *Molecular Genetics and the Human Personality* 232 (American Psychiatric Publishing, 2002).

Dr. Frederick Goodwin, for example, undertook a study of U.S. Marines receiving psychiatric discharges in an effort to determine whether any neurobiological anomalies existed.[132] Goodwin discovered that the discharged Marines each displayed one significant feature in common; all had low levels of the neurotransmitter serotonin—a chemical neurobiologists had long suspected as being able to influence one's ability to control behavior. Researchers had discovered decreased levels of this same neurotransmitter in a broad range of other violent people, including prisoners convicted of committing aggressive, impulsive acts, children who had tortured animals, and men who had scored unusually high on psychological exams for aggression, hostility, or psychopathic deviance. Goodwin hypothesized that the low serotonin levels handicapped the Marines' ability to control their impulsive tendencies. Once these intriguing patterns were noticed in humans, scientists began to manipulate serotonin levels in laboratory animals and found that decreased levels of serotonin apparently result in a tendency to be highly aggressive.[133]

Of course, while we may understand the function of serotonin in neurobiology, it is a major step to say that decreased levels of serotonin necessarily caused the behavior for which any of the former Marines were discharged from service or that the decreased serotonin levels predated the unbecoming behavior. In an interesting example of how this area can be almost infuriatingly complicated, researchers have also observed that non-surgically or chemically engineered monkeys could nevertheless have their serotonin levels increased or decreased merely by manipulating their rank order in the pack.[134] Based

---

[132] See Dean Hamer and Peter Copeland, *Living With Our Genes* 100, 102-106 (Doubleday & Co, 1998).

[133] The study of human behavior is ultimately the study of animal behavior. As a consequence, the same tools that researchers routinely use to study animal behavior can be adapted to studying human behavior. Professor E. Donald Elliot, a pioneer in analyzing the intersection of law and biology, has made the identical point, albeit in a slightly different context. See E. Donald Elliott, *Law and Biology: The New Synthesis?*, 41 Sr Louis U LJ 595 (1997).

[134] To substantiate this hypothesis of the effects of environmental manipulation on serotonin levels, Raleigh and McGuire subsequently tested college fraternity brothers, discovering that fraternity leaders had higher serotonin levels than recent pledges. This was a result that mirrored the studies involving monkeys, buttressing the notion that social hierarchy may itself have an effect on neurobiology. Thus social experience, individual health, and developmental factors may each affect serotonin function. Michael J. Raleigh and Michael T. McGuire, *Serotonin, Aggression, and Violence in Vervet Monkeys, in The Neurotransmitter Revolution: Serotonin, Social Behavior and the Law* 129, 129-45 (1994); see also Michael J. Raleigh and Michael T. McGuire, *Biodirectional Relationships Between Tryptophan and Social Behavior in Vervet Monkeys, in R. Schwartz, S.N. Young & R.R. Brown, eds, Kynurenine and Serotonin Pathways: Progress in Tryptophan Research, Advances in Experimental Medicine and Biology* 294, 289-98 (Plenum, 1991).

upon this research, it appears that environmental factors can themselves affect brain chemistry.

5. Age and Gender, and Crime

The single greatest predictor of violent criminality is the subject's gender. With some notable exceptions, violent behavior that results in homicide or injury is largely the providence of men.[135] Across cultures, men kill men 20 to 40 times more frequently than women kill women.[136] In the United States alone, men are eight times more likely than women to commit murder, nine times more likely to commit armed robbery and four to five times more likely to commit aggravated assault.[137] Most of these male killers are *young* men, between the ages of fifteen and thirty.[138] Interestingly, such violent behavior does not appear to be randomly distributed throughout this age-range. According to at least one estimate, roughly seven percent of young men commit some 79 percent of repeat, violent offenses.[139]

Is this necessarily rationally chosen behavior, or could there be something else at work? One long-standing theory for this striking gender difference involves the hormone testosterone, which is more abundant in men than in women.[140] But precisely how testosterone may trigger violent impulses in the brain is a mystery. Research does show that male sex offenders who are castrated are less likely to repeat their crimes and that men who take body-building steroids, which are chemically close to testosterone, can become aggressive. Studies of prisoners—both male and female—also suggest that aggression is linked to high testosterone levels. Similarly, considerable data show that aggression in animals is linked to high testosterone and that castration—particularly before the onset of sexual maturation—decreases aggression.[141] If that is true, what implications does that hold for freely chosen, rational behavior?

[135] Kristian Miccio, *Male Violence—State Silence: These and Other Tragedies of the 20th Century*, 5 J of Gender, Race & Justice 339 (2002).

[136] M. Daly and M. Wilson, *Homicide* (Hawthorne, 1988).

[137] FBI Uniform Crime Reports (2001).

[138] Id., J.Q. Wilson, and R.J Hernstein, *Crime and Human Nature* (Simon & Schuster, 1985).

[139] Quoted by Frederick R. Goodwin in R. Wright, *The Biology of Violence*, New Yorker 70 (March 13, 1995).

[140] Deborah W. Denno, *Gender Differences in Biological and Sociological Predictors of Crime*, 22 Vt L Rev 305 (1998); see also Anne Fautso-Sterling, *Myths of Gender* (Perseus Publ, 1992); D. Kimura, *Sex Differences in the Brain*, in *Mind and Brain: Readings from Scientific American* 78 (W H Freeman & Co, 1993).

[141] Michael S. Bahrke and James B. Wright, *Psychological Behavioral Effects of Endogenous Testosterone*, 10(5) Sports Medicine International Ltd., 303, 303-337 (1990).

6. The Special Problem of Addiction

Despite efforts to shoehorn addictive behavior into an ill-fitting paradigm in which it is shown to be the product of free and rational choice,[142] addiction seems to defy traditional notions of rationality. Addition is often compared to the heuristic devices of habit and tradition, yet such comparisons are difficult to sustain. It is widely known that individuals often repeat behaviors out of habit.[143] This has been viewed as a rational means of reducing the costs of decision making. Like other heuristics, decision making via habit may be rational, because it permits individuals to approximate utility-maximizing behavior at a reasonable cost.

Along a slightly different, albeit related, vein, behaviors that are driven by "tradition" approximate the status quo bias. If a person who is normally a non-drinker and in fact dislikes drinking nevertheless imbibes each New Year's Eve, like the status quo bias, the power of tradition results from the utility that individuals derive from conforming to shared practices, rather than from the inherent value of a given behavior. Tradition, generally understood as a specific practice of longstanding, reflects an ordering of preferences that may shift depending upon the context (the New Year's Eve party) in which they may surface.

Addictions, in a manner reminiscent of traditions, result when the fact that an actor has engaged in a behavior in the past makes him more likely to engage in that behavior in the future because the past behavior makes current behavior more pleasant. The heroin addict chooses to inject the drug because she has enjoyed the experience in the past. Thus, an addiction might be viewed as a type of tradition. The difference, however, is the physical or chemical compulsion that motivates an addict, and may in fact alter his brain chemistry, suggests that the effects of addiction are quite different from those of mere tradition. Thus, an individual's desire to shoot heroin is not merely motivated by the fact that he has engaged in those activities before, but a product of the chemical dependence created by the drug. Such a person belongs in a different category from that of a person whose desire to drink champagne at New Year's is motivated by the fact that he does so every year without fail.

The existence of addiction has important ramifications for public policy; namely, that policy makers seeking to discourage certain behaviors should realize that behaviors motivated by addiction are likely

---

[142] Gary S. Becker and Kevin M. Murphy, *A Theory of Rational Addiction*, 96(4) J of Pol Economy 675, 675-700 (1988).

[143] Korobkin and Ulen, 88 Cal L Rev 1051 at 1114 (cited in note 10).

to be much more difficult to manipulate than rational choice theory would predict. This may be why the severe penalties for drug possession (often a proxy for drug use) have not substantially eroded drug use among addicts. Even if the risk-adjusted expected cost of using an illegal substance exceeds the inherent benefit to an individual of doing so, the addict is unlikely to go straight. As a consequence, policymakers may be forced to find measures other than merely increasing the price of the undesirable behavior if they hope to eradicate it.

C. Irrationality and the Brain

Modern advances in neuro-biology suggest that many behaviors we perceive as being socially irrational are the product of cognitive defects and neurological malfunctioning. These seemingly maladaptive behaviors are neither random, nor entirely obscure, but rather appear consistently within populations. As brain imaging devices become ever more sophisticated, and our understanding of neuro-biology more complete, it is beyond peradventure that we will better be able to predict cognitive defects and socially irrational behavior in individuals. While it is plausible, as Owen Jones has argued,[144] that certain seemingly socially irrational behaviors were, in fact, rational from an evolutionary perspective, it is equally plausible that many observed irrational behaviors are in fact the product of organic brain damage from sources as varied as malnutrition, neglect, abuse, injury, or genetic defect. Such deficits in reason may not ultimately drive basic public policy, but they may be necessary to consider in refining the way in which we enact punishments and craft criminal law prohibitions.

IV. IRRATIONALITY AND PUBLIC POLICY

The importance of this discussion to public policy concerns should be readily apparent. To be useful for legal policy, behavioral theories need to predict (with some degree of accuracy) the likely responses to legal rules of the particular classes of actors to whom the rules are geared. If individuals commit many more errors in their attempts to maximize utility than the rational choice model posits, and those errors are not the result of garden variety market imperfections, but rather the result of systematic, widespread cognitive imperfections, then our analysis of the relative efficiency of legal rules is erroneous to the extent it fails to take those imperfections into account.[145] A model of

---

[144] Owen Jones, *The Evolution of Irrationality*, 41 Jurimetrics 289, 291 (2001).

[145] Thomas S. Ulen, *Cognitive Imperfections and the Economic Analysis of Law*, 12 Hamlin L Rev 385, 388 (1989).

human nature that fails to account for the central role of neurobiology and its effect on behavior inevitably results in an impoverished jurisprudence in a wide variety of circumstances. Legal policy makers rely upon those models when crafting legislative changes to modify incentive structures to influence human behavior. If policymakers, for instance, are considering revising penalties for violent offenders, they need a prediction of how such potential offenders will likely respond to competing sanctioning regimes. The struggle is that if a substantial number of violent offenders engage in such behavior because of the neurological or genetic defects discussed here, the traditional assumption that individuals will respond to increased sanctions may be inaccurate. New assumptions will needed to more accurately reflect the reality of human behavior.

This is not to imply that the rational choice model as expressed in optimal penalty theory fails to predict socially rational behavior.[146] This model has proven to be a powerful tool for conducting legal analysis. As with any tool, however, it may not be perfect for each intended application. Although public policy may often be based upon the assumptions employed by classical economics, it may need to take into account the fact that some individuals will not respond to utility maximization. That is not an indictment of the rationality assumption itself, rather it is a refinement of that assumption to address the growing body of empirical and neuro-science literature that calls certain of its core assumptions into question.

Most people recognize, in at least a conventional sense, that individuals are not rational all the time.[147] Yet, some law and economics scholars regard irrational behavior—to the extent they are willing to acknowledge that it even exists—as mere bumps upon the rationality highway. The neural mechanisms that define irrationality, however, ought to be considered a part of the assumption, and thus taken into account by public policy makers where possible.

If criminals are biased by availability when calculating (no doubt in an informal sort of way) the anticipated costs of crime, this analysis could change radically depending on what types of events are more salient to potential criminals. In order to determine which deterrence mechanism will be most efficient, policymakers need to understand whether criminals are likely to over- or underestimate the frequency and the severity of punishment that is actually meted out or if they are likely to respond to changes in penalties.

[146] Gary Becker, *Crime and Punishment: An Economic Approach*, 76 J Pol Econ 169 (1968).

[147] See generally Jon Elster, *Sour Grapes: Studies in the Subversion of Rationality* (1983).

It is at this point that the calculation of the optimal criminal sanction may become tricky. Increasing the severity or frequency of punishment necessary to reduce or to increase the incidence of any human behavior will correlate positively or negatively, respectively, with the extent to which the predisposition underlying that behavior is either the product of evolutionary forces or the result of neurological defects. The closer legislatures come to regulating high functioning reasoning, such as that akin to selecting stocks, the greater success they may have in deterring calculated behavior. The more legislatures are seeking to deter behavior that is akin to basic function, such as eating a chocolate bar, the greater the difficulty they may have.

Behaviors that are motivated by addictions, for example, bear a strong resemblance to behaviors that are motivated by visceral cravings such as hunger, thirst, sleep, or sexual desire. Unlike addictions, such cravings are generally evolved traits rather than desires that stem directly from past individual behaviors. But much like harmful addictions, visceral cravings can overpower actors, causing them to act in ways that fail to maximize utility. Hunger can make the dieter overeat, even though he would rather lose weight than enjoy a fattening meal. Sexual desire may tempt an individual to abandon his family, even though the costs of doing so clearly outweigh the benefits.

Rational choice models can fail in predicting behavior in these situations because actors tend systematically to underestimate the power of such visceral cravings before they occur, hampering advanced planning. In an interesting example of the power of craving, experimental subjects were recruited and told they would be compensated if they agreed to complete a quiz that would test their knowledge of history.[148] Some subjects were asked to choose, prior to completing the quiz, whether they would be compensated with a chocolate bar or a specified cash payment. Other subjects knew what their choice of compensation would be but were not required to make the choice until they had completed the quiz.[149] Subjects in the latter group were significantly more likely to select the chocolate bar than subjects in the first group, demonstrating that people are often not very good at predicting the power of their cravings before a temptation is imminent. This insight may explain why government policies seeking to quell addiction are sometimes less successful than rational choice theory would predict.

In situations of addictions, where individuals are especially likely to act in ways contrary to their more considered, stable judgments as to how to maximize their utility, an argument can be made for more

---

[148] Korobkin and Ulen, 88 Cal L Rev 1051 at 1118 (cited in note 10).
[149] Id.

aggressive *ex ante* government regulation. If rational choice theory provided sufficient behavioral predictions, the government would need to do no more to combat heroin use than to ensure that information concerning the risks of heroin were made widely available to the general public. Plainly, such is not the case.

V. A FINAL WORD

Economics tells us about incentives (nurture). Biology tells us about limitations that inhere in our being human (nature). The law's resistance to consider irrationality reveals a serious flaw in its ability to account for, and regulate or shape, human behavior. At the end of the day, *any* theory of human behavior is only as good as the assumptions upon which it is based. To be useful as a means of constructing public policy, those assumptions must be based upon empirical foundations. Simply to claim that no competing theories of behavior exist that have the same elegance as that of the rational actor, does not mean that the assumptions underlying that theory should neither be re-evaluated nor refined. A simple, elegant theory that systematically fails to account properly for human behavior is not a useful theory. Nor is a theory that refuses to permit modifications based upon empirical results of much more than decorative value. Science does not proceed smoothly, it often moves in fits and starts, but the theories of the natural sciences demand verification (or falsification) and refinement. The theories of social science must heed that same call.

We can understand social rationality by examining social statistics. It is for this reason that the insights provided by law and economics are so powerful. Economics, whether applied to law or not, is essentially a science of human behavior. It makes assumptions about how people will behave under given conditions. While it is powerful in its predictive ability when applied to groups, or even sometimes to individuals, it is not always accurate. More complete models, especially in criminal law, where the focus is on socially aberrant behavior, will need to take into account recent advances in neuro-psychiatry, genetics, and behavioral psychology in order to better shape public policy. To the extent researchers are able to posit theories that better explain, and predict, human behavior, they will be better able to assist policy makers.

Efficient Third Party Liability of Auditors in Tort Law and in Contract Law

Hans-Bernd Schäfer *

An audit and consequently auditor's liability has a different function in primary and in secondary capital markets. In primary markets the audit serves to reduce the problem of asymmetric information between the well informed seller and the uninformed outside investor. In secondary markets there is no asymmetric information between the sellers and buyers. The outside investor does not know ex ante, whether he will be a buyer or a seller. Consequently he does not know whether he might profit or loose from a wrong audit, which overvalues a company. This has consequences on the optimal level of protection, which should be higher in the primary market than in the secondary market. It is proposed that auditor's liability vis a vis shareholders should be restricted to cases of gross negligence in secondary markets and should be based on simple negligence in primary markets. The latter result can be achieved by assuming an implicit contract between the auditor and the investor in the primary market.

I. INTRODUCTION

A wrong audit can cause damages to shareholders in secondary markets, to buyers of firms, or shares in primary markets. This happens

* I thank Jochen Bigus, Robert D. Cooter, Guiseppe Dari Mattiacci, Fernando Gomez, Bruce Johnsen and Ria Steiger as well as the participants of the Olin workshop at the Berkeley School of Law and of the Levy workshop at the George Mason School of Law for helpful comments on an earlier draft. My thanks also go to the two anonymous referees. Financial support from the IQN-DAAD project is gratefully acknowledged. The usual disclaimer applies.

especially if outside investors base their decision on the audit and buy overpriced company shares. Liability of auditors is liability for pure economic loss. The main point of this paper is to give normative guidelines for the problem of whether or not the victim should be compensated for such losses. It proposes liability for disloyal and gross negligent behavior if a wrong audit caused damages in the secondary market. It proposes liability for simple negligence, if the audit was made for the primary market.

The legal forms of auditor's liability and of liability of experts in general differ widely across countries. Under tort law, most legal orders restrict or even exclude liability for pure financial loss. In contract law, pure economic losses are generally compensated in case of simple negligence. In some legal orders the plaintiff can base his claim either on tort law or on contract law or on both. Some countries (Germany) have a broad scope of (implicit) contract law, which covers case groups, which in other countries (Britain) are treated under tort law. The main concern is however not the legal form but a proposal for two liability rules, one based on simple negligence, one based on gross negligence. In principle these rules can be embedded in contract law, tort law, or both.

If damages caused by a wrong audit are recoverable under an implied contract between auditor and shareholder, the auditor is usually liable for simple negligence. In that case the auditor has negligently violated a contractual duty to the shareholder, even though the explicit contract was between the auditor and the corporation. If however, these damages are only recoverable under tort law, simple negligence will not lead to compensation because they are pure economic losses and because most legal orders restrict or exclude liability for pure economic loss in tort. For such damages, most legal orders grant compensation under tort law only if it is proven that the tortfeasor was willful, disloyal, reckless or grossly negligent.[1] In most cases, this excludes compensation. The economic literature on civil liability for economic loss has underlined the rationale for such restrictions.

However, the literature remains silent with respect to the borderline between contract law and tort law. There is general agreement that pure economic loss has to be compensated under contract law as the cost of this protection is internalized in the contract. If a wrong audit or a wrong and published balance sheet cause a pure financial loss to a shareholder, should this be regarded as a violation of contractual duties between the auditor and the shareholder, or just as a

---

[1] For surveys on the compensation of pure economic loss in tort see E. Banakas, ed, *Civil Liability for Pure Economic Loss* (Kluver Law International, 1996), and M. Bussani and V.V. Palmer, eds, *Pure Economic Loss in Europe* 75-93 (Cambridge, 2003).

tort? In civil law countries, this question is decisive for whether the plaintiff receives compensation or not. As judges lack the authority to introduce liability for pure economic loss in tort law, they can expand liability by expanding the scope of contract law to the respective group of cases. It is argued that this question should be answered in the affirmative, if the victim has an ex-ante willingness to pay for the costs associated with performing such a duty. In common law countries, such restrictions do not exist. Judges can impose a rule of simple or gross negligence in tort law or in contract law, depending on what they regard as reasonable.

It should be made clear, however that this argument is purely consequentialist as it reinterprets the problem of whether a certain victim's interest should be protected under contract or under tort only on the basis of their respective effects in terms of the injurers' equilibrium level of precaution. Contractual (or quasi-contractual) liability is called upon only as a way to remedy the lack of protection of purely economic interest under tort law in some jurisdictions.

It is argued that a wrong audit that causes damages to shareholders in secondary markets should generally be regarded as a tort case and compensation be restricted. It is also argued that a rule of gross negligence or of gross violation of professional standards in tort law can avoid the problems of underdeterrence as well as of overdeterrence in the compensation of pure financial loss in tort. However, a wrong audit should also lead to contractual liability for simple negligence, if it was made to prepare the sale in a primary market, (i.e. an initial public offering). Under this condition the economic rationale for restricting compensation for pure financial loss is not given.

The paper first analyses the social value of an audit. Then several liability rules with precise and vague levels of professional care are treated with respect to their incentive effects. This leads to the proposal of a rule of gross negligence in tort law. The last part analyzes the special conditions, under which the legal order should assume a contract with protective consequences for buyers of company shares, which leads to liability for simple negligence. The legal form of a contract with protective consequences for third parties (Vertrag mit Schutzwirkung für Dritte) is borrowed from German dogmatic scholarship, but may be interesting in this respect for an international audience as well.

This article draws from the literature on pure financial losses[2] and

---

[2] F. Parisi, *Recovery for Pure Financial Loss: Economic Foundations of a Legal Doctrine*, in M. Bussani and V. Palmer, eds, *Pure Economic Loss in Europe* 75-93 (Cambridge, 2003); see also M.Bussani, V.V. Palmer, and F. Parisi, *Liability for Pure Financial Loss in Europe: An Economic Restatement*, 51 Am J Comparative L 113, 113-162

from the literature on precise and vague negligence norms[3] as well as from the literature on the tort contract boundary.[4] The article does however not discuss the problem of joint and several liability and the strategic problems involved, which have been broadly discussed in the literature. The victim of a wrong audit might have a claim against the inside investor, the management, the firm and/or the auditor. This causes strategic interactions, which influence the level of care of all actors as well as the price of auditing.[5] These problems have been extensively dealt with in the literature and are left out here completely. The focus is exclusively on the question, under which conditions the victim should be highly protected by contract law or get a lower level of protection under tort law.

The problem of auditors' liability arises, given that the auditor certifies a financial report such as a balance sheet of a company. First, the auditor might cause damage to his contractual partner, the company and the company claims damages. The base of this claim is the contract with the auditor. Second, the auditor testifies a financial report and a balance sheet, which inside owners use for preparing a transaction, when they sell the company or shares to new owners or if a firm goes public in an initial public offering. By the auditors' overvaluation of the corporation, the buyer suffers a loss. Here typically asymmetric information between buyer and seller of the firm exists. The audit is made to reduce this asymmetry. Third, the auditor certifies a

---

(2003); E. Silverstein, *On Recovery in Tort for Pure Economic Loss*, 32 U Mich L Rev 404 (1999); E. Banakas, ed, *Civil Liability for Pure Financial Loss* (cited in note 1); W. Bishop, *Economic Loss in Tort*, 2 Oxford J Legal Stud 1, 1-29 (1982); V. Goldberg, *Recovery for Pure Economic Loss in Tort Following the Exxon Valdes Oil Spill*, 23 J Legal Stud (1991); M. Rizzo, *A Theory of the Economic Loss Problem in the Law of Torts*, 11 J Legal Stud 249, 249-275 (1982)

[3] See R. Crasswell and J.E. Calfee, *Deterrence and Uncertain Legal Standards*, 2 J L, Econ & Org 279, 281(1986); see also R. Schwartz, *Auditors' Liability, Vague Due Care, and Auditing Standards*, 11 Rev Quantitative Finance & Accounting, 183, 183-207 (1998).

[4] P.H. Rubin, *Torts and the Tort-Contract Boundary in Product Liability*, in F. Buckley, ed, *The Fall and Rise of Freedom of Contract* (Duke, 1999); Victor P. Goldberg, *A Reexamination of 'Glanzer v. Shepard': Surveyors on the Tort-Contract Boundary*, 3 Theoretical Inquiries in Law (Online Edition) No. 2, Article 6 (2002), online at http://www.bepress.com/til/default/vol3/iss2/art6.

[5] For a review of the strategic literature on accounting see R. Ewert, *Auditor Liability and the Precision of Auditing Standards*, 155 JITE 181, 181-206 (1999); see also S.A. Hillegeist, *Financial Reporting and Auditing Under Alternative Damage Apportionment Rules*, 74 The Accounting Review 347,347-369 (1999); Chi-Wen Jevons Lee, and Zhaoyang Gu, *Low Balling Legal Liability and Auditor Independence*, 73 The Accounting Review 533, 533-555 (1998); R.R. King, and R. Schwartz, *An Experimental Investigation of Auditors' Liability: Implications for Social Welfare and Exploration of Deviations from Theoretical Predictions*, 95 The Accounting Review 429, 429-451 (2000).

balance sheet, in which the net worth of the company is overvalued. This leads to an overvaluation of shares at the stock market until the bad company news reaches the market by other channels of information. Therefore, outside shareholders suffer losses. Here asymmetric information between buyers and sellers typically do not exist.

Now focus on the second and the third constellation, when the victims of such losses have no direct and explicit contractual relation with the auditor. It is argued that liability in the second case should be stricter than in the third case. The rationale for this is found in the literature on pure economic loss in torts. The basic argument is that pure economic losses contain a redistributive component. Therefore, the victims' loss is lower than the total societal loss, which might lead to overcompensation and overdeterrence of victims. The main purpose of this article is to show why this argument holds for the third, but not for the second constellation.

I first analyze the case in which the auditor's mistake leads to an overvaluation of shares at the stock market such that shareholders might suffer losses, a case that in recent years and months has occurred in many countries. As usual in the law and economics literature, the legal remedies are analyzed from a viewpoint of optimal deterrence. I first analyze the auditors' liability to shareholders and then proceed to the special case, in which the auditors' expertise is exclusively used for preparing the transfer of ownership from an inside to an outside investor and in which the buyers suffer a loss because the assets were overvalued. Throughout the article I assume that auditors as well as shareholders are risk neutral and maximize expected income.

II. THE OPTIMAL LEVEL OF CARE OF AN AUDITOR

A. The case of an information efficient capital market, the true yield parameter is known for every period

I begin the analysis with determining the efficient level of care of an auditor. The level of care is set equal with the costs of care (x). The question is which liability regime and which scope of liability provides incentives to reach the efficient level $(x = x^*)$.

I analyze a stock listed company, in which one share represents one unit of capital. a is the net yield per period per share and per unit of capital. The yield (a) is regarded as a parameter whose value might be either high or low. For simplicity's sake, the parameter can have only two possible values, which are common knowledge to shareholders, management, and auditors. Depending on the conditions of the market as well as on technical productivity, the parameter can take either a high or a low value in each period.

$$a \in \{a_l, a_h\}$$

r is the opportunity cost interest rate of capital. Then the net profit per period and per share is $a - r$.

If the capital market is information efficient in the strong sense the true parameter is known to the market and reflected in the market price. The market price is the discounted value of all future yield parameters. Consequently auditing cannot improve any decisions of shareholders or the management. Therefore mandatory auditing of annual reports, balance sheets and cash flow calculation is a mere waste as it creates additional costs to the shareholders without causing any benefits. Information efficient stock markets do not need mandatory auditing. Neither is there a rationale for any liability vis-à-vis stockholders, because by assumption auditors cannot cause losses to shareholders, regardless of the auditor's level of care.

B. The yield parameter is known only for the first period

To relax informational assumptions assume that the exact value of the yield parameter for the first period is common knowledge at the beginning of the first period. However, for all future periods the parameter is not known and cannot be revealed. There exists only a probability distribution. In other words, one knows the near future with certainty, whereas the distant future is uncertain.

In this case the price of one share (p) in period 1 is

$$p = a_h + R$$

if the yield parameter is high during the first period. R is a constant term, which reflects the discounted value of expected earnings in the periods 2 to infinity. If the yield parameter is low in the first period, two possibilities arise. First, $a_l > r$. In that case the price for the share is

$$p = a_l + R$$

Second, if $a_l < r$, shareholders are interested that the management shifts the capital to alternative uses outside the firm such that the yield is r. This asset shifting should be repeated in any future period, whenever $a = a_l < r$. This also includes the possibility of permanent liquidation of the firm, if $r/r = 1 > a_l + R$. This shifting requires that capital is not firm specific and can be transferred without a cost to productive uses outside the firm. Throughout this article I assume that this is possible, because the basic argument still holds if only fractions of the capital can be put to a different use outside the firm as a reaction to low yield within the firm.

Therefore, if the management acts in the shareholders interest, if the capital market is information efficient and if the parameter (a) is low an immediate reallocation of resources takes place. This generates a yield of $r - a_1$, compared to the situation, in which the capital stock is used inside the firm. The auditor can neither promote nor prevent this yield.

C. The yield parameter is not known

I now analyze a situation, in which the yield parameter for a particular period is uncertain at the beginning of the period, but reveals itself at no cost at the end of the period. The expected yield for any period is now the sum of the yield parameters, weighted with probabilities. Let the probabilities that the yield parameter is low be w and that it high be $(1 - w)$. The expected value (ā) of the yield parameter for the first period is then.

(1) $\bar{a} = wa_1 + (1 - w)a_h$

For the second and all other periods again add the constant term R to get the share price. The share price at the beginning of the first period is then

(2) $p = wa_1 + (1 - w)a_h + R$

The uncertainty reflected in this equation can have two reasons. Either nobody, neither shareholders nor management, know the true parameter or the insiders (management or inside owners) knows the true parameter, but conceals it successfully from the shareholders. The management might for instance know that the company just "burns money," and needs restructuring or even liquidation $(a = a_1)$ including dismissal of the management, but keeps this as a secret by fabricating positive news. Paradigmatic for such management behavior are the Holzmann bankruptcy[6] in Germany or the Enron scandal[7] in the USA. In both cases the management misinformed shareholders and was—for some time—able to keep share values up. In this case capital is used inside the firm even though the yield parameter is low and a loss of $r - a_1$ is caused which could have been avoided.

If at the beginning of a period the true value of the parameter is low and the management knows the true value and is loyal to shareholders,

---

[6] Business Week Online (January 28, 2002).
[7] Welt am Sonntag, (August 28, 2003).

it will shift resources to uses outside the firm. If shareholders know this the share price will—by the amount of $w(r - a_l)$—be higher than in equation (2). Equation (2) therefore presupposes that either the true parameter is not known to the management or that it is known to the management but not to the shareholders and that the management acts disloyal to shareholders by neither informing them nor shifting resources to uses outside the firm and continues "burning of money."

Under these assumptions the screening by an auditor can lead to a socially valuable information.[8] Auditors often have a broader knowledge than managers about the general conditions of the market. They might for instance see that a patent is valueless even though it is not yet expired or that housing prices in are likely to be depressed for a longer period, or that some of the main debtors of the company are close to bankruptcy etc. Or they can just see and make public what an disloyal management tries to conceal from the shareholders. In these cases their work can help to avoid further unproductive investment and losses.

It is now assumed that the auditor acts at the beginning of a period, that his effort might lead to a revelation of the true parameter for this period, and if so that this forces the management to stop losses by shifting resources to alternative use. Throughout this article the following sequence of actions and events is used

Sequence of events

1. At the beginning of the period the productivity parameter is unknown to shareholders. This is reflected in the price of shares.
2. The audit is made. The auditor either finds or does not find the true productivity parameter. The audit is published for the use of outside investors.
3. If the auditor finds that the true parameter is low $(a = a_l)$, this leads the management to shift   resources to uses outside the firm for the duration of the period.
4. If the audit does not reveal the true parameter, it reveals itself to the shareholders without cost at the end of the period.

The events 1.,2.,3. are all at the beginning of the period, the event 4. is at the end of the period. The company receives the yield (a_h, a_l or r).

---

[8] A socially productive information allows for an improvement of resource allocation, whereas a socially unproductive information does not have this capacity. A socially unproductive information can still be privately valuable, if it leads to a foreknowledge which can be used for a mere transfer of wealth, without improving the allocation of resources. See J. Hirschleifer, *Where Are We in The Theory of Information?*, 63 American Economic Review, Papers and Proceedings, 1-39 (1973).

To keep the analysis simple it is assumed, that the auditors effort cannot reveal the yield parameters for any future period t > 1. The value of the firm per share is therefore always the expected yield of the first period, which is partly dependent on the auditors' effort plus a fixed term R as the discounted net income of all other periods.

Now the optimal effort level can be calculated, which is set equal to the optimal cost level (x) of the auditor. The search costs of the auditor are x (per share). If in spite of his search the auditor does not find the true parameter value these costs are born by the shareholder and consequently the price of the share is reduced to.

(3) $p = wa_1 + (1 - w)a_h - x + R = \bar{a} - x + R$

This calculation of the price requires that the costs of auditing are common knowledge among shareholders, managers and auditors and are therefore reflected in the share price. If the auditor finds the true value of the parameter, three constellations can arise. The true value is high and immediately publicized, then the share price increases[9] to

(4) $p = a_h - x + R$

The auditor finds that the parameter is low. If it is low but still higher than r, the opportunity cost of capital, the share price reduces to

(5) $p = a_1 - x + R$

In this case the auditor has revealed the true value of the firm and found that it is lower than expected. But this does not lead to any improved allocation of resources. For a buyer of a company or a buyer of shares this might be a very profitable information. But socially this information is not productive as it does not lead to an efficiency gain. This case is therefore excluded from the further analysis.

If the auditor finds that the parameter is low and lower than r, an immediate reallocation of resources takes place to uses outside the firm for the duration of the period. The future "burning of money" is prevented by the activity of the auditor. In that case the value of the firm is

(6) $p = r - x + R$

In this case the auditor's work leads to a net efficiency gain of $(r - a_1) - x$.

Now the optimal costs of the auditor's effort can be calculated. It is assumed that the probability that the auditor´s search leads to the revelation of the true parameter is $q = q(x)$. Consequently the proba-

---

[9] It increases only if the costs of auditing are relatively small compared to the price increase due to the revelation the fact that the true parameter is high.

bility that the true parameter is not found is $1 - q(x)$. This function has the following properties: $q = 0$ if $x = 0$, $q \in (0,1]$ if $x > 0$, $q_x(x) > 0$ $q_{xx}(x) < 0$, and $q \to 1$, if $x \to \infty$.

Now the case in which the auditor's effort can lead to an efficiency gain is calculated, that is the case in which the low yield parameter is lower than the opportunity costs of capital $a_1 < r$.

The expected efficiency gain (eg) of the auditor's work is then the probability that the true parameter is detected multiplied with the prior probability that this parameter is low and below the opportunity costs of capital (r) in the first period multiplied with the efficiency gain that is made possible in this case minus the costs of auditing.[10]

$$(7) \quad eg = q(x)w(r - a_1) - x$$

The first order condition is $q_x(x)w(r - a_1) - 1 = 0$ or

$$(8) \quad q(x) = \frac{(1}{w(r - a_1) - x}$$

This is the Learned Hand formula for the optimal search costs of the auditor. It determines a unique optimal level of costs (x^*). Consequently the auditor acts negligently as long as his costs are below this level.

The expected social loss (SL) of negligent behavior of the auditor derives from (7). It is the expected social loss, if no audit takes place minus the expected loss reduction caused by the auditor plus the costs of auditing.

$$(9) \quad SL = [1 - q(x)]w(r - a_1) + x$$

III. CONSEQUENCES OF LIABILITY RULES

Now different tort liability rules which give the shareholder a claim against the negligent auditor are analysed.

---

[10] In this article I am only interested in the constellation, in which the true parameter is not found and turns out to be low. It is possible to extend the analysis to the symmetric case in which the auditor does not find the true parameter and the true parameter is high. The analysis of this case would emerge as a mirror image of this analysis. If the auditor finds that the yield parameter is higher than expected, that has no productive effect in the model. Consequently it should not lead to damage compensation in secondary markets. In primary markets, such cases are seldom because the seller has an incentive to reveal an unexpected high value of the firm. Legal economic problems in those cases arise if the seller in a primary market has no superior knowledge. These cases are seldom. They occur if the inside investor has no superior knowledge; for instance, if the seller is the heir of property, of which he knows as little as the potential buyer. In those cases the seller has a claim from an explicit contract with the expert. This does not cause conceptual legal or economic problems.

(1) Full liability and partial liability (on the European continent better known as difference principle or "Differenzprinzip") under negligence, if the level of due care is precisely defined. It is shown that these rules lead to overcompensation of shareholders, but not to overdeterrence.

(2) Liability under negligence, if the level of due care is not precisely defined and the auditor knows only a probability distribution of the due level of care. It is shown that this rule leads to overcompensation and to overdeterrence if overcompensation is sufficiently high.

(3) Full liability under gross negligence or under an obvious violation of professional standards. It is shown, that this rule leads to overcompensation, but that the problems of overdeterrence are reduced under this rule.

A. Full liability under negligence, if the level of care is precisely defined

1. The cost minimizing auditor

This rule gives every shareholder who suffers the loss of $(\bar{a} - x + R) - (a_1 - x + R) = \bar{a} - a_1$ at the end of the period a tort claim against the negligent auditor, who failed to detect the true value of the yield parameter at the beginning of the period. It is assumed that courts fix a due level of care, which is equal to the efficient level of care. Negligence is then defined by the condition $x < x^*$.

Under this rule the total costs of the auditor are TC. The expected liability costs are the damage compensation $(p - a_1 + R) = \bar{a} - a_1$ multiplied with the probability of compensation plus the costs of auditing (x). For the calculation of p see (3).

$$(10) \quad TC = \begin{cases} [1 - q(x)]w(\bar{a} - a_1) + x \text{ if } x < x^* \\ x \text{ if } x \geq x^* \end{cases}$$

Obviously the auditor does not choose an $x > x^*$.

Whenever he makes a choice in the range $x \in [0, x^*]$ he also must choose x^* as his private cost minimum. Whenever he reduces x by some arbitrary amount below x^* to save costs, the resulting expected damage compensation must be higher than the costs saved. As x^* is the socially optimal level of auditing costs, total social costs must rise if $x < x^*$. Damage compensation in case of damage $D = (\bar{a} - a_1)$ is higher than the social loss $(r - a_1)$.

Hence the additional damage compensation of the auditor from reducing auditing costs to a level below x^* are higher than the social losses for any level of $x < x^*$. As social losses of reducing the effort level below the optimal level (x^*) are higher than the cost reductions $(x^* - x)$, this proves that any cost reduction to a level below x^* increases total private costs, i.e. auditing costs plus liability costs for the auditor. And the auditor has an incentive to reach the optimal cost level. Therefore, even though damage compensation is higher than the total social damages $(r - a_1)$ in case a damage occurs, this does not lead to overdeterrence as long as the level of due care is precisely defined and efficient.[11]

B. Partial liability under negligence, if the level of care is precisely defined

1. The difference principle

Under partial liability[12] the damage award is the difference between the wealth of the victim with and without the negligent act. This rule, known in Continental Europe as the difference principle, (Differenzprinzip in German, § 249 BGB) would not lead to a full compensation $(p - a_1)$ of the shareholder by the auditor. To clarify this principle with respect to auditor's liability one must distinguish between three different cases.

(1) The buyer buys the shares before the beginning of period 1 and still keeps them after the end of period 1. The auditor fails negligently to discover and publish the low yield parameter at the beginning of period 1. At the end of period 1 the market reveals that the parameter is low (a_1). The buyer suffers a loss of $\bar{a} - a_1$. Under the difference principle the shareholder would however not be entitled to recover this loss. The defendant could argue that if he had been diligent and exercised due care and informed the public properly at the beginning of the period, the value of the shares would have dropped from p to $r + R$ and that he has caused only the damage $r - a_1$. This resulted from the fact that the auditors did not cause the management to shift resources to uses outside the firm where they could yield the opportunity costs

---

[11] This is in line with previous research, See J. Summers, *The Case of the Disappearing Defendant: An Economic Analysis,* 132 U Pa L Rev 145, 157-159 (1983), R.D. Cooter, *Prices and Sanctions,* 84 Colum Law Rev 1523, 1539 (1984), and S. Shavell, *The Judgement Proof Problem,* 6 Intl Rev L & Econ 45, 47-49 (1986).

[12] Partial Liability was discussed from an economic perspective by M. Grady, *A New Positive Economic Theory of Negligence,* 92 Yale L J 799, 799-829 (1983) and M. Kahan, *Causation and Incentives to Take Care under the Negligence Rule,* 18 Legal Stud 427, 427-447 (1989). They showed that deduction of losses that would have happened anyway from the liability of the injurer does not change the injurer's equilibrium level of precaution, a result claimed in this paper as well.

of capital. To my knowledge, this defense according to the difference principle would be accepted in most legal orders. Damage compensation in this case would therefore result not in full liability $(\bar{a} - a_1)$, but in partial liability $(r - a_t)$.

It is also noteworthy that in general the difference principle applies only, if the defendant shows that even without negligent behavior a certain damage would have occurred with certainty. The difference principle is however not applicable with respect to probabilities. If the defendant has reached a cost level of auditing of $x < x^*$ he cannot argue that even if he had reached the due level of care (x^*), the same damage might have occurred but with a lower probability. And he cannot argue that therefore the damage award should therefore be reduced to the damage $(r - a_1)$ multiplied with the probability differential of the damage probability with and without the due level of care. At least this defense seems not to be possible within Germany, where the difference principle is part of the Civil Code and generally—with some exceptions—accepted by jurisdiction. Therefore partial liability based on the difference principle is interpreted as a rule which reduces liability, if proof can be given that some of the damages would have occurred anyway, even if the defendant had reached the due level of care.

This means that—if the shareholder has bought the shares before period 1 and still holds them after the end of that period—the total costs of the auditor under this rule will be

$$(11) \quad TC = \begin{cases} [(1 - q(x)]w(r - a_1) + x \text{ if } x < x^* \\ x \text{ otherwise} \end{cases}$$

Is there overdeterrence in this case as under a rule of full liability? The shareholder receives a compensation equal to the social damage of $r - a_1$. The auditor cannot reduce his total costs by reducing his costs of care below the due level of care. This is due to the fact, that in case damage is paid, compensation is equal to the social loss

(2) The buyer buys the shares after the beginning of period 1 and keeps them until after the end of period 1. In this case the buyer buys at price p in period 1. The auditor failed to find and make public that the yield parameter is low. The buyer keeps the share until after the true parameter is revealed to the market at the end of period 1 and suffers a loss of $p - a_1 + R$. Now the use of partial liability under the difference principle does not lead to any reduction of the damage award. Had the auditor not acted negligently and had he found the true parameter, the drop in share prices by $(p - (r + R))$ would have happened before the buy. Therefore, the defendant cannot argue that if he had acted diligently the plaintiff would have suffered a loss of $(p - (r + R))$

anyway which would reduce the damage award to $(r - a_1)$. The difference principle leads to full liability and therefore—from a social point of view—to overcompensation. The total expected costs given that the shareholder bought the shares after the beginning of period 1 is then

(12) $\text{TC} = \begin{cases} [1 - q(x)]w(\bar{a} - a_1) + x, \text{ if } x < x^* \\ x \text{ otherwise} \end{cases}$

(3) The buyer sells the share after the beginning and before the end of period 1. Here the buyer sells shares at an overvalued price, because the auditor has failed to detect and publicize that the company is worth less than the market valuation. This resembles the case of an art collector who buys a painting at a high price, which is based on the expertise of an art expert, who negligently overlooked that the painting was a fake. The art collector resells the painting at a high price and only the second buyer discovers the fake and suffers the loss. To this shareholder the negligence of the auditor has caused a gain of $\bar{a} - r$ under the difference principle. Had the auditor not negligently failed to detect the true parameter, the shareholder would have suffered an equivalent loss. As this loss was avoided, the auditor has caused a gain to the shareholder. From an economic policy point of view this gain should be disgorged to the auditor according to the mitigation principle. But this is a practical impossibility. Therefore under the difference principle the private gains caused by the negligent behavior of the auditor are not disgorged, but the private losses of those who buy the shares within period 1 have to be fully compensated, which again leads to overcompensation.

2. Total expected damage compensation under the difference principle

Now the expected damage compensation under the difference principle is calculated. For this it is assumed that every shareholder who holds shares after period 1 has a constant probability of having bought the shares in period 1 (α) or before period 1 $(1 - \alpha)$.

The expected total cost for the tortfeasor (TC), damage compensation plus costs of auditing (x) is then

(13) $\text{TC} = \alpha[(1 - q(x))w(\bar{a} - a_1)] + (1 - \alpha)[(1 - q(x))w(r - a_1)] + x \text{ if } x < x^*$

The ratio Q between the private costs (TC) and the Social loss (SL) is then

(14) $Q(x) = \dfrac{\text{TC}}{\text{SL}} = \dfrac{[1 - q(x)]w[\alpha(\bar{a} - a_1) + (1 - \alpha)(r - a_1)] + x}{[q(1 - q(x))w[r - a_1] + x]} > 1$

It can easily be seen that this ratio is larger than one because $\bar{a} > r$ and that the private costs of the auditor of falling short of the efficient cost level x^* are larger than the social losses caused by this deviation. Thus overcompensation is inevitable even under partial liability. However, as only the social loss is compensated, if the shareholder has bought his shares before period 1, the difference between the auditor's private costs and social losses is smaller than under full liability.

Overcompensation does not lead to overdeterrence under partial liability, if the due costs of care are precisely defined at x^*. For the same reasons as explained under full liability the cost minimum must be the efficient and due level of care.

C. Overcompensation and overdeterrence under negligence, if the due level of care is unknown ex-ante

In this section the effect of overcompensation on deterrence is analyzed if the due level of care is not precisely known ex ante, neither to courts nor to tortfeasors.[13] Only during the judicial procedure, when the parties present the facts of the case and when the tortfeasor explains what he has done to reduce damages and when the plaintiff explains what could have been done the due level of care is fixed ex post. This is a realistic assumption for most of the cases. An ex ante precise level of care is to be found more often in regulatory law where experts can fix it beyond legal procedure. It is also to be found in those tort areas, in which a long accumulation of high court decisions has led to a precise rule. However in dynamic fields with changing technologies this is not to be expected and the due level of care is most likely known only as a probability distribution when the tortfeasor decides on his level of care. assumptions are changed as explained by the following graph.

Figure 1.

Here x is the cost of care. x_l denotes a lower threshold level of care for which negligence can be regarded as being obvious for an outside observer like a judge. If $x \leq x_l$ and a damage is caused, courts will assume

---

[13] For an analytical exposition without bounds for the range of the distribution function F. See R. Crasswell and J.E. Calfee, 2 J L, Econ & Org at 281 (cited in note 3), see also R. Schwartz, 11 Review of Quantitative Finance and Accounting at 183-207 (cited in note 3); and Ralf Ewert, 155 JITE at fn 1 (cited in note 5).

negligence and liability results with certainty. If $x \geq x_h$ it is equally obvious that the due level of care was reached and courts will always accept this level or a higher level as sufficient to exclude liability. It is assumed that tortfeasors know these threshold levels defined by the courts and therefore know all levels of care which exclude liability with certainty and all levels of care which will lead to liability with certainty.

Between x_1 and x_h the tortfeasor attaches a probability that he is held negligent to each possible care level. Denote this probability value with $F = F(x)$. F has the following properties.

$$
(15) \quad
\begin{aligned}
&F(x) \in [0,1] \\
&F(x) = 1 \text{ if } x \leq x_1 \\
&F(x) = 0 \text{ if } x \geq x_h \\
&F_x(x) < 0 \text{ if } x \in (x_1, x_h)
\end{aligned}
$$

To be able to analyze the effect of overcompensation, it is assumed that damage compensation is by a factor m (m > 1) higher than the social damages for all levels of $x < x_h$. In equation and (15) this ratio is shown for partial liability under the difference principle. From this equations it also follows that m can change with x, but that it is always larger than 1. However to avoid more complicated terms it is further assumed that m is a parameter (m > 1).

The further assumption is made, that the efficient level of care (x^*) is between x_1 and x_h. This is the most plausible assumption, if one assumes that the courts try to hit the efficient level of care when they fix the due level of care but for lack of information sometimes hit to the right and sometimes to the left of x^*. The tortfeasor minimizes his expected costs.

Assume that $0 \leq x \leq x_1$. Then his costs are mD + x, where mD reflects the damage compensation and D the social damages. In this range at every x an increase of x must decrease total costs, as by assumption the level of care is then smaller than the optimal level and any Δx leads to a higher reduction in damages ΔD and an even higher reduction in damage compensation $m\Delta D$, as m > 1. The cost minimum in this range is therefore at x_1. Assume now that x is increased by a small value at x_1, then again total costs must decrease, as by assumption the level of care is then still lower than the optimal level and the resulting reduction in damage compensation $m\Delta D$ is higher than the increase in x at x_1. Furthermore also the probability of being negligent decreases below 1 which leads to a further reduction of the expected damage compensation. Consequently, x_1 cannot be a cost minimum. If there exists a cost minimum it must be at a higher level of x than x_1. If $x \geq x_h$ total costs of the tortfeasor are x, as it is certain that the due level of care is reached. Consequently the cost minimum in this range is x_h. The cost minimum for all values of x must therefore be at at a level higher than x_l, and the highest possible cost minimum is x_h.

In the range total expected costs of the tortfeasor (TC) are TC = $F(x)mD(x) + x$. Differentiation with respect to x yields the first order condition $TC_x = m[F_x(x)D(x) + D_x(x)F(x)] + 1 = 0$, with $F_x < 0, D_x < 0, D(x) > 0, F(x) > 0$.

It is now easy to see that only by chance the tortfeasor gets incentives to reach the efficient level of care, if

$$(16) \quad F_x(x^*)D(x^*) + D_x(x^*)F(x^*) = -\frac{1}{m}$$

This depends on whether at x^* the joint effect of an increase of the costs of care on the probability of liability and on the damages just outweighs this increase. Otherwise the cost minimum is reached at some level of $x \neq x^*$ in the interior of the range or at $x = x_h$. The result is therefore either over- or undertederrence, if the standard of due care is known only as a probability distribution.

It is also easy to see that with an m high enough the value of $1/m$ must be higher than the value of the left hand side. That means that the equality can only be reached at an $x > x^*$ and that therefore overdeterrence results.

Proposition 1. If the level of due care is imprecise ex ante within a range and if the efficient level of care is within this range, there exists an m (m > 1) for which overcompensation in a negligence regime must result in overdeterrence. The same results for any number bigger than this m.

Overdeterrence of auditors is therefore a likely outcome under a rule of simple negligence, if

- the purely redistributive component of liability is high enough and
- it is not possible to define ex ante clear and efficient rules of behavior whose observation lead to an escape from liability and whose violation triggers liability with certainty. It is however questionable whether a complex task as auditing, which includes among other things asset valuation, can be efficiently prescribed by clear rules of behavior and due care. However, the problem of overdeterrence might still be solved or at least alleviated by a negligence concept of gross negligence.

IV. GROSS NEGLIGENCE AS A METHOD TO REDUCE OVERDETERRENCE

A. A concept of gross negligence to avoid overdeterrence as a result of overcompensation

For a solution or at least alleviation to this problem a concept of "gross negligence" or "gross violation of professional standards" is introduced, that should trigger liability instead of normal negligence.[14] First take a closer look at the distribution function $F(x)$. This function is defined over the interval $[x_1,x_h]$. Its value is 1 at the lower bound and 0 at the upper bound of this interval. The legal interpretation of the upper bound is that at these costs of care it is obvious that the tortfeasor was not negligent. The legal interpretation of the lower bound is that it is obvious that the tortfeasor was negligent. $F(x)$ is continuous and $F_x(x) < 0$, $F(x) \in (0,1)$ everywhere in the interior of the interval. Now assume that the legal system imposes a restriction on the court decision. This restriction is a rule which fixes an upper bound x_g which is strictly smaller than x_h. Liability is then excluded with certainty, if $x_g < x_h$ is reached, even if it is not obvious that the tortfeasor was not negligent.

With an $x_g < x_h$ one gets a new distribution function whose value is 1 at $x = x_1$ and whose value is 0 at $x = x_g < x_h$. Let this function be $G(x)$ and let it also be of the same type as $F(x)$. Then assume as a consequence:

(17) $G(x) < F(x)$ if $x \in (x_1, (x_1,x_g]$

(18) $G_x(x) < F_x(x)$ if $x \in (x_1,x_g]$.

This is illustrated by the following graph in which G and F are linear functions.

Here the absolute values of $G(x)$ and of $G_x(x)$ are strictly smaller than the values of $F(x)$ and $F_x(x)$ for any $x \in [x_1,x_g]$ I believe that this is a reasonable consequence also for other types of functions with the properties of $G(x)$ and $F(x)$ given as in (21) and (22).

The function $G(x)$ is interpreted as a definition of gross negligence. Under this definition the tortfeasor is liable in damages if it is obvious that his level of care was too low. But he can escape liability at a relatively low level of care at which it is not obvious that he was not negligent.

---

[14] Note that the problem is not only one of overdeterrence but also one of underdeterrece. If the law reacts with not granting damage compensation for pure economic loss at all, the necessary result is underdeterrence as long as damages are not purely redistributive.

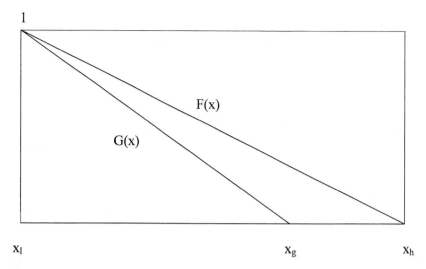

Figure 2.

Now ask, whether it is possible to find an x_g and thereby define a range of gross negligence, which leads to efficient incentives for the tortfeasor, even in the case of overcompensation. For this purpose regard x_g as a variable, which can run from x_l to x_h. This leads to a distribution function with the following properties.

$$G = G(x, x_g)$$

$$(19)\quad G = \begin{cases} 1 \text{ if } x = x_1 \\ 0 \text{ if } x = x_g \\ G \in (0,1) \text{ if } x \in (x_1, x_g) \end{cases}$$

in the latter case we also get

$$Gx < 0, G_{x_g} > 0$$

The total cost function for the tortfeasor in the range between x_1 and x_g is then

$$(20)\quad TC = G(x, x_g) m D(x) + x$$

For the first order conditions one gets

$$(21)\quad \begin{aligned} TC_x &= m[G_x(x, x_g)D(x) + D_x(x)G(x, x_g)] + 1 = 0 \\ TC_{x_g} &= m G_{x_g}(x, x_g)D(x) = 0 \end{aligned}$$

It is now possible to ask for the socially optimal upper bound $x_g{}^*$ of the distribution function $G(x)$. Now ask which x_g minimizes the total expected costs of the tortfeasor, given an optimal level of care $(x = x^*)$.

$$(22)\quad TC_x = [G_x(x^*, x_g)D(x^*) + D_x(x^*)G(x^*, x_g)] = -\frac{1}{m}$$

This yields an $x_g = x_g^*$. Proof: Assume as a starting point that m and x_g are high enough to lead to an overdeterrence at x_g i.e. $TC_x = [G_x(x^*,x_g)D(x^*) + D_x(x^*)G(x^*,x_g)] > - 1/m$. Now reduce the value of x_g continuously towards x_1. That reduces the values of $G > 0$ and of $G_{xg} < 0$. G_{xg} must decrease below all limits, as $G_{xg} \to -\infty$ if $x_g \to x_1$. This results because the value of G drops from 1 at $G(x_1)$ to 0 at $G(x_g)$. Consequently the first derivative of the function within this range, which is always negative must decrease below all limits. The range of the function then becomes smaller and approaches 0. The value of the function must always run from 1 to zero within this range, however small the range is. This must decrease the value of the derivative below all limits.

As $D(x^*)$ is positive and constant, there must therefore exist an $x_g = x_g^*$ at which $[G_x(x^*,x_g)D(x^*) + D_x(x^*)G(x^*,x_g)] = - 1/m$. Assume now that the legal system chooses the range $[x_1,x_g^*]$ over which the distribution function is defined. Then the tortfeasor minimizes his total costs when he chooses a care level which is equal to the socially optimal care level.

Proposition 2: Assume overcompensation for pure financial loss leads to overdeterrence under a level of due care which is known ex ante only as a distribution function $F(x)$ with a lower and an upper bound for the range of the function. Then there exists another distribution function $G(x)$ with the same lower bound and a smaller upper bound of its range, which induces the optimal level of care.

Such a distribution function can be called "Gross Negligence" or in the case of auditors "Gross Violation of Professional Standards." If courts stick to such a standard, when granting compensation for pure financial losses, it is guaranteed that overcompensation does not systematically lead to overdeterrence.

Of course the informational requirements for such a gross negligence standard can often not be met by the courts. If a concept of gross violation of standards is used, it might be to lax i.e. x_g too close to x_1 (the level of obvious negligence) and then even lead to underdeterrence. Or it might be too close to simple negligence, i.e. x_g too close to x_h, leading still to overdeterrence just as under a normal negligence standard. How often this happens, is dependent on the informational level of courts and cannot be analyzed here. But the systematic bias of overdeterrence as a result of overcompensation disappears, if the above concept of gross negligence is introduced.

B. Alternatives to gross negligence

Here the question arises whether a rule of gross negligence should be ranked best among existing alternatives.

The first alternative is, to stick to simple negligence but to make professional standards less vague and replace them by crystal-clear rules. A violation of such rules would then lead to overcompensation. But, as the accountant has a precise ex ante information about the condition of a violation of the rule, he has an extra incentive to meet the due level of care. Otherwise he would have to pay all damages including the purely redistributive losses. This is however not a recommendable option. It would be possible for courts to define clear rules of professional behavior, but it is unlikely that these would be efficient rules. First, courts would rely heavily on the expertise of interested parties. It is therefore likely that such precise standards become too low, leading to a level of care, which is also too low. Second, even if courts can solve the problem of biased expert opinion by relying on independent experts, it is questionable whether precise legal norms should govern the subtle and difficult task of producing or overseeing the production of true and reliable information on the value of a firm. Calculation of liability and related risks would be easier with precise rules, but probably at the expense of the quality of information produced. The complex task of asset valuation might degenerate into a useless exercise of a series of syllogistic accounting rituals. This might serve the vested interests of accountants but not the interests of shareholders in an efficient capital market. In this view, the set of legal norms of accounting should contain broad fiduciary duties in favor of shareholders and potential buyers, which give discretion to highly qualified accountants to decide what is in the best interest for them. These duties should be supervised by courts.

The second alternative to gross negligence is to lower the level of (over)compensation and to grant damage compensation for pure financial losses only for the resource losses, not for the purely redistributive damages. G. Israel[15] made this proposal. Under this norm courts would deduct the estimated redistributive damage component from the damage of the claimant when calculating the damage award. With an imprecise standard of care this solution could lead to both, underdeterrence and overdeterrence, but not to systematic overdeterrence. In general this rule would serve the same purpose as the rule of gross negligence and is therefore equally useful. The gross negligence rule can however be easier implemented into the existing body of legal doctrines. In most legal orders a rule of tort law could not be introduced by judge made law, if it denies full compensation to the victim, even if the victim has a claim, if comparative negligence did not occur, and causation is undebated. Even if parliament enacted this

---

[15] G. Israel, *Tort Law and Internalisation, The Gap between Private Cost and Social Loss,* 17 Intl Rev L & Econ 589-608 (1997).

rule, it would still be at odds with established routines of calculating damage awards. One could argue that the rule of gross negligence has the same consequentialist value as the rule of excluding redistributive damages from compensation, but takes better care of path dependency of the law. It can be easier implemented.

V. WRONG AUDITS IN PRIMARY MARKETS, SECONDARY MARKETS AND THE TORT-CONTRACT BOUNDARY

The above analysis would be of little value if it were restricted to tort law. The claimant has always the possibility to base his claim either on tort law or on contract law or on both. This is especially the case in the German civil law system (Anspruchskonkurrenz). With respect to the compensation of pure financial losses the difference between tort and contract is of fundamental importance, as in contract the usual restrictions to compensate pure financial losses do not exist. If within a contract an expert such as an auditor negligently delivers a wrong expertise and thereby causes a damage to the partner he is liable for the pure financial loss.[16] This is the general contractual default rule for consequential damages in Germany and in all major countries. If for instance an expert negligently overvalues a house in his expertise, which his contractual partner buys at a too high price, the expert is liable under contract law, even though he escapes liability under tort law. The fact that this has only led to a redistribution of wealth between the seller and the buyer of the house has no consequence in contract law. In a contract the partner has a willingness to pay the expert his costs of care x^* and his expected liability costs to such an extent that the sum total of his private damages from a wrong expertise and these costs are minimized. The contractual partner gets the liability he pays in the price of the expertise and his willingness to pay is related to the avoidance of private losses. Consequently, the problem of sorting out pure financial losses from compensation does in general not exist in contract law. The due level of care is clearly oriented to the avoidance of private losses and not of social losses. These costs are transactions costs, which allow the transfer of resources to the highest valued user. If under asymmetric information, a seller has signaling and bonding difficulties, the only possibility to facilitate efficient transactions is to collect additional information by the buyer.

The question here is, whether the shareholder has a contractual claim against the auditor. The auditor's contract is not with the share-

---

[16] In Germany contractual liability of the auditor is capped. § 323, 2 HGB.

holders but with the corporation. An explicit contract does therefore not exist. This however does not exclude contractual liability, as all legal orders have developed concepts and routines that lead to a contractual claim under an implicit contract or a quasi-contract. It seems however that in Germany the scope of contractual liability is larger than in Common Law Countries. In Germany the concept of a contract whose protective effects are extended to third parties exists on which a contractual claim can be based in such cases (Vertrag mit Schutzwirkung für Dritte).

Some authors[17] have proposed a liability concept sui generis, based on simple negligence, for the liability of experts whose legal consequences can however be taken either from contract law or from tort law. There exist different legal forms which have as a consequence, that the claim can be based on contract law even if the claimant has no explicit contract with the defendant. All these routines would lead to a compensation for pure financial loss under negligence. They therefore circumvent the restrictions of tort law with regard to pure financial loss.

It is neither possible nor necessary to deal with these concepts in detail. They have all one in common, which is crucial from an economic perspective.[18] They require that the protected person pays his protection in the price and that it can be assumed, that he has a willingness to pay for his protection.

With regard to shareholder liability it has already been shown, that the liability costs and the costs of care reduce the profits of the company and are therefore fully reflected in the value of a share. Therefore the shareholder always gets what he pays. This condition of quasi contractual liability is therefore given without any doubt. (See under B.)

The question is whether the shareholder is willing to pay for his protection and how much he would be ready to pay. Here it is now crucial to distinguish between shareholders in the secondary market and buyers of shares in the primary market or in initial public offerings. For both groups the willingness to pay for the protection is different. Therefore, the scope of liability should be different.

A. Shareholders willingness to pay for protection in the secondary market

The typical shareholder is an investment fund or pension fund or a private individual with a diversified portfolio. When he calculates his

---

[17] See C.W. Canaris, *Die Reichweite der Expertenhaftung gegenüber Dritten, ZHR*, 163, 206 (1999).

[18] H.B. Schäfer, *Die Haftung für Wirtschaftsprüfer aus wirtschaftswissenschaftlicher Perspective, AcP* (202), 808-840 (2002).

willingness to pay for the contractual liability and for the scope of his protection he is "behind a veil of ignorance." There are three possibilities for him to occur[19] but ex-ante he does not know which one it is.

(1) He has bought the shares before the audit, in which the company is overvalued. He still holds the shares after the bad news reached the stock market by other channels. The loss he suffered is therefore $r - a_1$. His private loss is then equal to the social loss, which the auditor caused.

(2) He has bought the shares before the balance was published and sells them after the wrong audit but before the bad news reaches the market, which is in period 1. The auditor has caused him a profit of $\bar{a} - r$ by his negligence. Had the auditor avoided the mistake the share prices would have dropped by this amount at a time when he was a holder of the share.

(3) He has bought the shares after the auditing took place (during period 1) and still keeps them, after the bad news reached the market anyway. Then he has suffered a loss of $\bar{a} - a_1$ Let the probabilities for the outcomes (1), (2) and (3) be u_1, u_2 and u_3. $u_1 + u_2 + u_3 = 1$

Then one gets for the expected loss of the shareholder (L), given a mistake of the auditor and given that the yield parameter is low including the costs of auditing is

(23) $L = u_1(r - a_1) - u_2(\bar{a} - r) + u_3(\bar{a} - a_1) + x$

From section A III. one can take, that the probability of a mistake of the auditor is $(1 - q(x))$ and that the probability that this will result in a damage because the yield parameter is low is $(1 - q(x)w)$. Therefore, if not the corporation but the shareholders themselves would conclude the contract with the auditor, they would ask for a level of care, which minimizes the sum total of the expected shareholders losses plus the costs of auditing, because that would maximize their shareholders value.

(24) $Min(1 - q(x))w[u_1(\bar{a} - a_1) - u_2(\bar{a} - r) + u_3(\bar{a} - a_1)] + x$

The shareholder would be interested that the auditor reaches the level of x that minimizes these expected costs.

Now follows an observation, which is crucial for the question of this article. Assume that the shareholder holds a diversified portfolio of stocks, bonds and money and neither plans to save nor to disinvest. The shareholder uses the dividends and interest payments for consumption. In that case, the only motivation for the selling and buy-

[19] See Part II.B.

ing shares is to improve the structure of the portfolio, to spread risks and to accommodate the portfolio to changing overall economic indicators. In that case the ex ante probability of buying and selling a particular share in any period must be equal. The shareholder therefore expects ex ante with a certain probability, that he will either buy or sell shares of a particular company in any period. If he buys, and the auditor overvalues the company this will cause him losses. If he sells the auditor causes him an equal gain. The probabilities of these two events are equal. Now call the probability that the shareholder will trade (buy or sell) shares of a particular company in a particular period u. Then the expected loss, given the audit led to an overvaluation in this period is $= u(\bar{a} - a_1 - (\bar{a} - r)) = u(r - a_1)$.

The probability that the shareholder will not trade in a particular period is then $(1 - u)$ and his expected loss in case the auditor overvalued the shares is $(1 - u)(r - a_1)$. Therefore the shareholder in a secondary market faces the following total expected losses, including the costs of auditing which he has to pay.

$$(25)\quad PL = (1 - q(x))w[(1 - u)(r - a_1) + u(r - a_1)] + x = (1 - q(x))w(r - a_1) + x$$

This is the expected private loss, if the damage occurs. Differentiating with respect to x yields the first order condition

$$(26)\quad q_x(x) = \frac{1}{w(r - a_1)}$$

This yields a cost level of care (x), which is optimal for the shareholder, but it is also socially optimal. (Compare with the first order condition in (8) in section BIII above). The shareholder's private interest in avoiding the loss is not larger than the interest of the society at large in an efficient organization of the capital market. One can therefore argue that there is no rationale to assume any implicit contract between shareholders and auditors, which would give rise to liability greater then that under tort law. Pragmatism recommends ruling out any contractual liability under these circumstances. The shareholder has no special willingness to pay for his protection which improves his legal position beyond that, which he enjoys under tort law. Under tort law liability should be triggered by gross negligence and disloyal behavior.

Admittedly, this result arises only if the shareholder plans neither to save, nor to disinvest continually over time. If for instance the shareholders are young they tend to save into their portfolio and therefore buy more shares in any period than they sell. If shareholders are old they disinvest and are likely to sell more shares in any period than they buy. There exist other conditions which might lead to a constellation under which shareholders face ex ante probabilities of

u_2 and u_3 which lead to a different willingness to pay for the auditor. But such considerations would be too artificial to have any effect on how the liability rule for auditors should be set up.

B. Buyers' of assets willingness to pay for protection in a primary market

These considerations however change if an audit is given for a firm for the reason to sell the firm or to go public and to inform potential buyers about the value of the firm. This constellation is not different from any asset valuation by an expert, which is made to inform the buying side and is therefore a transaction cost. This is a necessary cost if sellers, who are willing to reveal their superior knowledge, face signaling and bonding difficulties. Here the rationale of the audit and the expertise in general is to reduce the asymmetric information between the seller and the buyer. It is obvious that the buyer has a willingness to pay for the reliability of this expertise, which is determined by the private losses he incurs, when he buys an overvalued firm. He is therefore interested in a higher level of care of the auditor rather than a shareholder at the secondary market, where he is a buyer or a seller with equal probability. The only reason why in primary markets sellers and not potential buyers conclude the contract with the auditor is, that the expertise is a public good, valuable for all potential buyers and that free riding or unnecessary duplications of expertise would result if buyers concluded the auditing contract.

The buyer in a primary market wants the auditor to minimize the sum of his expected private losses and auditing costs, which are in this constellation

$$(27) \quad PL = (1 - q(x))w[\bar{a} - a_1] + x$$

This yields the first order condition of

$$(28) \quad q_x(x) = \frac{1}{w(\bar{a} - a_1)}$$

It also yields an x^* as the efficient cost of care, which is higher than in the previous analysis, when the shareholder has to determine his willingness to pay for the audit not knowing whether he will gain or lose as a result of the auditor's mistake. From an economic point of view, there is therefore no reason to restrict liability. The due level of care depends on the losses of the buyers in case they buy an overvalued firm. It is therefore conceptually higher than for the secondary market. Incentives should be given to reach this care level. Normal negligence should trigger liability. This is in the interest of the buyer who is willing to finance the auditing costs as part of his transactions cost.

This result can be obtained either by assuming an implicit contract between the buyer and the auditor or by extending the protective consequences of the contract between the firm and the auditor to the buyer or by a liability regime sui generis, which however leads to legal consequences as laid down in contract law. In Germany the result of liability for simple negligence can also be obtained within tort law (§ 823 Abs.2), if one interprets the regulatory statutes pertaining to the work of auditors as protection laws.[20] All these legal concepts would trigger liability in case of simple negligence with a negligence standard that reflects the possible private losses of the buyer as a consequence of an overvaluation.

To change liability rules by changing the branch of law that is applicable might seem to be artificially complex, and a concession of dogmatic restrictions in civil law countries. It is much simpler to have either a tort regime that exceptionally allows for the compensation of pure financial loss under simple negligence or a contract system that sometimes grants compensation for pure economic loss only under gross negligence.

Whatever legal form is chosen, the borderline between a stricter and a less strict liability rule for the auditor should be whether the expertise was made for the secondary or the primary market. In this context, it is now possible to give a comment on the much debated *Caparo v. Dickman* case in Britain.[21] Here a company had ordered an audit for the internal use of the management. An outside investor received this report. He noticed that the value of the firm given in the balance sheet was substantially higher than the market value at the stock exchange. He bought the majority of the company only to learn that the market value was correct and that the auditor had negligently overvalued the assets. The House of Lords denied compensation. Given the analysis in this article, this decision was in line with economic considerations, as the auditor did not know and could not know that his audit was used for a particular transaction. Therefore, the private loss of a buyer was not part of his price for the audit.

VI. CONCLUSION

Auditor's liability leads to a compensation of pure financial loss. It has been argued in the law and economics literature that the restriction of damage compensation in such cases is justified, as in this group of cases private losses of claimants are higher than the social losses. Compensation therefore might lead to overcompensation and

---

[20] Schutzgesetze in German.
[21] *Caparo Industries PLC v Dickman*, 1 All England Law Reports 568 (1990).

overdeterrence. In this article it is shown, that overcompensation of the victims leads to overdeterrence of the auditors, if the level of care for auditing is not strictly defined and only known as a probability distribution. However, overdeterrence can be reduced or even eliminated, if the liability for negligence is relaxed to a lower level such as gross negligence. It is also argued that this solution should be restricted to the activity of auditors in secondary markets, such as audit of the yearly balance sheet. A shareholder who operates in such a market has in general no willingness to pay for an auditing effort, which is higher than the optimal effort for a well functioning capital market.

If however the audit is exclusively made for the primary market (IPO or selling a firm) the level of care of the auditor should reflect the potential private losses and be higher than in secondary markets. Simple negligence should trigger liability. Here the buyers' willingness to pay for his protection is higher than in the secondary market. Consequently, liability should be stricter. One way of obtaining this result could be to extend contractual liability to the relation between the auditor and the buyer of a firm or of shares in a primary market.

The Supreme Court's Efficiency Defense

*Sheldon Kimmel**

Mergers that substantially lessen competition are illegal, but an efficiency defense may be reasonable when mergers sufficiently lower costs. Nonetheless, it is widely believed that the Supreme Court has never accepted an efficiency defense. However, this paper shows that the Supreme Court's failing firm doctrine is sensible only as an efficiency defense since it considers that mergers encourage failing firms to stay in the market, but without efficiencies, such mergers generally encourage exit. Indeed, the Court's failing firm holding originated "[i]n the light of" the efficiency defense it laid out in International Shoe.

I. INTRODUCTION

Some mergers that substantially lessen competition are bad for consumers and society as a whole, and are condemned by §7 of the Clayton Act. On the other hand, mergers between competitors may allow them to lower their costs (i.e., achieve efficiencies).[1] If a merger generates enough efficiencies that may indicate that it benefits consumers or society as a whole. Thus, in some cases it may be reasonable to accept an efficiency defense, meaning that the merger should

*Economic Analysis Group, Antitrust Division, U.S. Department of Justice. The views expressed are not purported to represent those of the Department of Justice. Andrew Dick, Russ Pittman, Alex Raskovich, John Sawyer, Lester Telser, Greg Werden and two referees provided helpful comments on an earlier draft, but any remaining errors are the author's.
[1] If we define efficiencies as cost reductions, that includes the ability of a merged firm to produce products that neither of the merging parties could have produced alone since the cost of producing such products pre-merger is effectively infinite.

be allowed because it generates enough efficiencies even though it would otherwise be condemned.[2] Indeed, courts began accepting efficiency defenses over 100 years ago.[3] In spite of that, it is widely believed that "the Supreme Court has not sanctioned the use of the efficiency defense in a section 7 case"[4] However, this paper shows that the *only* way to make sense of the failing firm doctrine that the Supreme Court introduced in *International Shoe v. FTC*[5] is to read it as being based on an efficiency defense—there is no other way to assert as broadly as the Court did that the firm's assets will likely leave the market unless it merges with a competitor, and that those assets will likely stay in the market if it merges.

As will be shown below, unless the Court assumed that the merger would produce efficiencies, the Court was completely wrong in concluding that the merger was necessary to keep the failing firm's assets in the market. Indeed, as shown below, those assets are all the more likely to leave the market post-merger. Since the Court's conclusion is completely wrong unless the merger produces efficiencies, but is perfectly reasonable if the merger generates enough efficiencies, the only reasonable conclusion is that the Court was talking about mergers that generate efficiencies.

Even though one can imagine economic models where a merger generates no efficiencies but a failing firm will exit unless its competitor acquires it, nothing in *International Shoe* suggests that the Court considered such a model.[6] Section II of this paper summarizes the case before the Court in *International Shoe* and the Court's ruling. Since, as the rest of this paper shows, the breadth of the failing firm doctrine requires that it be based on efficiencies, it is natural to

---

[2] Two distinct efficiency defenses are suggested in U.S. Department of Justice & Federal Trade Commission, Horizontal Merger Guidelines (1992, rev 1997), reprinted in 4 Trade Reg Rep (CCH) ¶ 13,104. If a merger generates so much efficiency that prices will not likely rise post-merger, then the merger does not hurt consumers, and the Agency will not challenge it. Footnote 37 in the Guidelines notes that the Agency will also consider the effects of efficiencies that have no direct effect on prices in the relevant market.

[3] The common law allows "co-operation between two or more persons to accomplish an object which neither could gain . . . alone . . . although, in a certain sense and to a limited degree, such co-operation might have a tendency to lessen competition." *Hoffman v McMullen*, 83 F 372, 376-77 (9th Cir 1897). While *Hoffman* is not an antitrust case, "The legislative history [of the Sherman Act] makes it perfectly clear that [Congress] expected the courts to give shape to the statute's broad mandate by drawing on common-law tradition." *National Society of Professional Engineers v United States*, 435 US 679, 688 (1977). Therefore, it is not much of a leap to go from *Hoffman* to an antitrust efficiency defense.

[4] *FTC v. HJ Heinz Co*, 246 F3d 708, 720 (DC Cir 2001).

[5] 280 US 291 (1930).

[6] See the appendix for such a model.

look for and to find efficiencies in *International Shoe*. As Section II shows, the *International Shoe* Court presented an efficiency defense and then made its holding on failing firms "[i]n the light of the case" in front of it, and the efficiency defense it had just presented.

Sections III-V of this paper consider the most commonly used economic models and find that in all these models, without efficiencies, mergers lead to exactly the opposite of what the Court predicted—assets that would have left the market without a merger are all the more likely to leave post-merger. Efficiencies, such as the ones the Court discussed in *International Shoe*, are the only possible support for the Court's broad failing firm doctrine.

Efficiencies are at the heart of the failing firm doctrine in two ways. First, as the rest of this paper shows, efficiencies are implicit in the environment that the failing firm doctrine assumes, where a merger between competitors is necessary to keep some assets employed in an industry. Second, efficiencies may be necessary to make sense of the failing firm doctrine's approach to that assumed environment. Indeed, the failing firm doctrine is a "mass of contradictions"[7] under the standard view that it trades off a merger's anticompetitive effects on consumers against harm to owners and employees from blocking the merger and having the firm fail.[8] However, the failing firm doctrine makes perfect sense if we view the *International Shoe* decision as recognizing an efficiency defense. Indeed, a close reading of two quotes from that decision suggests an efficiency defense. First, the Court in *International Shoe* was willing to lower the expected number of firms by allowing a merger that removed a competitor, even though its exit would otherwise have been only very likely: the failing firm faced not certain failure, but only "the grave *probability* of a business failure" (emphasis added).[9] Second, the Court, in *United States v. General Dynamics Corp.*, quoted *International Shoe* as supporting that reduction in the expected number of firms since "the effect on competition and the 'loss to [the company's] stockholders and injury to the communities where its plants were operated' . . . will be less if a company continues to exist even as a party to a merger than if it disappears entirely from the market."[10] Thus, the merger reduces the expected number of

[7] William F. Baxter, *Remarks: The Failing Firm Doctrine*, 50 Antitrust L J 247, 247-52 (1982).

[8] The legal problem with that view being that Court has never accepted such trade-offs. *National Society of Professional Engineers*, 435 US at 689.

[9] *International Shoe v FTC*, 280 US 291, 302 (1930).

[10] *United States v General Dynamics Corp*, 415 US 486, 507 (1973). The Court's concern with competition and stockholders and communities is stated more clearly and briefly in *General Dynamics* than in *International Shoe*, but *General Dynamics* is also noteworthy because it was written in 1974, after the 1950 Celler-Kefauver

competitors, but it increases the total welfare of consumers, stock-holders and society as a whole, just as in Williamson's efficiency defense.[11] Thus, *International Shoe* was proposing a trade-off, but not the one that legal commentators suggest (i.e., harm to competition vs. losses to shareholders and employees), but something close to Williamson's efficiency defense trade-off (i.e., harm to competition *and* stockholders *and* communities vs. harm to competition).[12]

Section III sketches the issues in general and shows that the *International Shoe* Court's analysis of the case in front of it had to include some indirect effect of the merger, such as the efficiency defense it laid out in that case. Section IV shows that the failing firm doctrine necessarily rests on efficiencies in the simple case of homogeneous consumers. Section V shows that the failing firm doctrine requires efficiencies where consumers are heterogeneous.

Thus, the standard view of the failing firm doctrine—that it trades-off a merger's harms to consumers against the harm to owners and employees from blocking the merger—makes no sense since the Court consistently rejects such trade-offs. More surprisingly, as is shown below, the *International Shoe* Court needed efficiencies for its factual conclusion that the acquired firm would likely stay in the market if and only if its competitor bought it. In fact a hybrid failing firm doctrine-efficiency defense makes perfect sense: a merger with a competitor does not lessen competition if it is likely the only way to keep the failing assets in the market because only that competitor can use them efficiently enough to make them profitable. For these reasons, *International Shoe* can be read sensibly only as an efficiency defense. Given all that, it should not be surprising to find that the *In-*

Amendments to the Clayton Act. That last point means that the Court had the last word, so we can ignore the debate over whether Congress revised the failing firm doctrine after *International Shoe*. While some authors conclude that Congress did not relate the failing firm doctrine to efficiency at all, Muris saw the failing firm doctrine as an example of Congressional support for mergers that appeared to lower costs (based on legislative history for those amendments that included concern that a failing firm be allowed to merge with a competitor that "can conduct the operation more efficiently"). Timothy J. Muris, *The Efficiency Defense Under Section 7 of the Clayton Act*, 30 Case W Res L Rev 381, 381-432 (1980).

[11] Oliver E. Williamson, *Economies as an Antitrust Defense: The Welfare Trade-offs*, 58 Am Econ Rev 18, 18-36 (1968). Williamson proposed balancing the loss from the higher prices that a merger might lead to against the costs it might save. McChesney argued that Williamson's trade-off does not apply to the failing firm doctrine, but McChesney's argument ignored the word "probability" in *International Shoe*. Fred S. McChesney, *Defending the Failing-Firm Defense*, 65 Neb L Rev 1, 1-20 (1986).

[12] While the language from *General Dynamics* cited above goes much of the way towards Williamson's trade-off, it may not fully follow Williamson (i.e., it is consistent with a merger that raises margins but lowers costs so much that both consumers and society as a whole benefit).

ternational Shoe Court described the case in front of it as an efficiency defense which it accepted.

II. *INTERNATIONAL SHOE*

The Supreme Court's *International Shoe* decision introduced the failing firm doctrine. The Court found that International faced more demand than it had capacity to fill, that McElwain faced so little demand that it was a failing firm, and that International wanted to buy McElwain in order to get additional factories quickly enough to fill the excess demand it faced.[13] The Court held "[i]n the light of the case thus disclosed" that if there are no other prospective purchasers, it "does not substantially lessen competition or restrain commerce" for a firm to buy a failing competitor "to facilitate the accumulated business of the purchaser and with the effect of mitigating seriously injurious consequences otherwise probable"[14]

Before considering the decision, it might help to consider a simple case: the merger of two firms, one (like International) that does not own enough productive capacity to fill the demand for the brands that it owns, and another (like McElwain) that owns relatively good but under-utilized plants. We should note that such firms were considered in both *International Shoe* and *Heinz*.[15] Indeed, one could generalize the efficiency here as "co-operation between two or more persons to accomplish an object which neither could gain . . . alone."[16] The complementary strengths that the two parties bring to such a merger may generate enough efficiencies that the merger raises output and therefore lowers prices (one thing leading to the other since the demand curve slopes downward). In such cases, the efficiency comes from combining one firm's trade secrets or copyrights (e.g., Beech-Nut's popular recipes or International's popular designs) with

[13] *International Shoe*, 280 US at 299-301.

[14] Id at 302-03.

[15] *Heinz*, 246 F3d at 723. According to the circuit court, "the principal merger benefit asserted for Heinz is the acquisition of Beech-Nut's better recipes, which will allegedly make its product more attractive and permit expanded sales at prices lower than those charged by Beech-Nut, which produces at an inefficient plant." Thus, both Beech-Nut and International (the shoe company that could not keep up with the demand for its popular brands) had plenty of demand for their products, but had too little or too expensive productive capacity to efficiently fill that demand. In both cases the other merging party (in the shoe case McElwain, in the baby food case Heinz) had that additional productive capacity.

[16] *Hoffman v McMullen*, 83 F 372, 376-77 (9th Cir 1897). Although this decision was written almost 100 years before Farrell and Shapiro (1990), it discusses what they refer to as a merger that generates "synergies": such a merger allows the parties to improve their joint production capabilities. Joseph Farrell and Carl Shapiro, *Horizontal Mergers: An Equilibrium Analysis*, 80 Am Econ Rev 107-26 (1990).

the under-utilized plant that the other firm owns.[17] This is not an economy of scale, but rather an increased use of the knowledge that the merger makes available throughout the merged firm.[18] However, the fact that a merger will generate efficiencies is not enough to defend it unless there are reasons to think, as the *International Shoe* Court concluded, that those efficiencies would not be likely without the merger.[19]

The simplest reading of *International Shoe* is that the Court intended its failing firm doctrine to be read "[i]n the light of" the efficiency defense that it had just laid out. However, whether that was the Court's intention or not, the fact remains that either *International Shoe* and the entire structure of the failing firm doctrine that has been built on it makes absolutely no sense at all, or it makes perfect sense as the efficiency defense that the Court has fairly explicitly accepted since 1930.

III.   THE ISSUE IN GENERAL

That the failing firm doctrine requires efficiencies may seem surprising since the doctrine sounds so plausible on its face: whether the merger generates efficiencies or not, the Court approves it since it seems to merely allow more production than there would otherwise be since it allows use of the failing firm's assets that no other firm wants and that will not return to the market after bankruptcy. However, the failing firm doctrine is not at all as simple as it seems. In fact, we now show that a failing firm doctrine makes no sense if we consider only the direct and immediate effects of a merger. Suppose we hold everything else constant except for the transfer of a failing

[17] One might loosely describe Beech-Nut as having tasty recipes and International as having stylish designs, but the point is that many consumers want to buy those recipes and designs, even given whatever added costs they entail. Thus, the key fact is that they are popular.

[18] Warren-Boulton gives an example of a similar type of efficiency. Suppose there are two laundries, one with relatively efficient washing machines, the other with relatively efficient dryers. A merger of the two laundries may increase output and lower costs. Frederick R. Warren-Boulton, *Implications of U.S. Experience with Horizontal Mergers and Takeovers for Canadian Competition Policy*, in Frank Mathewson, Michael Trebilcock, and Michael Walker, eds, *The Law and Economics of Competition Policy* (Fraser Institute, 1990).

[19] While the appellate court issued a preliminary injunction against Heinz, its only objection to the theory that *Heinz* shares with *International Shoe* is that the district court should have investigated whether Heinz needed to merge to get the efficiency benefits, whether Heinz could not have produced those same benefits without merging by developing better recipes on its own. *Heinz*, 246 F3d at 722. Similarly, one could have asked whether McElwain could not have developed better shoe designs on its own, but the *International Shoe* Court dismissed all such alternatives to the merger as "lying wholly within the realm of speculation." *International Shoe*, 280 US at 301.

firm's assets to one of its competitors. Pre-merger the failing firm's revenues would not cover all of its costs.[20] However, the only thing that changes post-merger is that the failing firm has become merely a profit center (a plant or collection of plants) owned by a competitor. That competitor has to value that profit center's output less than its previous owner did since the new owner internalizes what had been the external harm that the failing firm does to the new owner's other profit centers. In other words, since the new owner is a competitor, and since the demand curve slopes down, revenue from its other plants would rise if the failing firm shut down, so the total value the new owner places on the production of its newly acquired profit center has to be adjusted down to take account of the harm the failing firm does to the revenue it gets from its other plants. Thus, if we consider only the direct and immediate effects of a competitor's purchase of a failing firm, that merger will not preserve assets that would otherwise have exited, it will make those assets all the more unprofitable and thus make their exit all the more likely.

Thus, the only sensible interpretation of the Supreme Court's failing firm doctrine is that it has to consider indirect effects of a competitor's purchase of a failing firm that outweigh the direct effects considered above. The most obvious indirect effects the Supreme Court might reasonably consider are efficiencies that the merger is likely to create (such as those that it found in *International Shoe*). We now show that basing a failing firm doctrine on other indirect effects would be so difficult that the only reasonable presumption is that the Supreme Court's failing firm doctrine is based on a form of efficiency defense.

IV. IF CONSUMERS ARE HOMOGENEOUS, THE FAILING FIRM DOCTRINE IS BASED ON AN EFFICIENCY DEFENSE

A. Failing Firm Doctrine requires efficiencies if marginal cost is constant

This section considers two firms that produce a homogeneous product. Producing q_i at firm i's plant (where $0 < q_i \leq K_i$) incurs costs of $\alpha_i + cq_i$

---

[20] Even though it turns out not to affect the analysis, we should note the potential complication that bankruptcy may allow a firm to change its cost structure by defaulting on its obligations to pay above market prices for some inputs. Such a change in cost structure may be mostly a transfer (i.e., a pecuniary, but not real efficiency). That complication has no affect on this paper's analysis since the relevant cost structure of the failed firm is its post-bankruptcy cost structure. If a merger allows even further cost reductions, those cost reductions would be efficiencies which are being assumed away for the rest of the paragraph in the above text.

(i.e., operating the plant at any positive level of output incurs a marginal cost of c per unit of output and a fixed cost α_i that could have been avoided by shutting the plant down). We also adopt a standard stability assumption: these firms faced downward sloping residual demand curves for their output pre-merger, and they face a downward sloping residual demand curve for their output post-merger. The problem with the failing firm doctrine in this case is that if we had a real failing firm (one that will exit unless it merges) then the merger does no good since, as will be shown below, it will exit post-merger. Thus, the firm that claims to be failing may simply be trying to sell its plant to a competitor that offers more than it would get from a buyer that will not bid as much, but would be willing to keep it in business. To see the intuition for this result, this section maintains the assumption that both the failing firm's plant and its acquirer's plant will operate post-merger. That must mean that total output post-merger is more than either plant can produce by itself since otherwise the acquirer could save α_i by shutting down plant i, and consolidating production at plant j (that consolidation might have costs if $c_j > c_i$, c_j is not constant, or the merger allowed other efficiencies, but this section has assumed those issues away). Suppose we rearranged the post-merger production plan by moving as much production as possible into the acquiring firm's original plant—that rearrangement has no effect on profits since both plants have the same constant marginal cost. At that point we could consider closing the acquired plant, but apparently even the small amount of production it is left with is valuable enough to cover its costs. However, that situation (acquiring firm running at full capacity, "failing firm" producing more than enough revenue to cover its costs) is as bad for the "failing firm" as anything that could happen to it pre-merger, yet it is still profitable, contradicting the assumption that it was a failing firm.

Formally, let x_1 and x_2 be respectively the most profitable post-merger outputs. By assumption, $x_1 > 0$ and $x_2 > 0$. Since the post-merger outputs must be feasible, and since, the assumption that it is profitable to operate both plants post-merger implies that producing x_1 and x_2 is more profitable than consolidating all the output at one plant and shutting down the other (even though that saves the avoidable cost of a plant), it must be true that

(1) $K_1 + K_2 \geq x_1 + x_2 > \max\{K_1, K_2\}$.

The assumption that both plants would operate post-merger also implies that continuing in operation is more profitable than anything that could be done with just one plant. If Δ is the difference between the most profit the merged firm can make operating two plants and the most profit it can make operating just one plant, then

(2) $\Delta = (x_1 + x_2)p(x_1 + x_2) - c(x_1 + x_2) - \alpha_1 - \alpha_2 - \max_{i,x}[xp(x) - cx - \alpha_i] \geq 0$
where $x \in (0, K_i]$

and by assumption, $\Delta \geq 0$. Since K_i is a feasible choice of x, $\max_x[xp(x) - cx - \alpha_i] \geq K_ip(K_i) - cK_i - \alpha_i$ and since the residual demand curve slopes down, for any number $w > 0$ we might pick $\max_x[xp(x) - cx - \alpha_i] > K_ip(w + K_i) - cK_i - \alpha_i$ so from (2) $\Delta < (x_1 + x_2)p(x_1 + x_2) - c(x_1 + x_2) - \alpha_1 - \alpha_2 - [K_ip(w + K_i) - cK_i - \alpha_i]$. In particular, that is true for $w = x_1 + x_2 - K_i$ (since by (1) $x_1 + x_2 - K_i \in (0, K_i]$), so

(3) $0 \leq \Delta < (w + K_i)p(w + K_i) - c(w + K_i) - \alpha_1 - \alpha_2 - K_ip(w + K_i) + cK_i + \alpha_i$
$= w[p(w + K_i) - c] - \alpha_j$

The conclusion in (3) that $0 \leq \Delta < w[p(w + K_i) - c] - \alpha_j$ is useful since $w[p(w + K_i) - c] - \alpha_j$ is plant j's pre-merger profit if it produces w and i produces K_i (j's profits being even higher if i produces less). Since plant j could have produced w pre-merger and that would have given it profits of at least $w[p(w + K_i) - c] - \alpha_j > \Delta \geq 0$, that proves the following Proposition.

Proposition: Suppose two firms in a market face a downward sloping residual demand curve for the homogeneous product they produce with costs (both pre-merger and post-merger) of the form $\alpha_i + cq_i$ for $0 < q_i \leq K_i$. If it is profitable for a single firm to operate both plants, then it is all the more profitable for each independent firm to operate a single plant without a merger. A merger does not increase the number of plants that operate so there is no basis for defending the merger of these two plants; thus, no basis for a failing firm doctrine.

The intuition behind the proposition is that if both plants operate post-merger, it would be just as profitable for the merged firm to consolidate as much of its output as possible in its "non-failing" plant (since marginal costs are constant and the same at both plants). The fact that the merged firm chooses to operate both plants implies that the residual production at the "failing" plant would still be profitable, but the "failing" plant has to be at least that profitable pre-merger since no pre-merger environment can be as bad for it as one where its competitor produces at capacity, so the "failing" plant must be profitable pre-merger.

We note that so far this section has formally assumed that both plants have not only constant marginal cost, but the same marginal cost. However, the analysis will go through as above if the marginal costs are constant, but the "failing" firm has higher marginal costs than its competitor. The only difference between that case and the one described above is that if both plants operate post-merger, the non-failing plant will operate at full capacity post-merger while it is nevertheless profitable for the "failing" plant to operate, showing that it would have been at least as profitable for the "failing" firm to operate pre-merger.

While it is true, as the proposition notes, that a monopolist has relatively little interest in using a second plant, it is also true that a monopolist has more interest in acquiring a second plant than another firm would[21] because of the externality another firm would impose on it if it ran that plant.[22] Thus, a monopolist might want to buy and shut down its competition.

In order for a failing firm doctrine to make sense, we would need to modify the above example by adding either efficiencies (so that the merger lowers cost), upward sloping marginal cost curves (so that the merger can help rationalize production), product differentiation, or an upward sloping residual demand curve. It is straightforward for efficiencies to allow a sensible hybrid failing firm-efficiency defense: if a merger lowers the failing plant's costs enough, then its new owner may well want to keep it running. As the next section shows, the effect of upward sloping marginal cost curves is too ambiguous to justify the broadly stated failing firm doctrine that the Court introduced in *International Shoe*.

B. Failing Firm Doctrine Requires Efficiencies if Marginal Cost Increases

Appendix 2 considers a market where each plant's avoidable cost is α, its marginal cost is cq, there are one or two plants and the demand curve is linear: price is $A + BQ$ where $A > 0 > B$. Whether competition is Cournot or Bertrand, the results are the same as we have seen earlier: post-merger the monopolist is all the more likely to shut down the acquired plant than its original "failing" owner was. Thus, the presence of cost curves that slope up do not justify the failing firm doctrine. Of course, Appendix 2 considers only the simplest such cost curves, but even if other cost functions would allow a merged firm to profitably use a plant that had been failing pre-merger (without the merger producing efficiencies), that would not justify as sweeping a failing firm doctrine as the one the Supreme Court introduced (where *any* failing firm has such a defense available to it regardless of what cost function it has).

---

[21] Richard J. Gilbert, and David M. G. Newbery, *Preemptive Patenting and the Persistence of Monopoly*, 72 Am Econ Rev 514-26 (1982).

[22] Unlike the typical merger perspective where the interests of the merging firms by themselves tell us that they expect the merger to create market power and/or efficiencies, here the Court's acceptance of the failing firm doctrine tells us that the Court accepts an efficiency defense, but it does not immediately tell us the terms of the trade-off that the Court accepts.

V. IF CONSUMERS ARE HETEROGENEOUS, THE FAILING FIRM DOCTRINE IS BASED ON AN EFFICIENCY DEFENSE

This section considers Hotelling's model of spatial competition,[23] the only spatial model in existence in 1930 when the *International Shoe* decision was written. It would not be appropriate to use Hotelling's model to consider a failing firm doctrine since that model is not capable of handling all the relevant issues. However, we can extend Hotelling's model slightly so that it can be used to consider a failing firm doctrine, and again, we find that if we assume away efficiencies, the failing firm doctrine makes no sense.

Hotelling considered a road of length L, and two plants. One plant is at point A, the other is at point B, and both plants have marginal production costs of 0. Consumers pay shipping costs of c per unit distance which gives the plant at A a shipping cost advantage at one end of the road, let that end of the road be a units away from A. The plant at B is b units away from the other end of the road. Consumers are located uniformly on the road, are identical except for their location, and have perfectly inelastic demand. The total demand is for L units of the good. In that case, the only possible equilibrium prices are $p_a = c[L + \frac{1}{3}(a - b)]$, and $p_b = c[L - \frac{1}{3}(a - b)]$.[24] Those prices generate sales of $q_a = \frac{1}{2}[L + \frac{1}{3}(a - b)]$, and $q_b = \frac{1}{2}[L - \frac{1}{3}(a - b)]$ and profits of $\pi_a = \frac{1}{2}c[L + \frac{1}{3}(a - b)]^2$, and $\pi_b = \frac{1}{2}c[L - \frac{1}{3}(a - b)]^2$. Without loss of generality, we can take $a \geq b$, so $p_a \geq p_b$ and $\pi_a \geq \pi_b$.

Strictly speaking, we cannot apply Hotelling's model to a failing firm doctrine unless we modify the model to allow for a firm to be failing by, for example, allowing an avoidable cost $\alpha > 0$ (so that the firm at B is failing if $\alpha > \frac{1}{2}c[L - \frac{1}{3}(a - b)]^2$). An additional modification is also necessary since merging Hotelling's duopolists would produce a monopoly, and Hotelling's assumption of perfectly inelastic demand is not compatible with a monopoly (i.e., such a monopolist would keep raising its price and profits without ever reaching an equilibrium). However, it is possible to extend Hotelling's model so it can apply to a monopolist without affecting the way Hotelling's duopolists act. The simplest way to do that is to let demand be perfectly inelastic until price reaches p_a with demand falling off enough at prices above p_a for there to be finite prices that maximize a two-plant monopolist's profit (i.e., demand is as Hotelling assumed it when his duopolists compete, but a two-plant monopolist's price and profits are finite since demand is sufficiently elastic for prices above some level).

[23] Harold Hotelling, *Stability in Competition*, 39 Econ J 41, 41-57 (1929).
[24] Hotelling notes that is not an equilibrium if $p_a - p_b > c(L - a - b)$ (i.e., if $5a > 3L - b$).

Once again we assume away efficiencies, which in the current model means that a firm's total costs are α times the number of plants it operates, regardless of how many plants it operates. For a failing firm doctrine to make sense, a two-plant monopolist must be more profitable than a one-plant monopolist (i.e., a two-plant monopolist's optimal revenue must exceed that of a one-plant monopolist by more than α) and the failing firm's duopoly profit must be negative (i.e., its revenue must be less than α). To show that those conditions cannot hold simultaneously (i.e., the failing firm doctrine makes no sense in this extended Hotelling model), for the moment suppose that we actually had a legitimate failing firm doctrine. In that case, say the plants owned by a two-plant monopolist would produce Q_a and Q_b. Since the monopolist raises its prices until that starts cutting too much into the quantity demanded, $Q_b \leq q_b = \frac{1}{2}[L - \frac{1}{3}(a - b)]$. However, we now show that the monopolist can do better than that by shutting the plant at b down (saving that plant's avoidable cost, α) increasing its production at its original plant by Q_b, and then shipping those extra Q_b units to the customers that had been served by the plant at B. Since each of those customers is a different distance away, calculating the cost of the cheapest way to ship to those customers requires an integral, but the shipping costs are so far below α that we can dispose of the failing firm doctrine by considering only the simplest, albeit relatively costly, shipping plan: ship Q_b units from A to B and then let B's old customers take care of shipping from the site of the defunct plant at B as before. That plan raises the monopolist's shipping costs by $c(L - a - b)Q_b$, but that will turn out to be profitable since we will show that the savings in plant costs are bigger.

We now establish three inequalities that show that a firm that bought its failing competitor would shut it down because the avoidable cost α (saved by shutting down the plant at B) is more than the cost of shipping from A what the plant at B would have produced: $\alpha > \frac{1}{2}c[L - \frac{1}{3}(a - b)]^2 > c(L - a - b)q_b \geq c(L - a - b)Q_b$. That first inequality $(\alpha > \frac{1}{2}c[L - \frac{1}{3}(a - b)]^2)$ holds since the firm at B was failing as a duopolist pre-merger. The second inequality $(\frac{1}{2}c[L - \frac{1}{3}(a - b)]^2 > c(L - a - b)q_b)$ is straightforward.[25] The last inequality $(c(L - a - b)q_b \geq c(L - a - b)Q_b)$ holds since the monopolist produces less than the duopolists did since it keeps raising prices until that starts cutting too much into the quantity demanded. Combining all three inequalities shows that $\alpha > c(L - a - b)Q_b$, so the monopolist would profitably save α in avoidable costs by shutting down the failing plant, even at the cost of spend-

---

[25] To see that inequality, note that $\frac{1}{3}(a - b) < a + b$, so $L - \frac{1}{3}(a - b) > L - a - b$. We can multiply the left hand side of that by $\frac{1}{2}c[L - \frac{1}{3}(a - b)]$ and the right hand side of that by cq_b since $\frac{1}{2}[L - \frac{1}{3}(a - b)] = q_b$, and that gives the second inequality.

ing $c(L - a - b)Q_b$ on shipping. Thus, the failing firm doctrine makes no sense in the slightly extended Hotelling model.

VI. CONCLUSION

In 1930, the Supreme Court held that if there are no other prospective purchasers, it "does not substantially lessen competition or restrain commerce" for a firm to buy a failing competitor "to facilitate the accumulated business of the purchaser and with the effect of mitigating seriously injurious consequences otherwise probable". However, as shown above, unless the merger creates efficiencies, in the most commonly used economic models, a merger with a failing competitor will not "facilitate the accumulated business of the purchaser" or mitigate injurious consequences, but is all the more likely to remove the failing firm's assets from the market. While one can construct economic models that produce other results, the breadth of the failing firm doctrine does not suggest any models that do. Since the environment assumed by the failing firm doctrine requires that the merger produce efficiencies, since the Court's analysis and conclusions are a "mass of contradictions"[26] unless they are based on those efficiencies, and since the failing firm doctrine originated "[i]n the light of" a merger where the Court found efficiencies (even though it did not label them as such), the only reasonable way to read that doctrine is as an efficiency defense. Thus, the efficiency defense has always been at the heart of the failing firm doctrine. Alternatively, if there was no efficiency defense, then it would be very hard to "see any important economic justification for the very existence of [the failing firm] doctrine"[27]

Even though the failing firm doctrine makes sense only as an efficiency defense, one might argue that the Court meant to accept an efficiency defense only in this very limited case. While that may well be true, the same analysis applies whether the merger involves a failing firm or not, so it would be hard to see why that distinction should matter. One might argue that the efficiencies involved in the case of a failing firm are less speculative than they often are since if a firm really was failing pre-merger, a competitor would be, *a fortiori*, even less interested in running that firm post-merger unless the merger provided substantial efficiencies (i.e., one can infer efficiencies from the fact that the rival wants to operate a plant that had been failing). While that argument presumes two facts that may be hard to pin down (i.e., that the firm really is failing pre-merger, and that its pur-

---

[26] Baxter, 50 Antitrust L J at 247-52 (cited in note 7).
[27] Id.

chaser plans to keep it in operation post-merger), the *International Shoe* Court was confident that it knew both of those facts about the firms it had before it. Maybe the most likely possibility is that the failing firm doctrine was just the simplest version of the efficiency defense, and therefore the best version to begin with.

Appendix 1: Price Discrimination

Since the *International Shoe* Court had an efficiency defense in front of it, made its holding "[i]n the light of" that defense, and the whole decision makes perfect sense in that context, that is a natural and reasonable way to read that decision and the failing firm doctrine. Similarly, if we assume that the Court mentioned all the factors it considered relevant (i.e., we are not free to make up additional "facts"), then there is no other way to make sense of *International Shoe* or the failing firm doctrine. However, this appendix considers an additional "fact" that (while it has no basis in the record) would (if it was true) allow a different reading of *International Shoe*.

To illustrate the effects of price discrimination, suppose there are two firms that each have constant marginal cost of 1 up to a capacity of 25, and price is $4 - (Q/10)$. In that case surplus is maximized if each firm produces 15 so $Q = 30$, $p = 1$, and surplus is $\frac{1}{2}(Q)(4 - 1) = 45$. Alternatively, if the firms conform to Cournot's assumptions, the equilibrium would be $p = 2$, each firm produces 10 units and gets profits of 10 while consumer surplus is $\frac{1}{2}(Q)(4 - 2) = 20$, and total surplus is $10 + 10 + 20 = 40$. If we now introduce an avoidable fixed cost of 11 that a firm has to pay to stay in the market, the two Cournot firms would each get profits of -1. If those failing firms merged, and if the resulting monopolist could price discriminate perfectly, it could produce 15 at each plant, extract the entire maximum surplus of 45, and have profits of 23 left after paying the avoidable fixed costs. Alternatively, if the merger is blocked, a failing firm exits, the resulting 1 – plant perfectly discriminating monopolist produces 25, extracts the consumer surplus of $\frac{1}{2}(25)(4 - 1.5) = 31.25$, so total surplus is $31.25 - 11 = 20.25$. Thus, profits are either 23 (post-merger) or 20.25 (post-exit after merger was not allowed). Consumers are indifferent since they get no surplus in any case, so merger maximizes total surplus.

The point of the example is that merger to monopoly may allow price discrimination which may be the only way to cover fixed costs. In that case, even if the merger produces no efficiencies, it may keep assets in the market that may otherwise have left. Of course, consumers are indifferent about the number of plants that a perfectly discriminating monopolist operates, but if the monopolist can discriminate only imperfectly, such a merger can be good for everyone.

Appendix 2

Consider a market where each plant's avoidable cost is α, its marginal cost is cq, and the demand curve is linear: price is $A + BQ$ where $A > 0 > B$. In that case, a monopolist that uses n plants gets profits of $\pi = Q(A + BQ) - n[\alpha + \int_0^{Q/n} cx \, dx] = Q(A + BQ) - [cQ^2/2n] - n\alpha$. A monopolist maximizes its profit by producing $Q = An/(c - 2Bn)$, so its profits are $\pi = [nA^2/2(c - 2Bn)] - n\alpha$. Thus, a 1-plant monopolist values a second plant at $\Delta = \{[A^2/(c - 4B)] - 2\alpha\} - \{[A^2/2(c - 2B)] - \alpha\}$ which reduces to

$$(4) \quad \Delta = \frac{cA^2}{2(c - 4B)(c - 2B)} - \alpha.$$

Suppose there are two firms in this industry (each owning 1 plant), and one is failing (i.e., it will exit or merge). In that case, the most that the non-failing firm would be willing to pay to acquire the failing firm is the difference between the value of a 2-plant monopoly and a 1-plant monopoly, which is Δ. On the other hand, if both firms will survive, their profits will depend on the way they interact. It is easiest to consider Cournot competition, so we consider that first. Although the firms are identical, suppose one produces an exogenously given amount x, and the other produces q, an amount that it chooses to maximize its profits. Producing q gives it profits of $\pi = q[A + B(q + x)] - \frac{1}{2}cq^2 - \alpha$, so $d\pi/dq = A + 2Bq + Bx - cq$, $d^2\pi/dq^2 = 2B - c < 0$, so it chooses q to set $0 = d\pi/dq = A + 2Bq + Bx - cq$, so $q = (A + Bx)/(c - 2B)$. By symmetry, $x = (A + Bq)/(c - 2B)$ and those last two equations imply $x = A/(c - 3B)$, $Q = 2A/(c - 3B)$, and $p = A + B[2A/(c - 3B)]$ which reduces to $p = A(c - B)/(c - 3B)$. Therefore, $\pi_i = [A^2(c - B)/(c - 3B)^2] - \frac{1}{2}c[A/(c - 3B)]^2 - \alpha$ which reduces to

$$(5) \quad \pi_i = \frac{A^2(c - 2B)}{2(c - 3B)^2} - \alpha.$$

The difference between (4) and (5) is that (4) is the valuation that its competitor would place on the failing firm, while (5) is the valuation that the failing firm assigns to itself. Subtracting (4) from (5) and reducing gives $\pi_i - \Delta = [A^2/2(c - 2B)(c - 3B)^2(c - 4B)](-2Bc^2 + 11B^2c - 16B^3)$ which is positive since its only negative terms (B and B^3) appear only with minus signs. Thus, $\pi_i > \Delta$, so the plant is worth more to a Cournot competitor than it is to a monopolist: if the plant is failing pre-merger, it is even less profitable post-merger and all the more likely to exit. Thus, the failing firm doctrine makes no sense in this case.

Alternatively, the firms might compete Bertrand. In that case the obvious strategy of price equal marginal cost is not an equilibrium, since marginal cost slopes upward, and upward sloping marginal cost means that the only equilibria may be fairly complicated mixed strategies. However, whatever the equilibria are, they are more profitable than setting price at marginal cost.[28] Thus, while it is hard to calculate a firm's profit, we can calculate a lower bound on that profit by looking at the results of setting price equal to marginal cost pre-merger. In that case, $A + BQ = p = MC = \frac{1}{2}cQ$, so $Q = 2A/(c - 2B)$, $p = Ac/(c - 2B)$, $\pi_1 = \pi_2 = [A^2c/(c - 2B)^2] - \alpha - \int_0^{\frac{1}{2}Q} cx\,dx = [A^2c/(c - 2B)^2] - \alpha - c[A/(c - 2B)]^2/2 = \frac{1}{2}[A^2c/(c - 2B)^2] - \alpha > \frac{1}{2}[A^2c/(c - 2B)(c - 4B)] - \alpha = \Delta$. Since actual pre-merger profits will be higher than that (i.e., firms price above marginal cost), pre-merger profits will exceed Δ by even more. Thus, a monopolist's value of a second plant is less than the profit of a firm facing one Bertrand competitor. Therefore, if a Bertrand firm is failing and it merges with its competitor, the remaining monopolist is all the more likely to shut down the acquired plant. Again, the failing firm doctrine makes no sense in this case.

---

[28] Jean Tirole, *The Theory of Industrial Organization* 214-15 (MIT, 1989).